# Destabilizing Theory

# Destabilizing Theory

## Contemporary Feminist Debates

*Edited by*

Michèle Barrett and Anne Phillips

Stanford University Press
Stanford, California
1992

Stanford University Press
Stanford, California
This collection and Introduction
© 1992 Michèle Barrett and Anne Phillips,
  each chapter copyright the author
Originating publisher: Polity Press, Cambridge
  in association with Blackwell Publishers, Oxford
First published in the U.S.A. by
  Stanford University Press, 1992
Printed in Great Britain
Cloth ISBN 0–8047–2030–4
Paper ISBN 0–8047–2031–2
LC 91–67234
This book is printed on acid-free paper

# Contents

# List of Plates

Plate 1. Henri Matisse (1869–1954), *The Painter and his Model*, 1917. Paris, Musée National d'Art Moderne.

Plate 2. Brassai, *Henri Matisse in his Studio*. Photograph London, Victoria and Albert Museum.

Plate 3. Hans Namuth, *Jackson Pollock at Work*, 1950. Photograph New York, Studio Hans Namuth.

Plate 4. Ernst Haas, *Helen Frankenthaler at Work*, 1969. Photograph New York, Studio Ernst Haas.

Plate 5. Martin Charles, *Gillian Ayres in her Studio*, 1988. Photograph Isleworth, Studio Martin Charles.

# List of Contributors

**Michèle Barrett** is Professor of Sociology at City University, London. She is the author of *The Politics of Truth: From Marx to Foucault* (Polity and Stanford University Press 1991). *Women's Oppression Today* (Verso, 1980 and 1988), co-author with Mary McIntosh of *The Anti-social Family* (Verso, 1982 and 1991), and has written and edited other books and papers. At City University she is Head of the Sociology Division in the Department of Social Sciences and Director of the Centre for Research on Gender, Ethnicity and Social Change.

**Moira Gatens** lectures in philosophy at the Australian National University. She is the author of *Feminism and Philosophy: Perspectives on Difference and Equality* (Polity Press and Indiana University Press, 1991). A collection of her essays on gender, corporeality and desire will be published by Routledge in 1993. Her current research concerns philosophies of the body (Spinoza, Nietzsche and Freud) and their relations to theories of ethics.

**Biddy Martin** is Associate Professor of German Studies and Women's Studies at Cornell University. She is the author of *Woman and Modernity: The (Life) Styles of Lou Andreas-Salomé* (Cornell University Press, 1991) and has published numerous articles on feminist theory.

**Chandra Talpade Mohanty** teaches Women's Studies and the Sociology of Education at Oberlin College, and for 1991–92 is the Jane Watson Irwin Associate Professor of Women's Studies at Hamilton College. She has recently co-edited *Third World Women and the Politics of Feminism* (Indiana University Press, 1991), and is co-editor of a forthcoming reader on *Third World Feminisms* (Basil Blackwell). She is currently working on a manuscript on feminist theory and the politics of cross cultural analysis.

**Anne Phillips** is Professor of Politics at City of London Polytechnic. She is author of *Engendering Democracy* (Polity Press and Pennsylvania State University Press, 1991), and editor of *Feminism and Equality* (Basil Blackwell and New York University Press, 1987). She is currently working on democracy, citizenship, and the representation of group difference.

**Griselda Pollock** is Professor of the Social and Critical Histories of Art and Director of the Centre for Cultural Studies at the University of Leeds. She is co-author with Roszika Parker of *Old Mistresses Women, Art & Ideology* (Pandora 1981) and *Framing Feminism Art & the Women's Movement* (Pandora 1987). She is author of many books and articles on nineteenth and twentieth century culture, cinema and photography, including *Vision and Difference Feminism Femininity and the Histories of Art* (Routledge 1988). Forthcoming publications include *Sexuality and Surveillance Bourgeois Men and Working Women* Routledge 1992). She has two children.

**Rosemary Pringle** is Associate Professor of Sociology at Macquarie University. She is author of *Secretaries Talk: Sexuality, Power and Work* (Verso, 1989). She is currently working on gender and masquerades, using case studies from the professions.

**Gayatri Chakravorty Spivak** is Professor of English and Comparative Literature at Columbia University. She is author of *In Other Worlds* (Routledge, 1987) and translator of Jacques Derrida's *Of Grammatology* (Johns Hopkins, 1976). She is currently working on feminism and decolonization.

**Sylvia Walby** is Reader in Sociology at the London School of Economics. Books she has authored include *Patriarchy at Work* (Polity Press, 1986) and *Theorizing Patriarchy* (Blackwell, 1990), while she was recently co-editor of *Out of the Margins: Women's Studies into the Nineties* (Falmer Press, 1991). She is currently working on a book on the history of feminist thought.

**Sophie Watson** is Professor of Urban and Regional Planning at Sydney University. She is author of *Accommodating Inequality: Gender and Housing* (Allen and Unwin, 1988). She is currently co-writing a book *Rethinking Social Policy: Sex, Power and Knowledge*, and continuing her feminist research in urban studies.

# Preface and Acknowledgements

This collection of essays is focused on such dialogue as can exist between the current work of feminists on post-structuralist and postmodernist themes, and the political project of what for shorthand we call '1970s western feminism'. In our introduction we try to draw an outline of the characteristic assumptions of 1970s feminism, and explain how its project has been challenged both by a politics of difference (the charge that the specificity of black women's experience and the racism of white feminists had been ignored) and by the theoretical undermining of many of its paradigmatic assumptions. The essays in the book were commissioned around this theme, with the exception of one key article already published, which was revised in this context. The book does not aspire to be a total account of 'feminism' in its various political projects; it is far from global in its reference points; and its academic range is restricted to the arts, social sciences and philosophy. In this sense, it reflects the typical concerns of a western, academic feminist impulse, albeit one that has come to see 'western feminism' as an unstable and limited category. We have, however, addressed these problems beyond narrowly national or regional boundaries. Debates on these questions are occurring in different forms in Australia, Britain and the United States and we have sought to indicate some of the lines of commonality and disagreement in the way in which the underlying themes are addressed.

We are grateful to David Held at Polity Press for commissioning the book and to Catherine Hall, Ruthie Petrie and Sophie Watson for their comments and discussion.

# 1

# Introduction

## *Michèle Barrett and Anne Phillips*

Many of the essays in this collection draw attention to the need to 'destabilize' the founding assumptions of modern theory. Feminists have long criticized the pretensions of 'grand', 'high' and 'general' theory and have demonstrated the difficulties that attend any such enterprise. Universal claims have all too frequently turned out to be very particular, supposed commonalities false, abstractions deceptive. Feminists have become deeply suspicious of theoretical discourses that claim neutrality while speaking from a masculinist perspective, and have at times despaired of the possibility of 'gender-neutral' thought.

This long-standing critique has been carried further than ever with the current reappraisal of the grand schemas of modern western social, political and cultural theory. Here, in a sweeping attack on the falsely universalizing, over-generalizing and over-ambitious models of liberalism, humanism and Marxism, many feminists have joined sympathies with post-structuralist and post-modernist critical projects. In the context of these recognitions, many feminists have opted for an analysis of the local, specific and particular. Much of this work is 'deconstructive' in character, seeking to destabilize – challenge, subvert, reverse, overturn – some of the hierarchical binary oppositions (including those implicating sex and gender) of western culture. Thus we have a developing feminist theory whose intention is to destabilize.

There is a second construction of 'destabilizing theory' that runs through this collection. This is not so much the traditional ambivalence of feminism towards 'theory', based on a principled preference for activism, 'politics' or the experiential, although this is often present in some form. It concerns, rather, the fundamental nature of the critique that has been offered of the theoretical grounding and paradigmatic conventions of 'modernist' feminism. In the past twenty years the founding principles of contemporary western feminism have been dramatically challenged, with previously shared assumptions and unquestioned orthodoxies relegated almost to history. These changes have been of the order of a 'paradigm shift', in which assumptions rather than conclusions are radically overturned. So as well as exploring the question of feminism's relationship to theory *per se*, to theory in its worst moments of reckless abstraction and dangerous generality, the essays in *Destabilizing Theory* were written to highlight and debate the gulf between feminist theory of the 1970s and the 1990s. Whether or not a dialogue across that gap is possible, desirable or inevitable is a question on which the contributors have varying views – but all have addressed themselves to it.

These two themes are linked, to the extent that 1970s feminism was itself an instantiation of the 'modernist' impulse – and feminist critics of the 1980s and 1990s have indeed stressed this point. Looking back, we can see this period of western feminist thought as one of surprising consensus on the relevant questions, if not always on the answers that might emerge. Though now broken, this consensus should not be regarded as a symptom of underdevelopment – a 'prehistory' now well transcended in the sophistication of contemporary thought – for many of the issues posed in that period return to haunt the present. The sharp contrast we draw between what for shorthand we call 1970s and 1990s western feminism draws attention to the fundamental nature of the changes that have occurred, and helps us explore the extent of dialogue across these very different theoretical perspectives. The contrast is not intended as a marker of feminist 'progress'.

Our deceptively simple starting point is that 1970s feminism assumed one could specify a *cause* of women's oppression. Feminists differed substantially (and fiercely) as to what this cause might be – male control of women's fertility, a patriarchal system of inheritance, capitalism's need for a docile labour force – but did not really question the notion of a cause itself. Nor was there any difficulty with the idea of *oppression*, which seemed to have self-evident application. Important, too, was the assumption shared by most feminists that the cause being sought lay at the level of *social structure*. The structure might be posited as patriarchy, or an exploitative economic system, or a structural relationship between home and workplace, but in an emphasis that reflected the political context of the early women's liberation movement, the issues were typically cast in social structural terms. In the opening engagements of the late 1960s and early 1970s, conservative opponents tended to insist on arguments from nature or biology, relying on these for their defence of the existing sexual arrangements. Feminists united against them to stress the social and environmental instead. The distinction between sex and gender then became almost talismanic: symbol of a social rather than natural interpretation of the visible differences between women's and men's lives. Sexual difference was stripped down to its barest essentials, often only a recognition that women's reproductive capacities and rights were a salient political factor. And in an argument that dated back at least as far as Mary Wollstonecraft, feminists tended to see 'femininity' as a distortion of women's human potential, a major aspect of women's oppression, and a prime candidate for change.

In the taxonomies so beloved of the period – as of many commentators subsequently – feminisms were divided into their liberal, socialist and radical varieties, each offering its own package of answers to the undisputed central questions. Of these three, liberal feminism was perhaps the least enamoured of social structural explanation, tending to emphasize the power of prejudice, irrationality and discrimination. Women's oppression was typically conceived in terms of female socialization into a limited range of roles and assumptions, and the way these social roles were then reinforced by a cultural tradition that persisted in viewing women as very different from men. The implicit or explicit individualism was contested by socialist and radical feminisms alike, who queried both the analysis of women's oppression and the confidence it seemed to place in equal opportunities as the easy way out.

Socialist feminists argued that the key problems lay in a system that actively benefited from women's oppression. Their analysis thus stressed exploitation rather than sexist prejudice, the structure rather than the individuals who operated within it, and more specifically, the material benefits that capitalism derived from women's position and role. Against this, radical feminists stressed not capital but men – and not men as semi-innocent agents of capitalist oppression, but men as the ones who got the good deal. Radical feminism often began from an analysis of reproduction (a deliberate contrast to the socialist emphasis on production), but moved increasingly towards questions of sexuality and male violence. In the ensuing arguments, both radical and socialist feminists came to perceive the structures of oppression as stretching far back into the distant past: the analysis of causation involved a search for the original and founding cause.

In extensive debates between these shifting and often overlapping perspectives, 1970s feminists were concerned with where to put the explanatory weight: which elements to regard as the more fundamental;

what to pinpoint as the crucial source of oppression. Was women's oppression primarily located in the sphere of work or the sphere of the family? in the realm of production or the realm of reproduction? in economic structures or cultural representation? in sexuality or mothering or what? Such disagreements operated within the broader context of debates over the relative weight to be attached to structures of patriarchy (or sometimes the sex/gender system) versus capitalism; and either of these structural accounts versus social roles, or psychologies of power. The diversity of the answers helped conceal the consensus in the questions; yet behind all the sharp disagreements over what was primary or secondary, feminists united in the importance they attached to establishing the fundamentals of social causation.

This consensus has since broken up, and we offer here merely a sketch of what we see as key elements that aided this process. The first was the enormous and continuing political impact of black women's critique of the racist and ethnocentric assumptions of white feminists, which helped seal the fate of the original sex and class debate. The social structural models of society that had been organized around the two systems of sex and class found a third axis of inequality hard to accommodate; the already acute difficulties in developing a 'dual systems' analysis were brought to a head with the belated recognition that ethnic difference and disadvantage had been left out. One response to this – especially among feminists working on the sexual division of labour – was the shift to a more micro-level of analysis that lent itself better to the complex interplay of different aspects of inequality. Another was the increasing tendency to theorize the so-called 'triple oppressions' of gender, race and class in a more cultural and symbolic mode.

A second major source of unease lay in the confident distinctions between sex and gender that had characterized so much of the previous consensus. Sexual difference came to be viewed as more intransigent, but also more positive, than most 1970s feminists had allowed: a shift that was variously signalled in the growing interest in psychoanalytic analyses of sexual difference and identity; in the analysis of women's experience of mothering as forming the basis for alternative (and more generous) conceptions of morality and care; and in its most 'essentialist' moments, the celebration of Woman and her Womanly role. The arguments were partly conceptual, highlighting the theoretical problems in distinguishing between biology and social construction, and querying the previous sharp divide. They were also substantive, for alongside the philosophical difficulties in maintaining a sex/gender distinction went a shift in political direction. Many feminists came to challenge the quasi-androgynous visions (I want to be a person, not a woman or a man) of a future untroubled by significant differences of sex; the impulse toward denying sexual difference came to be viewed as capitulation to a masculine mould.

The third element involves the appropriation and development by feminists of post-structuralist and post-modernist ideas whose impulse was not first found in feminism, but whose impact has been outstanding. To say this is not to pose a clear distinction between the collapse 'from the inside' of the 1970s feminist consensus and theoretical developments 'outside' feminism, for (as Michèle Barrett's paper suggests) the interaction and dialogue have been far more profound than that would suggest. But it is to point to important parallel lines as well as links between feminist and not-feminist strands of contemporary social, political and cultural theory.

The issues involved here are well represented in the various contributions to this volume. If we consider the constellation of ideas that goes to make up the figure of 'Enlightenment' thought, we can identify a notion of a powerful and self-conscious political subject, a belief in reason and rationality, in social and political progress, in the possibility of grand schemes of social reform. Many of the contributors to this book develop a feminist inflection to the general arguments that constitute a major critique of this rationalist model. Anne Phillips, for example, begins her essay by recapitulating the literature of political thought that has revealed the 'man' lurking within humanity, and reviews the false universals that were mobilized in classic liberal thought. Chandra Talpade Mohanty explores, through a critique of a modern feminist variant of the syndrome, the problems of humanistic discourses that presume an underlying commonality between all people (in this instance all women), and thus develops the post-structuralist critique of ideas about experience and the subject. Biddy Martin considers the politics of 'authentic' and feminist lesbian identities, emphasizing the complexity of same-gender eroticism; she argues that we need to de-naturalize *hetero*-sexuality as part of destabilizing the powerful homo/heterosexuality opposition.

Rosemary Pringle and Sophie Watson, in their dissection of the problems underlying the notion of 'women's interests', illustrate well the critique of a grand Marxist theory that has hypostatized supposed interests within a framework that sees politics as the mere representation of, rather than – as Pringle and Watson argue – the constitution of, interests. Griselda Pollock, in a discussion of the iconic case of painting, shows to a new degree the gendering of modernity. That most central of modern, humanist figures, the expressive artist, is shown by Pollock to be one whose modernity and masculinity are irretrievably entwined. Gayatri Chakravorty Spivak, demonstrating in a feminist context the general point that language constructs rather than reflects meaning, shows how the notion of 'translatability' must be criticized if we are to have texts worthy of the designation of feminist writing.

These points illustrate the powerful critique that has been amassed – both within feminism and elsewhere – of the universalistic discourses of rationalism and the Enlightenment. Intervening across a range of politically and theoretically significant issues, the essays in this collection continue a tradition of critique of *soi-disant* grand theory, and in this sense are very much of the mood of contemporary feminist thought. But by putting them in the context of the almost paradigmatic shift from 1970s to 1990s feminism, *Destabilizing Theory* seeks also to engage a debate about the implications of these arguments. If, as we have suggested, the differences between the founding assumptions of the two periods are profound, this raises the question as to whether or how these developments might be thought of as intellectual 'progress'. Can the critical assessment of modernist theory be viewed as stages *en route* to a closer understanding of the problems confronted in an earlier decade, a re-theorization that unblocks previous obstructions, and clears the way to better analysis? Or have feminists simply changed the subject, turned away from what we had come to see as a theoretical cul-de-sac, abandoned a materialist discourse of causation, and given our attention to more refreshingly open fields?

The fear now expressed by many feminists is that the changing theoretical fashions will lead us towards abdicating the goal of accurate and systematic knowledge; and that in legitimate critique of some of the earlier assumptions, we may stray too far from feminism's original project. Susan Bordo, for example, has argued that 'too relentless a focus on historical heterogeneity . . . can obscure the transhistorical hierarchical patterns of white, male privilege that have informed the creation of the Western intellectual tradition';[1] while Christine di Stefano has reposed the question that ran through all 1970s debates: 'Are some differences more basic than others?'[2] One of the issues here is whether feminism can survive as a radical politics if it gives up on a hierarchy of theory. Feminists have moved from grand theory to local studies, from cross-cultural analyses of patriarchy to the complex and historical interplay of sex, race and class, from notions of a female identity or the interests of women towards the instability of female identity and the active creation and recreation of women's needs or concerns. Part of what drops out in these movements is the assumption of a pre-given hierarchy of causation waiting only to be uncovered. Do such developments then leave feminists with nothing general to say?

Such questions are not resolved by the essays in this collection. But all the contributions are informed by a clear sense of feminism as a politics as well as a theory, and together they do much to dislodge accusations that feminist politics has lost its way. At the theoretical level, they continue a dialogue across the 1970s and 1990s divide. Among the contributors, Sylvia Walby takes a position most clearly speaking 'for' the continued validity of the theoretical vocabulary of the modernist (macro-sociological) moment. But many others speak across the defining positions of the period, arguing, for example, that feminism must retain the political impetus implied in the aspiration towards universality; or noting the potential losses attached to any wholesale abandonment of those areas of study traditionally associated with sociology or political economy. One of the functions of presenting a debate of this kind is to show that to some extent there are issues that go back and forth over time, and that determining the novelty or originality of arguments can therefore be difficult.

In considering the relative strengths of 1970s and 1990s feminism, we do not put forward a single shared perspective, but would warn against two of the possible responses. We should certainly reject the simplistic teleology of assuming that later theory is therefore better theory, and that the best theory of all is the position from which we happen at the moment to be speaking. This model of theoretical progress, strongly influenced by a Marxist conception of thesis, antithesis and synthesis, is quintessentially nineteenth-century and modernist, and is one of which we will do well to be suspicious. On the other hand, we should also resist the strong view from the other side, which argues that nothing new is ever said and that what may look like a paradigm shift is in the end no more than the recycling of old debates in new terms. Neither of these two positions is satisfactory. To claim transcendence is to ignore our own position in history; to reduce debates to their essential content is to deny the power of context and discourse. As Foucault has shown, the question of what can be said, when, and by whom, is of crucial significance.

The question of theoretical progression has become particularly pertinent for contemporary feminism, because of the much discussed 'equality/difference' debate. It is easy enough to cast the 1970s position as a version of the 'equality' pole and the 1980s one as representing the 'difference' pole of the dichotomy. Much contemporary feminist thought has moved on from this to question the binary structures around which such arguments revolve. The critique of dichotomies, of dualisms, of falsely either/or alternatives, has become a major theme in feminist writing. Moira Gatens argues here, for example, that the school of *écriture féminine* is not (as is often said) an essentialist 'difference' position but seeks to make the much more radical move of destabilizing the binary opposition of equality/difference itself. Joan Scott, taking critique of the opposition itself further, has eloquently explained how the choice between equality and difference is a disabling one for feminists: 'the antithesis itself hides the interdependence of the two terms, for equality is not the elimination of difference, and difference does not preclude equality.' Scott concludes that we should *refuse* the opposition, in the name of an equality that rests on differences.[3]

Destabilizing the equality/difference opposition might also lead us to wonder at how busily feminists have constructed a false polarity over which to divide ourselves. For difference is not an absolute, but constructed in varying ways according to what is perceived as salient in a particular context. More intractable, however, has been the issue of whether, or how, feminists can or should destabilize the binary opposition between men and women that gives the category woman its meaning. As Denise Riley has pointed out, 'woman' is indeed an unstable category but one whose instabilities are none other than the subject matter of feminist politics.[4] To obliterate the men/women opposition is thus a move that pulls the rug from under feminist struggle, as such.

This point returns us to the ambiguous status of theory. The concepts and categories through which we appropriate, analyse and construct the world have a history within which we are ourselves implicated. Some of the resistance to the ideas and vocabularies of 'post'-structuralism, 'post'-modernism or 'post'-Enlightenment thought stem from this insight. For beyond the simpler resistance of those who have found all they need in the theorizations of an earlier moment lies a more troubled recognition that these theoretical discourses construct and are inscribed within the world they have helped to make. Feminism – as Griselda Pollock concludes her essay – is 'an intervention in history, informed by historical knowledges, which means not forgetting, in the act of necessary critique, the history of western feminism'. For feminism, there is no complete escape from a modernist history of an egalitarian, and emancipatory, movement.

Finally, the critique of modernist and universalistic thought does not reduce the importance of formulating a new basis for feminist political aspiration. Feminists have moved a long way from denying towards asserting specificity and difference, and have in the course of these shifts encountered the limitations as well as the value of a politics based on identities. Forging a commonality across difference now figures as a goal rather than a given: a process – as Chandra Talpade Mohanty puts it – of engagement rather than discovery. The strategic questions that face contemporary feminism are now informed by a much richer understanding of heterogeneity and diversity; but they continue to revolve around the alliances, coalitions and commonalities that give meaning to the idea of feminism.

### NOTES

1  Susan Bordo, 'Feminism, Postmodernism, and Gender-Scepticism', in Linda Nicholson (ed.), *Feminism/Postmodernism* (Routledge, London, 1990), pp. 133–56; p. 149.
2  Christine di Stefano, 'Dilemmas of Difference: Feminism, Modernity and Postmodernism', in Nicholson, *Feminism/Postmodernism*, pp. 63–82; p. 78.
3  Joan Scott, 'Deconstructing Equality-Versus-Difference', in Marianne Hirsch and Evelyn Fox Keller (eds), *Conflicts in Feminism* (Routledge, New York and London, 1990), pp. 138, 146.
4  Denise Riley, *'Am I That Name?': Feminism and the Category of 'Women' in History* (Macmillan, Basingstoke, 1988), p. 5.

# 2

# Universal Pretensions in Political Thought

## *Anne Phillips*

Early feminist arguments – dating back considerably before the French Revolution, but much strengthened by the events of 1789 – often conceived political priorities in terms of extending to women those rights and equalities that were being asserted as the birthright of men. Women applied to themselves rules that were originally formulated for a more limited constituency, and insisted on making universal what had started out far more particular. The case frequently rested on notions of a common humanity, some essential self all human beings share regardless of any differences by sex. And the arguments continually contrasted what men and women currently, historically, contingently are with what under different conditions they might hope to become. Feminists looked beyond the specificities of existing culture and society (cultures and societies in which women might well appear the inferiors of men) to a more transcendent rationality and justice.

This approach embraced key elements of Enlightenment thinking. The belief in an essential human equality despite all secondary differences; the scepticism towards prejudice and tradition; the confidence in external standards of rationality and justice against which to measure the world: all these formed an important context for feminist principles and debate. And while in this period – as it seems in every other – feminism contained within itself a double impetus towards both equality *and* difference, what we might term the universal aspiration towards an essentially human equality was always one part of the scene.

This kind of political argument has of course become increasingly contentious in recent discussion, with the Enlightenment turning into a code-word for everything we ought to distrust. Michel Foucault has taught us to view the autonomous and rational self as an insidious form of thought-police; Alasdair MacIntyre has trampled heavily over the pretensions of universal rationality, arguing that all notions of morality and reason are grounded in particular historical traditions;[1] Richard Rorty has freed us from the search for philosophical authority only to dump us on the ground of local contingency where anything or nothing goes.[2] In one way or another, most political theorists have had to deal with the critique of transcendent universals, the debate between classical and communitarian liberalism, the tension between Kantian and contextual moralities, the anti-foundationalism of post-modern approaches, the importance of grounding one's theories of justice in the value structures of the surrounding world. In a range of overlapping but not identical discussions, the Enlightenment has been getting itself a pretty bad name.

These moves against transcultural, transhistorical, transcendent rationality have their counterpart in recent feminist debate, for after so many sightings of the 'man' in humanity, many have come to view such abstractions as beyond redemption, and to regard any claims to universality as therefore and inevitably a fraud. Each candidate for universal status has presented itself in sharp contrast to the peculiarities and particularities of local identity, something that delves behind our specificity and difference and can therefore stand in for us all. But the 'individual' turns out again and again to be a male household head, the 'citizen' a man of arms, the 'worker' an assembly line slave. Each gender-neutral abstraction ends up as suspiciously male.

Feminist patience has worn thin, and there has been a significant (if by no means united) movement away from the abstract universals of the Enlightenment tradition and towards a new emphasis on heterogeneity, diversity and difference. Two crucial arguments have featured in this shift. The first is that in insisting on equality as something we claim *despite* all differences, women have been encouraged to deny aspects of themselves and to conform to some unitary norm; the second is that this norm was never gender-neutral. Thus Carole Pateman has argued, in a variety of influential texts, that 'citizenship has been made in the male image',[3] and that the belated inclusion of women operates very differently from the original inclusion of men. Sexual differentiation was built into the foundations of modern (that is, seventeenth-century onwards) political thought, in ways that have lasting consequences for the very categories through which we think our lives.

In *The Sexual Contract*, for example, Pateman notes that we have inherited a version of free contract between individuals as justifying anything these individuals might do. They can dispose of themselves and their bodies as they deem fit, and as long as the contracts they enter into can be shown to be voluntary, there is no legitimate basis for anyone's complaint. Applied to women, this then justifies prostitution, and in recent cases, the legal enforcement of surrogacy contracts even if the mother later changes her mind. The crucial point for Pateman is that contemporary notions of the individual, and by extension of free contract, express a masculine presumption that treats the body as separable from the self. So while some (mainly US) feminists have toyed with 'genuinely gender-free contract' as a weapon they might turn to their advantage, this is too much imbued with the assumptions of a masculine world.

> The logic of contract as exhibited in 'surrogate' motherhood shows very starkly how extension of the standing of 'individual' to women can reinforce and transform patriarchy as well as challenge patriarchal institutions. To extend to women the masculine conception of the individual as owner, and the conception of freedom as the capacity to do what you will with your own, is to sweep away any intrinsic relation between the female owner, her body and reproductive capacities. She stands to her property in exactly the same external relation as the male owner stands to his labour power or sperm; there is nothing distinctive about womanhood.[4]

One implication, Pateman argues, is that when feminists contest previous theories of what is appropriate to women or appropriate to men, they must be wary of the concepts they bring to their aid. Most importantly, they should resist the impulse towards denying that sex matters. Sexual differentiation is already writ large in political theory, in a manner that has so far served men. The solution is not to eliminate all such references, but to recast the story with both sexes on stage. Human identity is sexually differentiated, and exists in a bodily form. Those who seek to deny the body, who deal only in the abstraction of 'the individual' or 'the citizen', who think it should make no difference whether these individuals are women or men, will be writing in one sex alone as their standard. Women can be encompassed on an equality with men only if sexual difference is first of all acknowledged.

In the links that have been forged between feminism and postmodernism, such arguments have been pushed further along: emphasizing not so much sexual difference as the multiple differences that any theory must take on board. Nancy Fraser and Linda Nicholson see feminism as exposing 'the contingent, partial and ahistorically situated character of what has passed in the mainstream for necessary, universal, and ahistorical truths' and as leading us to query the kind of objectivity that resides in a transcendent 'God's eye view'.[5] They go on to argue that we must equally well question the notion of 'a' woman's perspective, 'a' feminist standpoint or 'a' root cause of women's oppression. If the universalisms of humanity are suspect, so too are the universalisms of gender, or those most dubious essentialisms of 'woman' or 'women'. The tendency towards universality sometimes crops up as unthinking assumption, sometimes as grand aspiration, but in either case it should be firmly resisted.

The arguments seem to overlap with issues that have arisen in mainstream political debate, and my starting point in this paper is to draw attention to these parallels. In particular, I want to comment on the common criticism that both these developments provoke. In each case, the move away from grand theory and towards a more specific, historically grounded, or else gendered, account, has laid itself open to complaints of incipient conservatism. In feminist literature, the danger most recurrently cited is that of losing the theoretical categories (gender, patriarchy, even women) through which we can understand and then challenge the world;[6] the subsidiary critique, which then applies preeminently to those who stress sexual rather than multiple differences, is that we may lose the capacity for transforming current gender relations. In mainstream theory, the emphasis has been more exclusively on the notions of justice or rationality that can give us any critical purchase on the communities within which we live. When people query the universalizing pretensions of previous traditions, do they thereby limit their radical potential, and blunt the edge of any critical attack?

I raise this problem without necessarily resolving it: partly because we need more work on exploring the precise degree of overlap between feminist and mainstream developments; partly because of the perennial difficulties in deducing politics from philosophical positions; partly because I want to query the sharpness with which the alternatives get posed. I argue, that is, against a polar opposition between what is abstract, impartial, gender-neutral, and what is specific, relational, engendered; and I suggest that the best in contemporary feminism is already steering a more middle route.

## COMMUNITARIAN AND POST-MODERN CRITICS

In the last decade of political theory, there has been a powerful move against 'grand theory', and especially against the kind of abstract theorizing that deduces principles of rights or justice from metaphysical assumptions that have their foundations only in thought. An increasingly preferred alternative is what has been described as the 'communitarian' approach, a perspective that grounds our moral and political beliefs in the experience of specific communities, and challenges the false abstractions of 'the' individual. Within this rather broadly defined (and by no means unitary) tradition, attention has shifted from establishing universally applicable standards of morality or justice towards elucidating the principles that are already present within any given society. The result is, to use Michael Walzer's words, 'radically particularist'.[7] Notions of justice are said to exist already as part of a community's shared intuitive beliefs, but they are often hidden or latent, and need to be brought into more direct light. Grounded as they are in historically specific communities, however, they cannot claim any universal relevance or scope. Nor do they need to. Richard Rorty argues, in his *Contingency, irony, and solidarity*, that human solidarity does not depend on a quaintly metaphysical notion of 'humanity' or 'human nature'. It develops rather in those widening ripples of sympathy that make it 'more difficult to marginalize people different from ourselves'.[8] People sympathize across difference, rather than because of some basic humanity we might like to think we all share.

The parallel between feminist and mainstream developments has been noted,[9] as has the major distinction, which is that only the feminists engage with the specific differences of sex. The comparison is instructive, for where feminists have employed their critiques of universality to radical effect, the work of mainstream theorists reveals a more conservative side. Think, for example, of Alasdair MacIntyre, who in his celebration of Aristotle or Aquinas is hardly the feminist's best friend.[10] His critique of liberalism seems well placed, if anything, to confirm the waverer in her commitment to Enlightenment ideals, for he manages to present the tradition in its most attractive light.

MacIntyre notes that the theorists of the Enlightenment expected reason to displace authority and tradition, and he describes the project of modern liberal, individualist society as 'founding a form of social order in which individuals could emancipate themselves from the contingency and particularity of tradition by appealing to genuinely universal, tradition-independent norms'.[11] This may not appeal to MacIntyre, but it holds obvious attractions for the social critic, who is impatient with the world as it is. Her interest in modernity is likely to be further enhanced by the contrast MacIntyre has drawn between the heroic and the modern age. In heroic society, he argues, people's sense of moral obligation is at one with their place in the social structure: 'for the given rules which assign men their place in the social order and with it their identity also prescribe what they owe and what is owed to them and how they are to be treated and regarded if they fail and how they are to treat and regard others if they fail.'[12] 'The self of the heroic age lacks precisely that characteristic which . . . some modern moral philosophers take to be an essential characteristic of human selfhood: the capacity to detach oneself from any particular standpoint or point of view, to step backwards, as it were, and view and judge that standpoint or point of view from the outside.'[13]

Against this attractive view of modernity, MacIntyre's main defence is that the project cannot and will not succeed. It sets up what is an impossible goal, and it is the failure to achieve what they should never have attempted that plunged modern theorists into the babble of emotivism and the trading in moral fictions. Through his historical investigation of different traditions of enquiry, MacIntyre claims to have established that our standards of judgement are always and inevitably formed within, and given their meaning by, the particular traditions of which we are part. For those who might think this a recipe for complacency (if we are stuck within our tradition how do we criticize its norms?) his response is that, in generating its own standards of rational enquiry, each tradition has engaged in self-criticism and revision – and sometimes defeated itself as a result.

Richard Rorty is equally dismissive of the search for universal, tradition-independent norms, though he goes much further than MacIntyre in accepting *no* authority for his most heart-felt beliefs. Neither capital-letter Reason, nor the rationality-of-this-particular-tradition: Rorty is happy to detach his liberalism from any kind of grounding and accept its force as just historically contingent. Liberals have relied too long – and unnecessarily – on a notion of the common humanity that human beings are said to share, and should now feel free to dispense with this prop. There is no more a universal human nature than there is a universal truth or a universal justice. Our beliefs are local and particular and contingent, but this does not mean we are stuck with no progress or change. For Rorty, it is imagination rather than reason that acts to extend our sensibilities and our understanding of others; it is literature rather than philosophy that increases our awareness of what causes people pain. Philosophy has sent us on a fruitless search for the 'something' that is common to us all – and then hardly knows where to turn when faced with extraordinary difference. Literature, by contrast, develops our skills in imaginative identification, helping us 'extend our sense of "we" to people whom we have previously thought of as "they".'[14]

The emphasis on literature is certainly compelling, as is the sensitivity to what is positive and progressive about difference. But as critics recurrently note, Rorty's imaginative acrobatics in the realms of theory seem to combine with the most commonplace complacencies when he turns to the western liberal tradition. 'How', as Nancy Fraser asks, 'can such critical metaphilosophical views sit so comfortably with complacent political attitudes?'[15] As one of those pursuing the links between feminism and post-modernism, Fraser finds Rorty's emphasis on the contingent and historically conditioned character of subjectivities and rationalities very much 'user-friendly' – something that seems 'open to the potentially transformative voices and aspirations of subordinated social groups'.[16] How can this combine with a smug 'bourgeois liberalism' that has so little purchase on feminist concerns?

The question becomes more pressing when we consider which of the strands in contemporary political theory have proved themselves most sensitive to issues of women's inequality. Despite the common ground that has been cleared between feminists and those bunched together under the rubric of communitarians (I do not include Rorty in this designation), the latter have been notable, if anything, for their incomprehension of feminist concerns. None of the leading figures in contemporary political theory has turned his critical eye on the structure of the family,[17] and it has been left to those more wedded to universalizing abstraction to raise the banner of equality between women and men. To give just one example, Will Kymlicka relies extensively on the situation of women when he defends liberalism against its critics, and uses this to make some telling points about the conservatism implicit in the communitarian approach.[18]

Kymlicka readily concedes the absurdities of abstract individualism, pausing only to observe how little foundation there is for believing that liberals ever held such a view. The crucial point for him is not whether we can imagine a self without attachments, but whether it is possible to detach ourselves from *particular* values or practices or goals. Are we so constituted by the traditions of our own society that it is for ever impossible for us to judge of their worth? Are we so constrained by the shared morality of our own period and community that our assertions on what is wrong only mean 'we don't do that sort of thing around here'? What then, he asks, of the Muslim woman in Egypt who says sexual discrimination is wrong? 'She does *not* mean "we don't do that around here". On the contrary, she is saying this precisely because it *is* done around there, and always has been done, and is very firmly embedded in all the myths, symbols, and institutions of their society and history.'[19]

In mainstream political theory, the move away from universal principles and values has laid itself open to the charge of incipient conservatism, and this worrying potential provides a backdrop to the discussion of feminist theory. Not that the criticisms that apply to one development necessarily apply to the other: we need much fuller exploration of the level of convergence before we can confidently comment on this. Nor indeed that philosophy and politics always go hand in hand: I have serious doubts as to how far one can deduce a political position from the conditions of a philosophical stance. But in considering current debates within feminist political theory, it is important to bear these parallels in mind. Those who seek to change the world will always need concepts that can give them a critical distance from the relations within which they live. If this is so, then how much is at risk in moves against abstract individualism, universal values, impartial justice? Is there a danger that such feminisms could lose their necessary distance?

### ENGENDERING OR DEGENDERING THEORY?

I commented earlier that the shift within feminism away from the abstract universals of the Enlightenment tradition, and towards a new emphasis on difference and differences, was significant but by no means united; and it would be seriously misleading to present 'sexual difference' as if it were the only or even dominant approach. There is substantial agreement that conventional political thought has offered us men in a gender-free guise, and that all the talk of universal rights or citizenship or rules has taken one sex alone as its standard, leaving the other one out in the cold. The starting point for much of this discussion is the distinction between public and private spheres, which, along with the relentless allocation of men to the first and women to the second, was early identified as the crucial underpinning to patriarchal political thought.[20] Feminist excavation in the classical texts showed this as the major sleight of hand that had excluded women from centuries of debate on citizenship, equality, freedom and rights, for having been subordinated to men in the private sphere they were then subsumed under men in the public. Women were thus rendered politically invisible. In text after text, the classical theorists equated the 'individual' with the male head of household, and gave him exclusive enjoyment of any subsequent rights or powers.

The question then arises: how to correct for this bias towards men?

While some feminists reject the unitary model altogether, others see the task as making the theories consistent with a genuinely gender-free world. Two examples from a recent collection on *Feminist Interpretations and Political Theory*[21] illustrate the range. In a devastating critique of John Rawls's *Theory Of Justice*, Susan Moller Okin takes him to task for the kind of substitution one might imagine that only the classical writers would make: talking of individuals, but then presuming they are male household heads.[22] Rawls postulated what he called an 'original position' from which individuals were asked to consider the kind of principles they would consider fair and just, no matter what their own social standing then turned out to be. If people were kept in temporary ignorance of their own class position, of their wealth, intelligence or strength, if they could not then anticipate whether they would end up in the top ten per cent or the bottom, what choices would they make about the best system for distributing social and economic advantage? Okin points out that sex is the notable exception in all the lists of attributes people are required to ignore; and that this sex-blindness is compounded when Rawls simply assumes that the family is just.

Despite her criticisms, Okin none the less defends the 'original position' as a brilliant idea that 'forces one to question and consider traditions, customs, and institutions from all points of view.'[23] This, she argues, could be pushed towards far more radical conclusions, for hidden within its distortions is something that can argue against gender differentiation, and become a way of challenging sexual subordination itself. If justice requires us to think outside of our own personal experience and perspective, then justice may not be compatible with a society that so systematically divides the experiences of women and men. A major precondition for a just society may be eliminating the inequalities between women and men.

Okin thus develops Rawls's argument to what she sees as a logical conclusion, and applies it to sexual relations as well. Yet in the same collection of essays, Moira Gatens stresses the problems Mary Wollstonecraft encountered when she tried to do just this to eighteenth-century principles of equality. Wollstonecraft neglected to note 'that these principles were developed and formulated with men as their object.'[24] From Gatens' perspective, there is limited mileage in a paradigm that posits sexual equality only at the price of sexual neutrality – and she regards neutrality more as 'neutering', as trying to wish bodily difference away. In a particularly striking phrase, she describes the liberal paradigm as offering fair and equal treatment only 'to those activities that *simulate* the neutral subject',[25] and thus having little to say on such matters as rape, domestic violence or enforced pregnancy, where it is precisely women's bodies that are involved. In both political and moral theory, Gatens argues, we have to come to terms with bodily specificity.

The contest these examples indicate has been conducted on a number of terrains – including equality, justice, political representation – and in each case one of the main objections to those who emphasize difference is that they have overplayed their hand. If universal values do indeed impose a masculine norm, then this may be admitted as a problem. But is this really the case? Defending the concept of equality as a central component in feminist thought, Richard Norman, for example, argues that there has been too much confusion of 'equality' with 'identity' or 'uniformity', and that being equal never meant all people being regarded as the same.[26] Defending the universal scope of justice, Onora O'Neill likewise argues that feminists have misrepresented justice as 'not merely universal but uniform', and have failed to see how much it already embraces and acknowledges difference.[27] As should become clear, I have considerable sympathy with these points, and do not see the issue as an either/or choice. But the feminist debate on difference has been more nuanced than such criticisms suggest, and it deals with important substantive concerns.

EQUALITY, JUSTICE, REPRESENTATION

The first of these refers to an issue that has long been a focus of feminist concern, which is whether women can achieve social and economic equality with men by insisting that sex should not matter. What, for example, should be the principles that inform equality legislation, and particularly any legislation for achieving equality at work? Should women be calling for sex-specific legislation that builds in protections for (say) pregnant women; or should they be opposing discriminatory legislation that makes any difference between women and men? In the United States this dilemma has arisen most recently over the issue of maternity leave; in Britain it has emerged in considering the remnants of nineteenth-century 'protective' legislation; in virtually any history of the nineteenth- and twentieth-century women's movements it comes out in a tension between those who ground their policies in equality and those who ground them in difference.[28]

In *The Female Body and the Law*, Zillah Eisenstein argues that such dilemmas arise because the man is being taken as the norm, from which the woman deviates at her peril.[29] The male has been the reference point in all our phallocratic discourse, and discussions of even sexual equality continue to privilege his body. Women can say they want to be treated the same – but this means being treated as if they were men; or they can demand laws that are specific to their needs – but this means being compensated for their lesser abilities or role. The fact is that the norm is already sexually specific; and Eisenstein argues for a new version of equality that no longer depends on us all being the same. One point she stresses is that we do not resolve the problem by going only for 'the' sexual difference. We should think rather of a plurality of many differences, so that equality becomes compatible with diversity instead of forcing us into the self-same mould. It is not that all men are different from all women ('women get pregnant, men don't'), for there are multiple differences between women as well as multiple differences between men. It does not help to define women through their capacity for childbearing, and the dichotomy of male *or* female can be as destructive as having to fit within a male-defined norm.

The argument suggests a very radical pluralism, in which seemingly endless differences by sex, race, age, class, culture . . . all have to be taken into account. An obvious complaint would be that this emphasis leads us away from being able even to think of equality, for if people are so complex and diverse it seems impossible to conceive of them as in any sense being treated the same. Eisenstein tries to steer a careful middle way, however, between two options, arguing that equality 'must encompass generalization, abstraction and homogeneity as well as individuality, specificity, and heterogeneity'.[30] It is not a matter of ditching all the abstract universals and putting concrete difference in their place. We cannot do without some notion of what human beings have in common; we can and must do without a unitary standard against which they are all judged.

This seems to me the right approach, though I am left with an uneasy suspicion as to whether it is so radically different from what people already practise and believe. As Onora O'Neill observes, we are all equally liable to taxes but we pay differently according to what we earn: the notion of a unitary standard which is then varied in its applications is not such a novel idea. It may be that the legislative and judicial debates in the USA have been peculiarly blinkered in applying a unitary norm; and that experience elsewhere (in countries, for example, where the equal right to work is thought perfectly consistent with provision for maternity leave) already indicates a more complex approach.

The second set of debates, around the concept of justice, centres on a contrast between male abstraction and female specificity, and draws much of its sustenance from Carol Gilligan's *In A Different Voice*. From a series of studies that look at the way children and adults respond to both real and hypothetical dilemmas, Gilligan has suggested that men and women have different conceptions of morality. The former, she argues, are typically guided by an ethic of rights that rests on a fair application of abstract rules, while the latter are guided by what she terms an ethic of responsibility, that tries to enter into each person's dilemma and contextualize differences in need.

> The morality of rights is predicated on equality and centered on the understanding of fairness, while the ethic of responsibility relies on the concept of equity, the recognition of differences in need. While the ethic of rights is a manifestation of equal respect, balancing the claims of other and self, the ethic of responsibility rests on an understanding that gives rise to compassion and care.[31]

Much previous work in this area had operated with a developmental hierarchy, which treated the ethic of responsibility as a lesser stage, and Gilligan turns this round to argue that these express different notions of what justice is about.

Gilligan does not treat the differences as innate (though her work can certainly lend weight to a more essentialist feminism that then accepts such differences as given), nor does she necessarily assert one ethic as superior to the other. In a sympathetic review of her position, Seyla Benhabib argues that we need both.[32] The notion of impartial justice (the 'male' standpoint of what Benhabib calls the generalized other) implies being able to put oneself in another's shoes, and hence acknowledge his or her entitlement to whatever rights or considerations we might claim for ourselves. But this makes no sense unless we can also take the standpoint of the concrete other, for until we know the individual's concrete and specific history, we are not yet in a position to say whether it is like or unlike our own.

This is the point at which Onora O'Neill's reservations become relevant again, for is this a radically new position or a restatement of what people already try to do? If we think of a typical jury trial, for example, the jurors are surely required to take both these standpoints together, for while they are enjoined on the one hand to lay aside their prejudices and act as impartially as is within their power, they are provided on the other with often detailed accounts of the defendant's position. They are usually expected to take these into account. More precisely perhaps, the jury is supposed to operate by impartial rules, while the sentencing can be tailored to difference. But as O'Neill puts it: 'Justice is not uniform; care is not unprincipled.'[33] If this is right, then instead of transforming existing assumptions, feminism may just be helping to make them more explicit.

I think this is partly true, and that there *is* an element of misrepresentation in the way some feminists have analysed conventional notions of what is just. Iris Young, for example, rightly argues that 'feminist analyses of the dichotomy between public and private in modern political theory imply that the idea of the civic public as impartial or universal is itself suspect';[34] but perhaps overstates her case when she suggests that justice is normally thought of as something totally opposed to feeling. Being impartial is indeed associated with being dispassionate, but not with 'being entirely unaffected by feelings in one's judgement'.[35] On the contrary, feelings provide much of the substance of our notions of right and wrong ('I don't know why I feel like this, but it just seems wrong to me'); though in most notions of justice (whether they are taken from common sense or from high theory) we are then expected to examine these feelings for special pleading or inconsistency. This is not a matter of 'expelling' feeling, but it does mean recognizing that people can be too much swayed by their own personal experience. As one of the recurrent objects of unthinking prejudice, women would be ill-served by any 'justice' that gave up on that.

Feminists have not on the whole argued *against* impartiality, but for a more complex and balanced appreciation of the relationship between emotion and abstract reason, as well as between what makes us different and what it is we all share. But then the critics may be right: that this is not such a novel position as it is sometimes claimed to be; and that while it illuminates weaknesses in some contemporary political thought, it does not reverse all existing positions. If feminists take up the high ground of empathy and emotion versus abstract and impartial reason, they are, I believe, wrong. If they situate themselves more firmly in the middle ground, they may be right but not so profoundly original. To link this back to Zillah Eisenstein's arguments on equality, if feminists argue that we should concentrate on the differences between us *instead* of those things we all share, they risk losing the language for even talking about people being equal. But if they argue (as she does) that equality must encompass homogeneity as well as heterogeneity, they may not be saying anything dramatically new.

I have been discussing this as if there were unanimity among feminist political theorists, but positions on justice in particular reflect varying positions about whether sexual difference should be made explicit or else expunged. In her discussion of Rawls, Susan Moller Okin describes a wonderfully pertinent cartoon. 'Three elderly, robed male justices are depicted, looking down with astonishment at their very pregnant bellies. One says to the others, without further elaboration: "Perhaps we'd better reconsider that decision".'[36] The question she raises is what makes it possible for people to enter imaginatively into the position of others, and whether we can fully do this while society is still structured by gender? Her own conclusion goes against the growing emphasis on sexual difference: 'that not only is gender incompatible with the attainment of social justice, in practice, for members of both sexes, but that the disappearance of gender is a prerequisite for the *complete* development of a nonsexist, fully human *theory* of justice.'[37]

An obvious point of criticism would be that pregnancy is a 'difference' that cannot be eliminated, and that, however much we might welcome the disappearance of those structures that direct women to certain kinds of work and men to others, no amount of equalization within household and wage work is going to make the male judges have babies. Is Okin then just capitulating to the notion that difference is the problem, instead of accepting it as a reality and getting the theories to adjust? I think not, for as long as people are scheduled from birth into the range of possibilities deemed appropriate to their sex, then the dominant notions of justice and fairness will be *more* dictated by difference than anyone could reasonably desire. It is one thing to argue for heterogeneity and diversity to be written into our theories of equality and justice; it is quite another to accept 'the' difference and rearrange our thinking around that. And one of the things this indicates to me is that, notwithstanding the conceptual difficulties feminists have raised around the distinction between sex and gender, we will continue to need some way of disentangling the differences that are inevitable from those that are chosen, and from those that are simply imposed.

The final area of debate I want to comment on relates to issues of political representation. Feminists have frequently noted the extraordinary under-representation of women within both elected and non-elected elites, and here they come up against a powerful swathe of opinion that says sex should be an irrelevant consideration. At the simplest level, this surfaces in arguments that say we should choose our representatives by the way they reflect our views, and that whether these people are male or female should not figure as a legitimate concern. At a more complex level, it surfaces in what is otherwise a radically democratic view: the idea that citizenship should transcend the privatized and fragmented interests of the dominant corporate world.

In another of her works, Iris Young argues that radical democrats often uphold the most transcendent of universal views, and that they thereby reveal themselves as being as much untouched by gender as the orthodoxies they set out to demolish.[38] This is at its most apparent when writers appeal to a notion of universal *rather* than particular interests, and argue that politics should be dealing with what are common rather than private concerns. Those who develop such arguments may be primarily concerned to criticize the subservience to private economic interest, but when they present the public realm as the antithesis to the differentiated 'private' world, the argument gets extended to all other aspects of the private sphere.[39] Any kind of local affiliation is then seen as a problem, and group interest or identity are thought of as something we should be trying to transcend. When citizens participate in political decisions, they are expected to aim at the kind of impartial general will that will take them beyond their own personal concerns. As Iris Young puts it, they are being called upon to leave their selves behind.

The crucial point she makes is that this celebration of universal against particular values can all too easily serve the interests of dominant groups. 'In a society where some groups are privileged while others are oppressed, insisting that as citizens persons should leave behind their particular affiliations and experiences to adopt a general point of view serves only to reinforce that privilege: for the perspectives and interests of the privileged will tend to dominate this unified public, marginalizing or silencing those of other groups.'[40] It is, that is, the old, old story. Appealing to the grandest principles of abstract rationality and universal concern, political theorists write in men once again.

Iris Young then draws on the notion of group difference to present an alternative view. As long as some groups are privileged and others oppressed (she offers a range of criteria by which we might judge whether a group is oppressed), then there should be mechanisms for representing the distinct voices and perspectives of those who are at a political disadvantage. Not for the privileged: they are already well served by the existing structures and mechanisms of power. But public money should be made available to support the 'group' representation of the others. They should be given the means to organize themselves as a group; they should be guaranteed a voice in social policy-making when decisions are being taken that may affect their group; and – most controversial of all – they should have veto power over those decisions that specifically and directly affect their group.

An alternative version of introducing group difference into the political realm has been suggested by those who look to quotas as a way of getting more women elected. This is considerably more developed (both in discussion and implementation) in parts of northern Europe like Norway, Sweden and Denmark, where women have achieved marked success in persuading their political parties to operate either a formal or an informal quota, thus guaranteeing women a substantial share of those seats that the party wins. Mechanisms for increasing women's representation in politics fall a long way short of what Iris Young proposes, and most obviously in leaving out any procedure through which these women then 'represent' a group. They are less open, on the other hand, to the difficulties in ascertaining what any group 'really' wants.[41] Both approaches, however, reject the dominant convention that politics is a matter for abstract individuals, for persons of insignificant sex.

If there is some uncertainty as to how much the focus on difference transforms existing perspectives on justice, there is no such question mark here. Substantial and practical implications would flow from treating people as members of variously privileged or oppressed groups, and from stressing the things that differentiate them rather than the abstract humanity or citizenship they might be said to share. But as with issues of equality and justice, the difficult questions turn on how far one would want to go; and in this case what balance one might hope to achieve between the ideals of the universal citizen and the reality of group differentiation. There is a powerful attraction in the notion of politics as an activity in which we get outside of ourselves, putting our own personal and group interests into a more general perspective. Any alternative approach suggests a battle between vested interests which the larger groups will inevitably win. Iris Young explicitly contests this implication, arguing that her own emphasis on group representation is entirely compatible with, and indeed will enhance, a revitalized public life. Existing interest groups, she argues, tend to press their own interests as forcibly as they can, without any acknowledgement that they need consider others. In contrast to this, her 'heterogeneous public' would be constantly reminding people that social justice means considering the position of each oppressed group, and would thereby encourage them towards those decisions that are the most just. In this sense, it would not become a matter of universal values versus group difference, but of building unity without denying social difference.

### THE ASPIRATION TOWARDS UNIVERSALITY

Commenting recently on the debate between liberalism and its communitarian critics, Michael Walzer has suggested that the two strands exist in an almost symbiotic relationship, and that 'insofar as liberalism tends towards instability and dissociation, it requires periodic communitarian correction.'[42] The one, that is, recurrently calls forth the other, in a cycle that has no victor and can anticipate no ultimate end. Much the same can be said of debates within feminist theory. In one version or another, there has been a perennial see-saw between the universalizing aspirations of equality ('my sex does not matter, for I am human, just like you') and the assertion of sexual difference ('I am a woman, and that does not make me less equal'). This endlessly recycled opposition is currently transposed into the language of universality versus specificity, but the issues remain broadly the same. Each generation of feminism throws up and debates these competing approaches, each side then moderating the other's extremes.

Yet what strikes me in considering the debates on equality, justice or representation is that feminist arguments have been considerably less polarized than critics sometimes suggest. There is of course a great deal of unfinished business between those who view the inadequacies of modern politics in terms of the illegitimate intrusion of gender, and those who see sexual neutrality as a fraud; and we can anticipate much fruitful discussion in the continuation of these debates. But even among those feminists who start from the centrality and intransigence of sexual difference, the arguments are no simple reversal of Enlightenment beliefs.

Some of contemporary feminist theory *does* overplay its hand, presenting the orthodoxy as more straightforwardly abstract and universal than is in fact the case. Some does read as an affirmation of sexual differentiation *against* universal concepts or ideals, and where it does this, I believe it risks losing what has been a powerful weapon against women's subordination or exclusion. But of the writers I have considered in this essay, Carol Gilligan has no need to set the ethic of responsibility *above* the ethic of rights, even if she sometimes seems to be doing just this; Zillah Eisenstein explicitly identifies with a version of equality that embraces both the abstract and the specific, both homogeneity and heterogeneity; and with all her celebration of heterogeneity and differences, Iris Young none the less associates herself with the kind of public life in which groups try to build on an understanding of each other, and do not just press their own specific claims. Those feminists who challenge the universalism of traditional political or moral thought do not just fly off in the opposite direction, and they are at their most persuasive not in counterposing the particular to the general, the sexually specific to the universal, but in emphasizing the interplay between the two. This approach, I believe, substantially alters the pattern of political debate. But it does not alter it as much as we might like to suggest – and if it did so, it would more probably be wrong.

When the orthodox notions of citizenship or equality have incorporated a masculine body, when the very 'individual' of political discourse has been for so long a man, then it is far too risky to carry on uncritically as if these old-style abstractions can express women's highest goals. But as we turn from this towards a greater emphasis on sexual and other kinds of difference, we do not thereby abandon all the universal pretensions of political thought. We can do well enough without an abstract, degendered, 'neutered' individual as the basis for our aspirations and goals. We cannot, however, do without some notion of stretching outside of ourselves, some capacity for self-reflection and self-distance, some imaginative – and more importantly, some practical – movement towards linking up with those who have seemed different. This remnant of the old pretensions is perhaps best described as an aspiration or an impulse towards universality: a recognition of the partial, and potentially confining, nature of all our different and specific identities; a commitment to challenging and transforming the perspectives from which we have previously viewed the world; a politics of greater generality and alliance.

The mistake of much conventional theory has been to see this process as one of delving behind the insignificant differences of being to come up with a purified core. The problem is better approached from the opposite direction: of being able, partly through comparison with those who are different, to reconceptualize what we had considered our essential characteristics as if they were accidents themselves. We do have to detach ourselves (however imperfectly and temporarily) from the crucial facts of our sex, our religion, our nationality, our class, our beliefs, so as to enter imaginatively into experiences that can seem so different from our own. This is not to say that we have to deny these features, but important as sexual/bodily identity is, it is never our only or even essential characteristic. What is central in one context is marginal in another – which is what makes it possible for us to change our perspective.

The pretensions towards a universal truth or universal humanity have been rightly criticized, and the work of many recent feminist theorists has revealed how persistently such abstractions confirm the perspectives of a dominant group. The arguments go further, to cast severe doubt over the possibility of any better abstraction, and to warn against the potentially fruitless pursuit of a genuinely degendered universal. What I call the aspiration towards universality none the less remains. In the reworking of contemporary political theory and ideals, feminism cannot afford to situate itself *for* difference and *against* universality, for the impulse that takes us beyond our immediate and specific difference is a vital necessity in any radical transformation.

NOTES

1  Alasdair MacIntyre, *After Virtue* (Duckworth, London, 1981), and *Whose Justice? Whose Rationality?* (Duckworth, London, 1988).
2  Richard Rorty, *Contingency, irony, and solidarity* (Cambridge University Press, Cambridge, 1989).
3  Carole Pateman, *The Disorder of Women* (Polity Press, Cambridge, 1989), p. 14.
4  Carole Pateman, *The Sexual Contract* (Polity Press, Cambridge, 1988), p. 216.
5  Nancy Fraser and Linda J. Nicholson, 'Social Criticism Without Philosophy: An Encounter Between Feminism and Postmodernism', in Linda J. Nicholson (ed.), *Feminism/Postmodernism* (Routledge, London, 1990), pp. 19–38; p. 26.
6  See, for example, the essays by Nancy Hartsock, Susan Bordo, Christine di Stefano, in Nicholson, *Feminism/Postmodernism*.
7  Michael Walzer, *Spheres of Justice: A Defense of Pluralism and Equality* (Basic Books, New York, 1983), p. xiv.
8  Rorty, *Contingency, irony, and solidarity*, p. xvi.
9  Marilyn Friedman, for example, notes the striking similarity between feminist and communitarian critiques of the abstract individual, but goes on to explore what she sees as more fundamental areas of divergence. See Friedman, 'Feminism and Modern Friendship: Dislocating the Community,' *Ethics*, 99 (1989), pp. 275–90.
10  Nor I think a 'post-modernist', as suggested by Sabina Lovibond in her critical review of his work: see, Lovibond, 'Feminism and Postmodernism', in Roy Boyne and Ali Rattansi (eds), *Postmodernism and Society* (Macmillan, Basingstoke, 1990), pp. 154–86. For a fuller critical discussion, see Susan Moller Okin, *Justice, Gender, and the Family* (Basic Books, New York, 1989), ch. 3.
11  MacIntyre, *Whose Justice? Whose Rationality?*, p. 335.
12  MacIntyre, *After Virtue*, p. 116.

13  Ibid., pp. 118–19.

14  Rorty, *Contingency, irony, and solidarity*, p. 192.

15  Nancy Fraser, *Unruly Practices* (Polity Press, Cambridge, 1989), p. 5. For other critiques of Rorty, see, for example, Richard J. Bernstein, 'One Step Forwards, Two Steps Backward: Richard Rorty on Liberal Democracy and Philosophy', *Political Theory*, 15 (4) (1987), pp. 538–63; Rebecca Comay, 'Interrupting the Conversation: Notes on Rorty', *Telos*, 69 (1986), pp. 119–30; Richard Flathman 'Review of Rorty', *Political Theory*, 18 (2) (1990), pp. 308–12.

16  Fraser, *Unruly Practices*, p. 5.

17  See Okin, *Justice, Gender, and the Family*, for an excellent discussion of this.

18  Will Kymlicka, *Liberalism, Community and Culture* (Clarendon Press, Oxford, 1989). Similar issues are raised by Philip Green in his discussion of Michael Walzer, where he comments that radical particularism might seem less attractive to those who are excluded from the dominant community; and that when it comes to matters of racial and gender inequality, there is a lot of mileage in the old-fashioned universals that stress our right to be treated the same. Green, 'Equality Since Rawls: Objective Philosophers, Subjective Citizens, and Rational Choice', *Journal of Politics*, August (1985), pp. 970–97.

19  Kymlicka, *Liberalism, Community and Culture*, p. 66.

20  For example, Jean Bethke Elshtain, *Public Man, Private Woman: Women In Social and Political Thought* (Princeton University Press, Princeton, N.J., 1981); Carole Pateman, 'Feminist Critiques of the Public/Private Dichotomy', 1983, reprinted in Pateman, *The Disorder of Women*, pp. 118–40.

21  Mary Lyndon Shanley and Carole Pateman (eds), *Feminist Interpretations and Political Theory* (Polity Press, Cambridge, 1991).

22  Susan Moller Okin, 'John Rawls: Justice as Fairness – For Whom?', in Shanley and Pateman, *Feminist Interpretations and Political Theory*, pp. 181–98. This essay is extracted from Okin, *Justice, Gender, and the Family*.

23  Ibid., p. 190.

24  Moira Gatens, '"The Oppressed State of My Sex": Wollstonecraft on Reason, Feeling and Equality', in Shanley and Pateman, *Feminist Interpretations and Political Theory*, pp. 112–28; p. 113.

25  Ibid., p. 127.

26  Richard Norman, 'Socialism, Feminism and Equality', in Peter Osborne (ed.), *Socialism and the Limits of Liberalism* (Verso, London, 1991), pp. 121–138.

27  Onora O'Neill, 'Friends of Difference', *London Review of Books*, 11 (17) (1989).

28  See, for example, Olive Banks, *Faces of Feminism* (Martin Robertson, Oxford, 1981); or, specifically on Britain, Anne Phillips, *Divided Loyalties: Dilemmas Of Sex and Class* (Virago, London, 1987).

29  Zillah Eisenstein, *The Female Body and the Law* (University of California Press, Berkeley, Cal., 1989).

30  Ibid., p. 221.
31  Carol Gilligan, *In A Different Voice* (Harvard University Press, Cambridge, Mass., 1982), pp. 164–5.
32  Seyla Benhabib, 'The Generalized and Concrete Other', in S. Benhabib and D. Cornell (eds), *Feminism As Critique* (Polity Press, Cambridge, 1987), pp. 77–95.
33  O'Neill, 'Friends of Difference'.
34  Iris Young, 'Impartiality and the Civic Public', in Benhabib and Cornell, *Feminism As Critique*, pp. 56–76; p. 66.
35  Ibid., p. 62.
36  Okin, 'John Rawls: Justice as Fairness', p. 190.
37  Ibid., p. 193.
38  Iris Marion Young, 'Polity and Group Difference: A Critique of the Ideal of Universal Citizenship', *Ethics*, 99 (1989), pp. 250–74. See also her *Justice and the Politics of Difference* (Princeton University Press, Princeton New Jersey, 1990).
    of Universal Citizenship', *Ethics*, 99 (1989), pp. 250–74.
39  One of the arguments developed by Carole Pateman is that political theorists frequently talk of a distinction between public and private when referring to the distinction between political and economic; they rarely notice the further distinction that divides both of these from the other private, household, sphere. See, for example, her introduction to *The Disorder Of Women*.
40  Young, 'Polity and Group Difference', p. 257.
41  For a fuller discussion of these issues see Anne Phillips, *Engendering Democracy* (Polity Press, Cambridge, 1991), ch. 3.
42  Michael Walzer, 'The Communitarian Critique of Liberalism', *Political Theory*, 18 (1) (1990), pp. 6–23; p. 21.

# 3

# Post-Post-Modernism?
# Theorizing Social Complexity

## Sylvia Walby

Post-modernism in social theory has fragmented the concepts of sex, 'race' and class, denying the pertinence of overarching theories of patriarchy, racism and capitalism. The post-modernist tendency has a double aspect: it is both a mode of theorization and a form of substantive analysis of gendered, ethnic and class phenomena. This reaction to modernist attempts to capture the nature of the social world in spare, elegant formulations is understandable given some of the simplicities and denials of important differences entailed in the old approach. I shall argue in this paper, however, that the fragmentation has gone too far, resulting in a denial of significant structuring of power, and leading towards mere empiricism.

The fragmentation of macro-analytic concepts in the theorization of 'race', gender and class is a typical part of the post-modernist project. Within each of these fields, there has been a recent move towards arguing that the central category is too internally differentiated to be utilized as a significant unitary concept. Sometimes this has been argued with reference to the other categories, for instance, that women are too divided by ethnicity for the concept of 'women' to be useful.[1] Sometimes the point is made more generally about the number of divisions between women being too great to enable us to utilize the concept of 'patriarchy'.[2] In the field of 'race' and ethnicity it has been suggested that ethnic groups need to be finely differentiated and that the division into black and white hides more than it reveals, since some ethnic minorities do not appear to share the same disadvantages as others. In the debates on class, it has been argued that other divisions – for example, 'consumption cleavages' based on housing – are more important than social class in explaining political behaviour such as voting patterns.[3] Here it has been suggested that divisions over housing tenure, such as owner occupation or tenancy, are better predictors of politics and voting than the 'classic' social divisions over the means of production. The post-modernist aspect of social theory focuses on complexity and denies the coherence of classic analytic concepts such as 'woman', 'class' and 'race'.

There is a substantive as well as a theoretical resonance of post-modernism in social analysis. One instance of this is the argument about a supposed change from organized to disorganized capitalism.[4] Here it is suggested that the social divisions within capitalism are no longer centrally organized in terms of class divisions in the sphere of production, but have become both fragmented and decentralized beyond production into 'consumption'. A related debate is that about the increasing flexibilization of the workforce, where it is argued that monolithic forms of the capital labour relation are being replaced by flexible utilization of various categories of labour.[5] In Britain the journal *Marxism Today* has attempted to catch these themes under the heading, 'new times'.[6]

A further use of the concept of 'post-modern' in social analysis has been its application to particular cultural forms, especially those of architectural design. I have no quarrel with the distinctions between modernist and post-modernist drawn here, which, for instance, contrast the elegant simplicities of modernist skyscrapers with playful post-modernist pastiches which mix different architectural styles. This is not my concern here, but its usage in this context is not inconsistent with other usages of the concept of 'post-modern'.

I use the concept of 'post-modern' broadly to refer to changes which lead to fragmentation on a number of different levels, from substantive social reality to modes of social analysis. It is my claim that these have common features. I am not arguing that post-modernism simply follows on temporally from modernism. Rather it catches an analytic grouping of themes which are current in contemporary social science, the main aspect of which is fragmentation. The reality of or necessity for fragmentation has been argued empirically, and epistemologically. I shall argue that this tendency has been taken too far.

I shall be arguing that while the social relations involved in gender, 'race' and class have indeed changed, and while the notion of 'new times' does have some purchase on the world and the concept of 'flexibility' has some uses, the post-modernist argument has been taken too far in the attempt to disintegrate the concepts of gender and 'race' and to see capitalism as disorganized. Gender and 'race', or more precisely, patriarchy and racism, remain potent social forces, and capitalism has not withered away despite its new form. Rather than support the idea of the declining significance of 'race'[7] or patriarchy,[8] I shall argue that they remain virulent social divisions. However, I do not wish to argue for a return to the totalizing framework of traditional Marxism, which attempted to tuck all other forms of social inequality under that of class. This extreme modernist meta-narrative I reject as well. I am arguing for mutual determination among the three systems of 'race', class and gender. Despite the call for complex accounts of social change, however, most sociologists in practice analyse at best only two out of the three of gender, 'race' and class, and often only one of these.

Finally, I am arguing for an international perspective. Neither class, nor 'race' nor gender can be understood within one country alone. We live in a world system, which is limited only marginally by national sovereignties. However, this world system is one not only of capitalism (as Wallerstein would argue),[9] but also of racism and of patriarchy.

## POST-MODERNISM AND THE CONCEPTS OF 'WOMAN', 'RACE' AND 'CLASS'

### *Woman and patriarchy*

Within feminist analysis there has been a debate about whether the concepts 'woman' and 'patriarchy' necessarily imply a problematic essentialism. The strongest criticism has been reserved for the concept of 'patriarchy' with its implicit theory of gender inequality; but the notion of 'woman' too has come under attack for similar reasons. The concept of 'patriarchy' is criticized for implying that women's oppression is universal and for being unable to handle historical change.[10] Analyses which use the concept of 'patriarchy' are criticized for being unable to deal with the differences between women, especially those based on class and ethnicity. This criticism is not reserved for those radical feminist analyses which use the concept, but has been extended to Marxist feminist and liberal feminist theory more generally. This wider body of feminist work has been criticized for inadequate appreciation of the significance of ethnic differences and inequalities.[11]

Analyses from the perspective of women of colour have raised a number of important issues for theories of gender relations. First, the labour market experience of women of colour is different from that of white women because of racist structures which disadvantage such women in paid work. This means that there are significant differences between women on the basis of ethnicity, which need to be taken into account. Secondly, ethnic variation and racism mean that the chief sites of oppression of women of colour may be different from those of white women. This is not simply a statement that women of colour face racism which white women do not, but also a suggestion that this may change the basis of gender inequality itself. The best example of this debate is that on the family, which has traditionally been seen by white feminist analysis as a major, if not the major, site of women's oppression by men. Some black feminists, such as hooks,[12] have argued that since the family is a site of resistance and solidarity against racism for women of colour, it does not hold the central place in accounting for women's subordination that it does for white women. This warns against generalizing from the experience of a limited section of women (white) to that of women as a whole. A third issue is that the intersection of ethnicity and gender may alter ethnic and gender relations. Not only is there the question of recognizing ethnic inequality, and the different sites of oppression for women of different ethnicities, but the particular ways in which ethnic and gender relations have interacted historically change the forms of ethnic and gender relations.

Arguments about the differences between women have been taken a step further in the work of cultural studies' post-structuralist theorists. Some post-modernists argue that not only is the concept of patriarchy essentialist but so also is that of 'women'. These post-modern feminists draw theoretically upon the deconstructionism of Derrida,[13] the discourse analysis of Foucault[14] and the post-modernism of Lyotard.[15] For instance, the project of the journal *m/f* was to argue that not only is there no unity to the category of 'woman', but that analyses based on a dichotomy between 'women' and 'men' necessarily suffer from the flaw of essentialism. Instead, there are considered to be a number of overlapping, cross-cutting discourses of femininities and masculinities which are historically and culturally variable. The notion of 'women' and 'men' is dissolved into shifting, variable social constructs which lack coherence and stability over time.[16]

The project for many feminist post-structuralists is to explore the variety of forms of femininity and masculinity. The substantive focus is usually an investigation of the forms of representation of gender in cultural texts such as film, literature, magazines and pictures. These writers try to catch the nuances of different forms of femininities. Following Derrida[17] and Foucault,[18] these writers make a break with the restrictions of the Freudian tradition and its deep structures of the psyche. As in the Lacanian tradition, there is a focus on language and subjectivity. There are two main types of analysis, one following Derrida with a focus on 'difference', and one Foucault with a focus on 'discourse'. Derrida's concept of difference does not allow much conceptual space for power inequalities, while Foucault's notion of discourse has power through knowledge at its heart.[19] Feminist interventions attempt to criticize and rework rather than simply adopt these approaches.

The deconstructionist emphasis, common in the journal *m/f*, takes as its project the breaking down of the unitary notion of 'woman' because of the essentialism it sees behind such a concept.[20] The intellectual project is to examine how the category women is constructed.[21] Early Coward[22] pursues this through an investigation of the multiplicity of discourses of femininity which can be found in contemporary women's magazines. There are many different ways in which 'femininity' is represented. In some, such as *Women's Own* and *Good Housekeeping*, femininity is seen in relation to family roles of cooking, cleaning and child-care. In others, such as *Cosmopolitan*, the focus is on the sexualization of the body of women in the context of successful careers and sexual and economic independence, and references to family roles are almost non-existent. In *Cosmopolitan* the glamour image is continued through the advertisements for related products such as make-up, soaps and body lotions. The film *Emmanuelle* offers yet another form of femininity, in which female sexuality is presented for the voyeuristic male gaze. Coward suggests that *Cosmopolitan* is a site of competing definitions of female sexuality, while that of *Emmanuelle* is foreclosed.

Adams and Minson argue that the subject of feminism is not simply women, since this is an essentialist concept.[23] The emphasis on deconstructing femininity implies that the categories of men and women have no use in a social analysis. Indeed Barrett and Coward argue that the project amounts to denying their existence as categories at all.[24] It is as if only representations can be analysed.

The post-modern critics have made some valuable points about the potential dangers in theorizing gender inequality at an abstract and general level. However, they go too far in their dispersal of identity and power and consequently there are many limitations to their accounts of gender relations. First, they typically neglect the social context of power relations.[25] In so far as power is discussed it is represented as highly dispersed, so dispersed as to preclude the possibility of noting the extent to which one social group is oppressed by another. This dispersal together with a de-emphasis of economic relations makes analyses of gender within a Foucauldian tradition overly free-floating. (Power is not

neglected in the analyses by Foucault himself, since for him the knowledge at the base of each of his discourses is also power, but it is very
dispersed.)

Secondly, the post-modern critics go too far in asserting the necessary
impossibility and unproductive nature of investigating gender inequality. While gender relations could potentially take an infinite number of
forms, in actuality there are some widely repeated features and considerable historical continuity. The signifiers of 'woman' and 'man' have
sufficient historical and cross-cultural continuity, despite some varia-
tions, to warrant using such terms. It is a contingent question as to
whether gender relations do have sufficient continuity of patterning
to make generalizations about a century or two and a continent or so
useful. While the answer to this cannot be given at a theoretical level, I
would argue that in practice such generalization is possible. There are
sufficient common features and sufficient routinized interconnections
for it to make sense to talk of patriarchy.

The post-modernists are correct to point out that many of the existing
grand theories of patriarchy have problems in dealing with historical and
cultural variation. But their solution of denying causality itself is unnecessarily defeatist. The problems in many theories of patriarchy are
due to a contingent, not necessary, feature in the analyses. Their problem is that they utilize a simple base–superstructure model of causal
relations. In a theory in which there is only one causal element it is
not surprising that there are difficulties in understanding variation and
change. This problem can be solved by theorizing more than one causal
base. I have argued at greater length elsewhere that the solution to this
problem is to theorize patriarchy as composed of six structures rather
than one and to theorize the different forms of patriarchy which are
produced as a consequence of their different articulation.[26] The six main
structures which make up a system of patriarchy are: paid work, housework, sexuality, culture, violence and the state. The inter-relationships
between these create different forms of patriarchy. The ability to theorize different forms of patriarchy is absolutely necessary to avoid the
problems of simple reductionism and of essentialism. In private patriarchy the dominant structure is household production, while in the
public form it is employment and the state, though in each case the
remainder of the six structures is significant. In the private form the
dominant mode of expropriation is individual, by the husband or father;
in the public it is collective, by men. In the private form the strategy is
exclusionary; in the public it is segregationist. This model is more fully
developed elsewhere.[27]

Using such a model for Britain over the last a hundred and fifty years, two main forms of patriarchy may be identified: the private based on the household; and the public based on the subordination of women in the public sphere. These forms are found in different periods and among different ethnic groups. There has been a historical shift from public to private. In contemporary Britain, Asian women are more likely to be subordinated within private patriarchy; Afro-Caribbean women by public patriarchy; with white women in between. These are differences in form and are contingently, not necessarily, related to degrees of patriarchy. This point is important in that it enables us to theorize the different forms of patriarchy which are specific to different ethnic groups, without this getting conflated with the question of degree of patriarchy. For instance, the presence of women in the public sphere, especially paid work, may be associated with greater freedoms, but it may not, and may merely indicate a longer working day. I shall come back to this point.

### *'Race'*

A parallel argument to post-modernist accounts of gender has been advanced in the case of 'race'. It has been argued that the distinction between black and white is too simplistic and does not capture the range of experiences of people of different ethnic minorities.[28] It is suggested that we need to differentiate between, in Britain, Afro-Caribbeans and Asians and, indeed, to subdivide Asians into Hindu and Muslim. (Asians in Britain are from the Indian subcontinent, India, Pakistan and Bangladesh, unlike many Asian-Americans who are of Chinese or Japanese ancestry.) The Council for Racial Equality in Britain recommends a three-fold ethnic categorization of black, Asian and white. Similar arguments are made in the US with distinctions of Black, Hispanic, Native American Indian, and sometimes further differentiation according to nation of origin.

The argument is similarly about the diversity of experience, in particular that some ethnic minorities are 'successful' in terms of education and employment. The implication of this is that racism should not be treated as the main determinant of the disadvantage of some ethnic groups if others can 'succeed'. Thus again the import of the fragmentation of the ethnic categories is to criticize the more radical writings for their emphasis on discrimination as the most important determinant of the disadvantaged position of ethnic minorities or women. Again this may give rise to the substitution of analyses of difference rather than inequality.[29] A further differentiation within specific ethnic groups is made by some class analysts, who analyse the relative success of some members of an ethnic group and the disadvantage of others. For instance, Wilson analyses the growth of a black middle class and a black underclass of the truly disadvantaged.[30]

## *Class*

There have been two main forms of post-modernist argument in relation to class. First, that class is no longer the main social and political divide because of the growth of internal class divisions. This argument has been advanced particularly in relation to 'consumption cleavages', such as that of housing. For instance, Saunders argues that differences in housing tenure, especially the movement into home ownership out of renting from the public sector, have had a significant impact on social and political location.[31]

A second version is the 'new times' thesis, particularly the argument that capitalism has changed from an organized to disorganized form in recent years.[32] The 'new times' writers have argued variously that capitalism has changed from being organized to disorganized;[33] from corporatist to post-corporatist; from Fordist to post-Fordist; that the labour process has become flexibilized;[34] that labour markets have become more segmented;[35] that there has been a decline in the degree of homogeneity of the working class and working-class organizations;[36] that the main focus of politics has changed from production to consumption;[37] and that culture has changed from modernist to post-modernist.[38] These theses have been grouped together to form a composite 'new times'.[39] While there are significant differences between these writers on a number of issues, they share some important themes. They agree that there has been a disintegration of the mid-twentieth-century bargain between capital and labour, which is considered as the origin of the welfare state. They share a belief in an increasing complexity in political and cultural cleavages, and a movement away from the politics of the capital–labour struggle over production being the most important political struggle.

These writers have caught something, but I would argue that their view of the fragmentation of capitalism and their failure to see any overall pattern other than disintegration are results of their insufficiently theorizing gender and ethnicity. If they were to theorize these sufficiently, then they would see not disorganization but rather a new form of organization, which played the elements of gender, ethnicity and class in a slightly different format, but not so dramatically differently as to warrant the term 'disorganization'. Aspects of these new forms of organization are considered more fully later in the chapter in the context of a discussion of the new international division of labour.

Gender and ethnicity are absent from most of these accounts, apart from the occasional footnote, though in a few the arrival of women is seen to herald the breakup of the corporatist bargain. The latter occurs with the reference to the apparently new 'feminization' of the labour force, the development of so-called 'new social movements' such as feminism, and the related apparent decline in the degree of homogeneity of the working class and working-class organizations. However, gender and ethnic divisions within the workforce are not new. Women have always been a disadvantaged minority within the workforce. Ethnic minorities, of different origins, have always been a significant component in the workforces of not only the USA but also Europe (the UK utilized Irish labour before that from the 'Commonwealth'). The leadership of the labour movement has always been drawn from the native white male group; the other groups have always contested this. These divisions are ever present, as are the social and political struggles around them. They do not represent a new, post-modern phenomenon.

So far I have argued against the tendency to fragment the categories of 'race', gender and class. However, there are forms of 'modernist' social theorizing that I think reduce the complexity of the social structures too far. In particular I want to argue that this occurs when the determination of these social forms is discussed within a Marxist-influenced framework. I shall argue below that the tendency to reduce social determination of gender and ethnicity to class should be resisted, while not wanting to argue that class is not an important element.

## HIERARCHIES OF DETERMINATION

Post-modernist analyses are often constructed in reaction to totalizing frameworks, which attempt to reduce the complexity of the social world to one or two structural principles. Structural Marxism, in particular, has been a major theoretical system against which the post-modernists have reacted. However, recent class analysis has typically been much more nuanced in its appreciation of the complexity of the social world. The question remains whether it has sufficiently responded to the challenge of the desire to catch complexity rather than to build simple, if powerful, theory.

While contemporary changes in gender, 'race' and class cannot be understood outside of an adequate theorization of each and their mutual interaction, most literature looks at either one or two of these – rarely at all three – and is necessarily flawed as a consequence. Yet there are some highly sophisticated analyses of the intersections between class and 'race', and between class and gender, which engage with both theoretical and empirical issues of these intersections in carefully nuanced ways.[40] An example of this is the superb account of the intersection of 'race' and class by Wilson.[41] Indeed this account is unusually comprehensive in discussing gender relations, though this dimension of his account is not as sophisticated as the other two.

Wilson argues that 'race' alone cannot explain the disadvantaged position of black people in US society. The structure of the economy, in particular unemployment, must also be taken into account; thus 'race' cannot be understood outside of a class analysis. Equal opportunity and affirmative action programmes provide routes through which those black people who are educated can gain access to middle-class jobs. However, they do not provide such a route for those who are not well educated. There is increasing polarization between the better-off black people and the truly disadvantaged. Wilson argues that the black 'underclass' or 'truly disadvantaged' is perpetuated over time by a number of mechanisms. He argues that the structural isolation of the ghetto plays an important role in this. However, he is clear that this is not the same as a self-perpetuating subculture of poverty. It is primarily structural rather than ideological.

Wilson introduces gender into his analysis during his consideration of the structure of the black household. One of the most important proximate causes of poverty is the increasing proportion of female-headed families. Wilson unequivocally refers to this as 'social pathology'. He describes the significant increase in the proportion of black families which are female headed, and correlates this with the increasing poverty among the black underclass. Wilson considers whether welfare payments are the cause of the increase in children born to women living without husbands, and uses evidence from comparable surveys to show that welfare payments are not an incentive to have children out of wedlock. Wilson suggests instead that the proximate cause of this increase in female-headed households is the decline in the pool of marriageable black men. This itself is caused by the increase in black male joblessness. Wilson assumes that men without jobs are unmarriageable.

Thus the problem is ultimately traced back to employment issues, with family structure as the mediating factor.

Wilson's argument is consistently buttressed by extensive reference to empirical studies. It is a most impressive piece of scholarship. His correlations are impeccably established. His theoretical account of the relationship between 'race' and class is sophisticated and subtly nuanced. However, while his account of the relationship between 'race' and class draws upon a range of analytic considerations, that of the intervening variable, gender, is much more crudely dealt with. His use of the term 'social pathology' to describe female-headed families invokes a disease metaphor, which implies that the only 'normal' family is one in which a husband and wife are co-resident where there are dependent children. This naturalistic account of gender relations is in striking contrast to his refusal to naturalize 'race' differences. A further surprising element is the suggestion that among white people the increasing rate of divorce is a sign of women's emancipation, in contrast to the pathology of black families.

Wilson does successfully establish an empirical correlation between low household income and the household being headed by a lone female. He does not address the issue of whether the women in two-parent households have equal access to the family income. While he explores the question of whether higher welfare payments affect the propensity of women to have children without a resident husband, he does not address the impact of the structure of welfare payments on the propensity of fathers to stay with their children and the mothers of their children. The question of whether the refusal to pay benefits to families which have a man present is an incentive for the man to desert and for a woman to leave a man is not addressed. Yet the main US benefit of paying Aid to Families with Dependent Children does appear to be such an incentive. High male joblessness is more likely to lead to a high proportion of female-headed families if the benefit structure makes it difficult for such men to stay with these families. Such a structure of welfare payments is not a given, since most European countries have benefit structures which do not encourage male desertion. The benefit structure is an intervening variable, but not in the way that Wilson explores.

Finally, the empirical correlation which is the main basis of Wilson's claim that male joblessness leads to female-headed households does not hold across all disadvantaged ethnic minorities. While the correlation is real for Afro-American households, and for Afro-Caribbean households in Britain, it does not hold for Asian households in Britain. In Britain

both the major ethnic minorities, Afro-Caribbean and Asian, are economically disadvantaged relative to white people as evidenced by a
series of indicators, such as that the rate of unemployment of both the
Afro-Caribbean and Asian populations is twice that of the white population, and that average Afro-Caribbean and Asian male wage rates are
significantly lower than that of white men.[42] However, while the
Afro-Caribbean population has a higher proportion of female-headed
households than the white, Asian households in Britain have a lower
proportion of female-headed units in comparison with the white
population. Asian households are more likely to have a man and woman
present than those of any other ethnic group in Britain, black or white.
High jobless rates among Asian men in Britain do not lead to high rates
of female-headed households. The implication of this is that Wilson's
thesis that a high rate of female-headed households is a result of economic disadvantage is contradicted by the experience of Asians in Britain.
Gender relations in households are not simply determined by economic
class position. Ethnically variable structures of gender relations are more
important and more autonomous as an intervening variable than Wilson
suggests.

A debate with a parallel theoretical structure is that about the relationship of gender and class within Marxist theory. There are many
examples of Marxist writers who, while wishing to maintain that gender
inequality is an important feature of contemporary society, argue that it
is primarily determined by class relations. The instance of the reserve
army of labour debate is a classic instance of this. Here Marxist writers
argued that women's rate of labour force participation was principally
determined by the boom and slump of the capitalist economy.[43] Women
were differentiated from men in the labour market by their position
in the family, which meant that they could be constituted as a labour
reserve. In times of economic expansion women would be pulled into
the economy, while in times of economic recession they would be 'let
go' and returned to the family, where they had other things to do and
forms of economic support to depend on. Some writers in this school
did note that women were one possible labour reserve and that there
were others that capital could call upon, such as immigrant Third World
people.[44]

There are empirical problems with this account that stem from its
theoretical reductionism in relation to gender. The data on women's
employment patterns in the recent recession in Britain and those in the
OECD countries show that women did not leave paid employment in
larger numbers than men in this period in the way that the theory

predicted. It was men, not women, who were more likely to lose their jobs; women's employment in Britain grew throughout this period, unlike that of men.[45] The failure of the explanation stems primarily from a refusal to recognize the autonomous nature of gendered power from that of class. Women are segregated from men because of forms of patriarchal closure in the labour market and have been concentrated in the sectors of the economy which are least affected by the recession. That is, women's position in the labour market is crucially determined by patriarchal structures within employment. It is insufficient to turn to capital and the family as the sole causal agents.

## THE INTERNATIONAL DIMENSION

My third main argument is that gender, ethnicity and class cannot be successfully explained within one country, but that the international dimension is of crucial significance. Most internationalist analyses have taken capital as the dominant force. Following from my discussion in the previous section I argue that this is wrong, and that we need to theorize ethnicity and patriarchy on a world scale as well.

The international dimension is of importance, not only as a form of variation in gender relations in employment, but also for its effect on gendered employment relations in Britain.[46] Most basically, the standard of living in nations such as Britain depends upon the labour of those in the Third World, through unequal exchange relations.[47] Further, the specific forms of industrial restructuring, which have had different effects upon male and female workers in the metropoles such as Britain, the US and West Germany, have depended upon new international forms of capital.[48] The new international division of labour has an intensely gendered form, although this is not often recognized.[49] A strong case for the interconnectedness of the exploitation of First and Third World women by patriarchal capitalism is made by Mitter and by Mies.[50]

Mitter's book integrates a concern with class, gender and 'race' on an international level. She argues that the new international division of labour has involved new forms of exploitation of workers, and that the labour of black women has been particularly central to this process. Mitter sees the new international division of labour developing as a result of a two-way movement of capital. In the first instance capital moves to the Third World in search of labour cheaper than that in the First World. The labour of women is particularly exploitable because of

the conditions of subordination in which women live. Hence one
increasing labour pool for capital is that of Third World women. The
evidence for this is especially strong in the newly industrializing countries of Asia, in particular Taiwan, South Korea, Singapore and Hong
Kong. This exploitation is associated with the repression of trade unions
and the militarization of the state. The exploitation of women is not
confined to factory work but extends into the sale of their sexuality
through organized prostitution and sex-tourism. Here Mitter's account
moves beyond the simply economic level into an appreciation of the
significance of sexuality as a terrain of women's subordination.

The second instance is in the capitalist heartlands where new forms of
'flexible' working practices involve increases in the exploitation of the
labour of certain sectors of the workforce. These forms of economic
restructuring are facilitated, though not determined, by new forms of
technology. Capital demands a cheap, flexible and disposable workforce,
and this need is met by women. Mitter draws particularly on the
examples of electronics and clothing workers to illustrate her case. For
instance, the branch plants of the electronics industry in the peripheral
regions of the UK have particularly recruited married women with little
prior experience of factory work. They are preferred for similar reasons
to those of capital in the Third World: that they have 'nimble fingers'
and are cheap, patient and docile. The employers have the power to
define the work as not skilled, despite the dexterity needed. In these
new forms of working arrangements there is an increasing tendency to
subcontract work away from the main employer, so that the subcontrac-
tor rather than the main employer bears the brunt of fluctuations in
product demand, and also to ensure a greater degree of control for the
main employer. Mitter argues further that racism in Europe makes it
difficult for ethnic minorities to obtain employment in the mainstream
primary sector of the economy. Hence ethnic minorities are likely to
end up in vulnerable positions in the ethnic businesses which are concentrated in precarious niches in the secondary sector of the economy.
The most extreme version of this is outworking, in which individuals
work at home and are self-employed rather than employees. It is more
often women who engage in this form of labour, a practice not discour-
aged by their men who see it as a way to ensure that the women
perform the full range of domestic labour.

In both instances the new forms of capitalist economic organization
involve the increased polarization of the workforce and particularly
utilize the labour of black women in the newly created 'flexible', casual
jobs. Mitter argues that this gives black women across the world a

common economic position despite national boundaries, and thus a common political interest. Hence her thesis of the common fate and common bond of women in the newly globalized economy.

Mitter's book represents a tremendous synthesis of a mass of research detail and activists' reports on the new international division of labour and women. Its central thesis that the new international division of labour is as much a strategy about gender as it is about capital is extremely well substantiated by a wealth of detail. Mitter has captured the structure of the changes without losing the nuances of local specificity. However, questions remain. First, the general thesis of the new international division of labour has come under critical scrutiny. Gordon argues that the thesis is massively overstated.[51] While the movements of capital have occurred in some industries, such as the textile industry which is the focus of the work of Froebel et al.,[52] they have not occurred in others. Further, the movements are merely fluctuations which do not necessarily represent long-term trends. Hence, the thesis should not be overstated as a universal feature of contemporary capital. Secondly, Mitter details the position of women but does not theorize it. We are left unclear as to the structures which determine women's subordination. Is it the result of patriarchy, or simply the outcome of a concatenation of events? Is it structured or is it merely a historical accident? At places Mitter emphasizes the importance of the family and of men's active resistance to women's movement beyond it. In the absence of a theorization of gender inequality we are left with capital as the main motor of change and gender relations as the background. Yet given the foregrounding of women's experiences by Mitter this would not appear to be her intention. Perhaps we should say it is a wonderful account of the changes and how they fit together, but the theorization of gender and its interrelationship with 'race' and class is left undone.

Mies engages in a more explicitly theorized account of women on a global scale.[53] Like Mitter she is concerned with the recent restructuring of capital and with the interconnections between class, gender and 'race' on an international level. An important difference is that Mies seeks to theorize gender relations in terms of patriarchy. Patriarchy, like capitalism, is a world system. Patriarchy is maintained by a series of structures and practices including the family, systematic violence and the expropriation of women's labour. Mies uses the term 'capitalist-patriarchy' to refer to the current system which maintains women's oppression. She argues that we need to go beyond the old usage of the term 'patriarchy' which refers to the rule of the father since, she argues, many other categories of men – for example, male bosses – are involved in the subordination of women. Capitalism, for Mies, is the latest form that patriarchy takes. Thus she reverses the more conventional hierarchy between the two systems and argues that patriarchy predates capitalism and has analytic priority. She resolves the dilemma of dual systems theory, as to how systems of 'patriarchy' and 'capitalism' might inter-relate, by theorizing capitalism as an expression of patriarchy.

Mies argues that the dependency of women in the industrialized countries is only possible because of the exploitation of women in non-industrialized countries.

> It is my thesis that these two processes of colonization and housewifiza-tion are closely and causally interlinked. Without the ongoing exploitation of external colonies – formerly as direct colonies, today within the new international division of labour – the establishment of the 'internal col-ony', that is, a nuclear family and a woman maintained by a male 'bread-winner', would not have been possible.[54]

Mies argues that the domestication or, as she calls it, the housewifiza-tion, of women in the metropolitan capitalist nations is dependent upon the exploitation of the Third World. She argues that the development of this family form was historically specific and was restricted to the rise of imperialism during the nineteenth century. It started with the bourgeoisie and was spread to the working classes. The first stage is the process of forcible colonization and the development of the luxury trade. The second stage is the development of an internal colony, in which women are colonized by men in Europe. The relations within the industrialized countries provide only half the account; the other is that in the colonies and ex-colonies.

Mies argues that there has been a shift in the international division of labour, from the old one in which raw materials were exported from the colonies for processing in the industrialized world and then marketed world-wide, to a new international division of labour. In the new division industrial production is transferred to the developing countries, producing unemployment in the industrialized countries. The general account is not new,[55] but Mies argues that the gender dimension is more important than was previously recognized. It is women who are the new industrial producers in the Third World, and it is women who are the consumers of these items in the First World. Women are the optimal labour force in the Third World since their designation as dependent housewives enables them to be paid low wages. Women in the First

World, fired from their jobs as a result of the transfer of industry, are the consumers.

Mies's account is rich in detail and further manages to integrate a concern with issues as wide-ranging as violence against women and movements for national liberation. Mies has provided a far-reaching, provocative account of the interconnections between the First and Third Worlds and, unlike most previous attempts to do so,[56] has integrated an analysis of gender relations. The strengths of her analysis are its view of the economy as internationally linked, of the relations of exploitation, of developments over time, and the sensitivity to the different ways in which women can be oppressed and exploited. The weaknesses stem from problems in some of the supporting evidence and theoretical silences; not unexpectedly, given the scope of the project. First, her argument that women in the First World are currently subject to house-wifization following the transfer of industry to the Third World is empirically incorrect. Women are entering paid employment in greater proportions than ever before, despite having higher unemployment rates than men in almost all western countries bar Britain.[57] This process is not complete, but nevertheless the direction of change is the opposite from that argued by Mies. Secondly, the nuclear family form was not unique to modern capitalism. Laslett and MacFarland have shown that it predated the rise of capitalism, so could not have been caused by it.[58] Even the more intensely domesticated version in which the women are not allowed to take outside employment is not unique to the Victorian middle classes since it can be found among Islamic societies, especially among their urban middle and upper classes. In short, Mies places too much explanatory emphasis upon changes in capitalism, despite her stated interest in a world system of patriarchy.

A synthesis of the strengths without the weaknesses of Mies and Mitter would ideally take their impressive grasp of the international interconnectedness of recent economic changes and the significance of the inter-relationship of class, gender and ethnicity for understanding this. However, it would need to produce a theorized account of gender and of ethnicity, not only of capital (taking more from Mies than Mitter), and would have a more accurate account of the actual changes in the patterns of women's paid and unpaid work (taking more from Mitter, but as qualified by Gordon). That is, it would produce a theorized notion of capital, patriarchy and racism as analytically autonomous systems of social structures, which are closely interconnected in practice. There is a new international division of labour, though this affects some branches of industry more than others, especially manufacturing rather than services. Women are being increasingly recruited into waged labour by capital, thus changing the nature of the patriarchal relations in which women (and men) are enmeshed. Black women, whether resident in the First or Third World, bear the brunt of the labour to a disproportionate extent, while receiving a disproportionately small part of the rewards.

We are seeing a change in the form of patriarchy in many, though not all, parts of the world: a shift from a relatively privatized form of patriarchy, in which women primarily labour in the home unpaid, to a relatively public form of patriarchy, in which women do waged work.[59] These forms of patriarchy are to be found to differing extents in different ethnic groups.

CONCLUSION

Post-modernist arguments for the fragmentation of the concepts used in 'modernist' social theory have produced a tendency to shift the central theoretical concept away from 'structure' into 'discourse'. This is represented in the increasing significance of Foucault rather than Marx in social theorizing. The consequences of this are to conceptualize power as highly dispersed rather than concentrated in identifiable places or groups. In the face of the complexity of the social world the post-modernist response is to deny the possibility of causality and macro-social concepts. This newfound complexity is sometimes the result of taking seriously the issues of gender and ethnicity. But rather than abandoning the modernist project of explaining the world, we should be developing the concepts and theories to explain gender, ethnicity and class. Not only is the concept of 'woman' essential to grasp the gendered nature of the social world, but so is that of 'patriarchy' in order that we do not lose sight of the power relations involved. The analysis of the new international division of labour shows most clearly the need to maintain the use of the structural concepts of patriarchy and capitalism and not to neglect racism.

To conclude, I have argued that the post-modern tendency to fragment the categories of woman, 'race' and class is misplaced, but that we should not return to the old version of the modernist meta-narrative which reduced these social inequalities to class. There is a significant possibility in between which enables us to theorize rather than merely describe gender and ethnicity independently from capitalism. We do not need to abandon the notion of causality in the face of the complexity of the social world. We do not have to move from analysis of structure to that of discourse to catch that complexity; neither do we have to resort to capitalism as the sole determinant in order to have a macro-social theory.

## NOTES

This paper was first presented to the American Sociological Association annual conference in San Francisco in 1988. I am grateful to the organizer of the session and its participants for helpful comments, and also to Celia Lury and to the editors of this volume.

1   Floya Anthias and Nira Yuval-Davis, 'Contextualizing Feminism – Gender, Ethnic and Class Divisions', *Feminist Review*, 15 (1983), pp. 62–75; bell hooks, *Feminist Theory: From Margin to Center* (South End Press, Boston, Mass., 1984).

2   Michèle Barrett, *Women's Oppression Today: Problems in Marxist Feminist Analysis* (Verso, London, 1980); Sheila Rowbotham, 'The trouble with "patriarchy"', in Feminist Anthology Collective (eds), *No Turning Back: Writings from the Women's Liberation Movement 1975–1980* (The Women's Press, London, 1981), pp. 72–8.

3   Peter Saunders, *A Nation of Home Owners* (Unwin Hyman, London, 1990).

4   Scott Lash and John Urry, *The End of Organized Capitalism* (Polity Press, Cambridge, 1987); Claus Offe, *Disorganized Capitalism* (Polity Press, Cambridge, 1987).

5   NEDO, *Changing Working Patterns: How Companies Achieve Flexibility to Meet New Needs* (NEDO, London, 1986); Michael Piore and Charles Sable, *The Second Industrial Divide: Possibilities for Prosperity* (Basic Books, New York, 1984).

6   *Marxism Today*, October 1988; Stuart Hall and Martin Jacques (eds), *New Times: The Changing Face of Politics in the 1990s* (Lawrence and Wishart, London, 1989).

7   William Julius Wilson, *The Declining Significance of Race: Blacks and Changing American Institutions* (University of Chicago Press, Chicago, 1978).

8   Michael Mann, *The Sources of Social Power*, volume 1, *A History of Power from the Beginning to A.D. 1760* (Cambridge University Press, Cambridge, 1986); Bryan Turner, *The Body and Society* (Basil Blackwell, Oxford, 1987).

9   Immanuel Wallerstein, *The Capitalist World Economy* (Cambridge University Press, Cambridge, 1979).

10  Barrett, *Women's Oppression Today*; Rowbotham, 'The trouble with

"patriarchy"'; Lynne Segal, *Is the Future Female? Troubled Thoughts on Contemporary Feminism* (Virago, London, 1987).

11 Valerie Amos and Pratibha Parmar, 'Challenging Imperial Feminism', *Feminist Review*, 17 (1984), pp. 3–20; Michèle Barrett and Mary McIntosh, 'Towards a Materialist Feminism?', *Feminist Review*, 1 (1979), pp. 95–106; Arthur Brittan and Mary Maynard, *Sexism, Racism and Oppression* (Blackwell, Oxford, 1984); Hazel Carby, 'White woman listen! Black feminism and the boundaries of sisterhood', in Centre for Contemporary Cultural Studies, University of Birmingham, *The Empire Strikes Back: Race and Racism in '70s Britain* (Hutchinson, London, 1982); Angela Davis, *Women, Race and Class* (The Women's Press, London, 1981); bell hooks, *Ain't I a Woman?* (Pluto Press, London, 1982); Gloria Joseph, 'The Incompatible Ménage à Trois: Marxism, Feminism and Racism', in Lydia Sargent (ed.), *Women and Revolution: The Unhappy Marriage of Marxism and Feminism* (Pluto Press, London, 1981); Sue Lees, 'Sex, Race and Culture: Feminism and the Limits of Cultural Pluralism', *Feminist Review*, 22 (1986), pp. 92–102; Cherrie Moraga and Gloria Anzaldua (eds), *This Bridge Called My Back: Writings by Radical Women of Colour* (Persephone Press, Watertown, Mass., 1981), especially Audre Lorde, 'An Open Letter to Mary Daly', pp. 94–7; Pratibha Parmar, 'Gender, Race and Class: Asian Women in Resistance', in Centre for Contemporary Cultural Studies, University of Birmingham, *The Empire Strikes Back: Race and Racism in '70s Britain*.

12 Hooks, *Feminist Theory*.

13 Jacques Derrida, *Of Grammatology* (Johns Hopkins University Press, Baltimore, 1976).

14 Michel Foucault, *The History of Sexuality*, volume 1, *An Introduction* (Pelican, Harmondsworth, 1981).

15 Jean-François Lyotard, *The Postmodern Condition: A Report on Knowledge* (University of Minnesota Press, Minneapolis, 1978).

16 Linda Alcoff, 'Cultural Feminism versus Post-structuralism: The Identity Crisis in Feminist Theory', *Signs*, 13 (1988), pp. 405–36; Barrett, *Women's Oppression Today*; Michèle Barrett, 'The Concept of Difference', *Feminist Review*, 26 (1987), pp. 29–41; Rosalind Coward, 'Sexual Liberation and the Family', *m/f*, 1 (1978), pp. 7–24; Nancy Fraser and Linda Nicholson, 'Social Criticism without Philosophy: An Encounter between Feminism and Postmodernism', *Theory, Culture and Society*, 5 (1988), pp. 373–94; Chris Weedon, *Feminist Practice and Poststructuralist Theory* (Blackwell, Oxford, 1987).

17 Derrida, *Of Grammatology*.

18 Foucault, *The History of Sexuality*; Michel Foucault, *The Use of Pleasure*, volume 2, *The History of Sexuality* (Penguin, Harmondsworth, 1987).

19 Barrett, 'The Concept of Difference'.

20 e.g. Parveen Adams, 'A Note on Sexual Divisions and Sexual Differences', *m/f*, 3 (1979), pp. 51–9.

21 Parveen Adams, Rosalind Coward and Elizabeth Cowie, 'm/f', *m/f*, 1

(1978), pp. 3–5; Elizabeth Cowie, ' "Woman as Sign" ', *m/f*, 1 (1978), pp. 49–64.

22  Coward, 'Sexual Liberation and the Family'.

23  Parveen Adams and Jeff Minson, 'The "Subject" of Feminism', *m/f*, 2 (1978), pp. 43–61.

24  Michèle Barrett and Rosalind Coward, 'Letter', *m/f*, 7 (1982), pp. 87–9.

25  See also on this point Alcoff, 'Cultural Feminism versus Post-structuralism: The Identity Crisis in Feminist Theory'; Fraser and Nicholson, 'Social Criticism without Philosophy: An Encounter between Feminism and Postmodernism'.

26  Sylvia Walby, *Theorizing Patriarchy* (Blackwell, Oxford, 1990).

27  Sylvia Walby, *Patriarchy at Work: Patriarchal and Capitalist Relations in Employment* (Polity Press, Cambridge, 1986).

28  See Anthias and Yuval-Davis, 'Contextualizing Feminism – Gender, Ethnic and Class Divisions' on a dual argument on this point.

29  These arguments should not be overstated. For example, the deconstructionist Gayatri Chakravorty Spivak is extremely critical of those deconstructionists who underestimate gender inequality: see Spivak, *In Other Worlds: Essays in Cultural Politics* (University of Chicago Press, Chicago, 1987).

30  Wilson, *The Declining Significance of Race*; William Julius Wilson, *The Truly Disadvantaged: The Inner City, the Underclass and Public Policy* (University of Chicago Press, Chicago, 1987).

31  Saunders, *A Nation of Home Owners*.

32  Lash and Urry, *The End of Organized Capitalism*; Offe, *Disorganized Capitalism*.

33  Lash and Urry, *The End of Organized Capitalism*; Offe, *Disorganized Capitalism*.

34  NEDO, *Changing Working Patterns*.

35  Richard C. Edwards, David M. Gordon and Michael Reich, *Labour Market Segmentation* (Lexington Books, Lexington, Mass., 1975).

36  Lash and Urry, *The End of Organized Capitalism*.

37  Manuel Castells, *City, Class and Power* (Macmillan, London, 1978); Manuel Castells, *The City and the Grass Roots: A Cross-Cultural Theory of Urban Social Movements* (Edward Arnold, London, 1983).

38  Lyotard, *The Postmodern Condition*.

39  *Marxism Today*, October 1988; Hall and Jacques, *New Times*.

40  e.g. John Rex and Sally Tomlinson, *Colonial Immigrants in a British City: A Class Analysis* (Routledge, London, 1979); Wilson, *The Declining Significance of Race* and *The Truly Disadvantaged*, on race and class; and Barrett, *Women's Oppression Today*, on gender and class.

41  Wilson, *The Truly Disadvantaged*.

42  Colin Brown, *Black and White Britain: The Third PSI Survey* (Heinemann, London, 1984); *Employment Gazette*, March (1988), p. 172.

43  Veronica Beechey, 'Some Notes on Female Wage Labour in Capitalist Production', *Capital and Class*, 3 (1977), pp. 45–66.
44  Ibid.; Swasti Mitter, *Common Fate, Common Bond: Women in the Global Economy* (Pluto Press, London, 1986).
45  Walby, *Patriarchy at Work*.
46  Diane Elson and Ruth Pearson, ' "Nimble Fingers make Cheap Workers"': An Analysis of Women's Employment in Third World Export Manufacturing', *Feminist Review*, 7 (1981), pp. 87–107; Maria Mies, *Patriarchy and Accumulation on a World Scale: Women in the International Division of Labour* (Zed Books, London, 1986); Mitter, *Common Fate, Common Bond*; Olive Schreiner, *Woman and Labour* (Fisher Unwin, London, 1918).
47  A. Gunder Frank, *Capitalism and Underdevelopment in Latin America* (Monthly Review Press, New York, 1967); Wallerstein, *The Capitalist World Economy*.
48  Folker Froebel, Jurgen Heinreichs and Otto Kreye, *The New International Division of Labour: Structural Unemployment in Industrialised Countries and Industrialisation in Developing Countries* (Cambridge University Press, Cambridge, 1980); Doreen Massey, *Spatial Divisions of Labour: Social Structures and the Geography of Production* (Macmillan, London, 1984); Mitter, *Common Fate, Common Bond*.
49  Ibid.
50  Ibid.; Mies, *Patriarchy and Accumulation on a World Scale*.
51  David M. Gordon, 'The Global Economy: New Edifice or Crumbling Foundations', *New Left Review*, 168 (1988), pp. 24–64.
52  Froebel et al., *The New International Division of Labour*.
53  Mies, *Patriarchy and Accumulation on a World Scale*.
54  Ibid., p. 110.
55  See Froebel et al., *The New International Division of Labour*.
56  e.g. Frank, *Capitalism and Underdevelopment in Latin America*; Froebel et al., *The New International Division of Labour*.
57  OECD, 'Women's Employment during the 1970s Recession', in A.H. Amsden (ed.), *The Economics of Women and Work* (Penguin, Harmondsworth, 1980); Walby, *Patriarchy at Work*.
58  Peter Laslett, *Family Life and Illicit Love in Earlier Generations: Essays in Historical Sociology* (Cambridge University Press, Cambridge, 1977); Alan McFarland, *The Origins of English Individualism* (Basil Blackwell, Oxford, 1978).
59  Walby, *Theorizing Patriarchy*.

# 4

# 'Women's Interests' and the Post-Structuralist State

## Rosemary Pringle and Sophie Watson

We killed the Queen. We picked our way through a series of state-rooms and stabbed Her. It was all very abstract: no blood or noise. We left, taking any papers that might incriminate us. Apparently we had Her cremated – there was no sign of a body – but we had trouble getting rid of the ashes. We gave them to a priest-like figure to dispose of but he couldn't do so without giving us another set in its place. So we had this urn, which we had exchanged several times for different sets of ashes. Though we'd freed ourselves of the original we were still carrying around an urn full of ashes.

Then we found ourselves in court amongst a large group of women who were dressed in sackcloth and demonstrating with placards. All were chanting, 'I killed the Queen', which created a great deal of confusion.

These are fragments of a dream produced by one of us as we started thinking about this paper. It encapsulates our key themes and dilemmas. Sovereignty, as theorized by the classical political theorists, was assassinated a long time ago and the sovereign was displaced by a bureaucratic/legal/coercive order. The state became complex and differentiated; no longer embodying the will of the sovereign, it was rather the arena, or set of arenas, in which the action takes place. While this is a familiar enough story to mainstream social scientists, many socialists and feminists invoke the older model: they are still carrying the sovereign's ashes around. The question we take up here is why those ashes are so difficult to bury, and why we cling to them. Given that the dream represents both the sovereign and her assassins as *female*, it is clear that feminism is heavily implicated. Why then are we in 'sackcloth and ashes' when we should be celebrating?

The reasons have to do with the threats and confusions posed by post-modern and post-structuralist thought. While their relation to feminism has been widely discussed in the area of cultural politics, less has so far been said about the state. Yet essentialist notions of women's political 'interests' and of 'the state' are under challenge just at the point when feminist political scientists are gaining a hearing in their discipline, on the importance of gender as a central analytic category.[1] We argue here that while the ashes of sovereignty do need to be buried, the state itself remains an important focus. But the state, the interests articulated around it, and feminist political strategies need to be reconsidered in the light of post-structuralist theory.

For feminists there are both risks and gains in these new emphases. In treating gender as discursively constructed rather than objectively or structurally given, there is a danger of its being decentred or trivialized, with the fundamental quality of gender domination being lost. Wendy Hollway has expanded on discourse theory to show how gender-differentiated meanings and positions are made available to men and women.[2] All discourse is gendered but this point is systematically ignored outside of feminism. In the work of Foucault,[3] and of Laclau and Mouffe,[4] gender identity is no more than a subject position within a discourse. The latter pay lip-service to feminism, but treat the women's movement merely as one amongst many new social movements which can be recruited to the project of 'radical democracy'. Women might well complain that just at the moment when they are achieving 'identity' and articulating 'interests', these fundamental categories are being rejected by a group of predominantly male theorists. While these are real problems, we none the less argue that they are outweighed by the benefits of engaging with post-structuralist approaches to the state. These include an ability to respond more contextually and strategically to shifting frameworks of power and resistance; and a fuller recognition of multiplicity and difference amongst women. A consideration of the ways the state has been discursively constructed creates the possibility of deconstructing existing discourses, including feminist ones, as well as an assessment of the strategic possibilities open to feminists in different frameworks.

'The state' has been one of the major casualties of recent social theory. While behaviourists have always seen it as too broad a conceptual category to be subjected to empirical analysis, it was the focus of considerable intellectual activity within both Marxism and feminism in the 1970s. Since then it has been so reduced in status in these same circles that not only its relevance and centrality but its very existence have been questioned. Where the concept remains in everyday use, it is used descriptively, mostly by the 'practitioners' of social policy and social welfare.

Marxists and many feminists had assumed that the state has an objective existence as a set of institutions or structures; that it plays a key role in organizing relations of power in any given society; that it operates as a unity, albeit a contradictory and complex one; and that there is a set of coherent interests, based on underlying economic or, in the case of some feminisms, sexual relations, which exist outside the state and are directly represented by or embodied in it. As key concepts like the mode of production and the labour theory of value came under challenge, along with the objective reality of the 'economic' and the 'social', it was inevitable that 'the state' would have to be either reformulated or rejected.

Feminists unmoved by the Marxist and post-Marxist projects have in any case ignored the state as an object of theoretical concern.[5] In stressing that 'the personal is political' they had already emphasized the omnipresence of power and the continuities between men's power in the state and in other domains. The collapse of Marxist certainties and the emergence of discourse analysis has provided a certain intellectual vindication for this position. In a recent paper, Judith Allen argues not only that feminists don't need a theory of the state but that the retention of the concept actually obscures many of the connections which they want to make.[6] Reflecting on the history of prostitution and abortion, she claims that the state is 'a category of abstraction that is too aggregative, too unitary and too unspecific to be of much use in addressing the disaggregated, diverse and specific (or local) sites that must be of most pressing concern to feminists'. Since 'the state' is not an 'indigenous' category of feminist thought, it should, she believes, be abandoned. Leaving aside for a moment the question of the 'indigenous', we can see that Allen's concern echoes that of many thinkers on the left for whom Marxist accounts of capitalism and the capitalist state appeared too general, too rigid and too functionalist to explain the nature of power relations in the late twentieth century.

Foucault's much-quoted writings on power have been of obvious importance in this transition. He argues that power is not imposed from the top of a social hierarchy nor derived from a fundamental opposition between rulers and ruled.[7] It is relational rather than owned or seized, and it operates in a capillary fashion from below. Power finds a shifting and unstable expression in networks and alliances that permeate every aspect of life. 'The state' is an overall effect of all these relations and cannot be assumed to act coherently as the agent of particular groups.

Foucault shifts the emphasis away from the intentionality of the state to pose questions about its techniques and apparatuses of regulation. Though he starts with the localized and specific mechanisms and technologies of power he is no pluralist. He aims to show how these mechanisms and technologies get annexed and appropriated to more global forms of domination. But these interconnections are not to be read off from a general theory; in each case they have to be established through analysis. To place the state 'above' or outside society is to miss its main significance and to insist on a homogeneity in the operations of power which simply is not there. He warns that we should not assume that 'the sovereignty of the state, the form of the law or the over-all unity of a domination are given at the outset; rather, these are only the terminal forms power takes'. Power does not reside in institutions or structures, and rather than there being a 'unity of state power' there is a 'complex strategical situation in a particular society'.[8]

Foucault deliberately makes few direct references to 'the state' because he wants to confront the view of it as Leviathan, a sovereign being from which power emanates. Yet as a historian of power Foucault remains much more interested in discourses and practices concerning the state than other post-structuralists who have concentrated more exclusively on language and culture. In particular he is concerned with the discourses on 'governmentality',[9] including social science and statistics, and the diplomatic-military techniques of policing and surveillance of populations that characterize the modern state. Though he does not say so, these domains are clearly masculine. 'Governmentality' was originally conceived on the model of (a father's) management of a family, and family remains an important instrument of government.

It is possible to distinguish between the discourses that in some sense found the modern state and those that produce 'the state' as it appears in feminist discourses. The former assume a masculine subject rather than self-consciously defending or creating 'men's interests'. Here we can include not only 'governmentality' but 'fraternity' as evoked by the social contract theorists. Pateman argues that the original social contract was in reality a sexual-social contract, in which men overthrew the rule of fathers but only to institute a fraternal agreement which guaranteed men access to women's bodies.[10] She argues that while fraternity has evoked less attention than liberty and equality, its specific gender connotations largely explained away, it 'does not appear by accident as one of the basic liberal and contractarian principles, and it means exactly what it says – brotherhood'.[11] This cannot be dismissed as a fairy story, for 'fraternity' underpins liberalism, and the 'social contract' forms a powerful mythical basis of the contemporary state.

The discourse of 'fraternity', we suggest, presumes and evokes the notion that men alone are the political actors, that state and civil society have been established by men, who act on behalf of the population as a whole. Political differences tend to be constituted as differences between men, reinforcing at a more fundamental level the notion of the public, political domain as a masculine one. In modern 'fraternal' discourse, like the specifically patriarchal ones that preceded them, women are treated as the objects or recipients of policy decisions rather than full participants in them. What feminists are confronted with is not a state that represents 'men's interests' as against women's, but government conducted as if men's interests are the only ones that exist. Claims to be representing 'women's interests', however disunified they may be, may actually be tossed around among groups of men and used as a strategy for achieving their own goals. In the 1990 Australian election campaign, for example, the major parties competed for 'the women's vote' with substantial child-care packages, particularly after the polls showed that more women than men were undecided about which way to vote. Even the reactionary National Party, after being attacked by Prime Minister Hawke for being 'sexist', entered the fray, offering increased funding for breast cancer testing.

Before taking up the question of interests we must go back to consider more concretely some key feminist discourses around the state and the contexts in which they operate. Our concern is not with how 'accurately' they describe or theorize the state, but with the political implications of particular theories. We draw in particular on Britain, Australia and Scandinavia.

## FEMINISMS AND THE STATE

The state only became an object of feminist theoretical concern in the late 1970s when Marxist feminists attempted to adapt current Marxist theories of the state to women. Within this paradigm, a feminist analysis of social reproduction, the family and gender was grafted on to an analysis of the capitalist state, which was still seen as acting predominantly in the interests of preserving the dominant class relations and assisting the accumulation of capital. At the level of the state, the emphasis was on how the capitalist state created and reproduced patriarchal relations. Elizabeth Wilson[12] and Mary McIntosh[13] analysed the ways in which the welfare state reproduces the capitalist modes of production and women's dependence upon men within the family. In this account gender domination is seen as functional to capitalism:

> Capitalist society is one in which men as men dominate women, yet it is not this, but class domination that is fundamental to the society. It is a society in which the dominant class is composed mainly of men; yet it is not as men but as capitalists that they are dominant . . . the state must be seen as a capitalist one.[14]

Such accounts overemphasized the effectiveness with which the welfare state reproduces the capitalist mode of production through women's dependence upon men within the family. And they were unable to explain convincingly just why the state should need to reinforce masculine dominance and privilege. Zillah Eisenstein attempted to solve the problem by treating the state as the mediator between the dual systems of patriarchy and capitalism.[15] This raised another set of difficulties in establishing where these systems began and ended, and produced an analysis that was overly functionalist. Most tended to focus on the oppressive aspects of the state.[16]

The 'capitalist state' view was particularly dominant in British feminism, reflecting the importance of class divisions in British political life and the tendency of radicals to interpret inequality and oppression in terms of class. Attempts to work within the state arenas were viewed with suspicion and likely to be dismissed as co-option. The influential text *In and Against the State*[17] treats the state as a form of social relations which acts in the interests of capital. Though it discusses working within the institutions, it exhorts people to build a culture of opposition. As a result of adopting such a position feminists were ambivalent about working within state institutions, which retained their masculinist and exclusionary culture of white male and class privilege.

It was only after the Thatcher government came to power that the picture began to change. Provoked by the increase of central government control over local government expenditure and the privatization of public services, many became involved in local government as a significant site of resistance and reaction. Women began to enter these local political and bureaucratic arenas. The Greater London Council set up the first women's committee in 1981 and other local authorities followed. 'Local' came to symbolize 'humanitarian', in opposition to the privatization policies of the Thatcher government. Even at this level, working with the state was regarded as 'tainting'. Feminist interventions retained a marginal character and focused on the 'interests' of particular disadvantaged groups rather than the more general policy issues. There was suspicion of local government workers and concern about accountability. As open meetings were held and working parties set up, particular efforts were made to secure the representation of black, disabled, older and lesbian women. Yet open or co-ordinating meetings were always susceptible to domination by well-organized groups (such as the 'Wages for Housework' group) and by those women who were articulate and had the time and resources to attend.[18] Women who were co-opted on to committees as lesbian or black women found themselves having to represent the interests of women from their respective constituency or local area. Membership of a particular group thus allowed a speaking position as, say, lesbian, which had direct impact on the way certain policies were formulated. In some instances this meant that one woman could define the issues for the group in question with little or no accountability to her own constituency. While such problems may be seen as endemic to participatory democracy, the 'against the state' discourse gave them a sharp edge. This discourse is still alive and well. A recent review dismissed feminist bureaucrats in Australia as a group whose lives are lived out 'on the borderland between radicalism and conservatism', as they uncritically embraced a pragmatic form of social democracy.[19] Nevertheless, feminist interventions into the state arenas are now gaining headway after years of the Thatcher government. The Labour Party has committed itself to a Ministry for Women and appointed a shadow minister on women's affairs.

In Australia and Scandinavia the problems have been of a rather different order. The Australian working class has had a long pragmatic tradition of expecting the state to be concerned with the welfare of its citizens and to act as an arbitrator of conflict. This is reflected particularly in the wage fixing of the arbitration and industrial relations commissions. The bureaucracy has been perceived as more open and less under the control of the establishment. Despite a relatively small welfare state, a positive value has been placed on state intervention. The more diverse bases of feminism in Australia combined with the political culture to create a space where feminist interventions were possible and not immediately subject to widespread criticism.

In the early 1970s, the liberal feminist Women's Electoral Lobby (WEL) grew up alongside Women's Liberation. By the time the Whitlam Labor government was elected in 1972, WEL was well placed to lobby for women's advisers, anti-discrimination legislation, equal opportunity programmes, an integrated child-care policy and so on. The Whitlam government was committed to opening up the public service and creating bureaucratic structures which reflected changing community needs, and feminist interventions were constituted by and through such discourse. Throughout the seventies a number of feminists entered key positions within the bureaucratic and ministerial staff. Many of the personal links made in the seventies have been maintained and developed. The channels of intervention, the interests represented and the policies initiated reflect the players, their histories and their connections. This is not to deny the importance of feminist pressure groups and networks outside. But the particular flavour of Australian feminism, its strengths and its limitations, lie in this relation to the bureaucracy.

Two problematic areas can be identified. One concerns the positioning of the 'femocrats' as mediators of the 'interests' of all Australian women. There is an issue here not only about how representative they are, but of the discursive practices within which 'interests' are constructed. Where British feminists might be suspicious of the procedure, there is in Australia a recognition that femocrats are actually articulating interests that are by no means pre-given, and which have to be constructed in the context of the machinery of government. Whatever the debates and conflicts, they have played an important part in securing funding for a range of women's services, even if this has involved tensions for the feminist groups involved, trying to maintain feminist principles as well as being accountable to the funding authority.[20]

A second question concerns the relationship between the feminist bureaucrats and the Australian Labor Party (ALP). The Hawke Labor government, which was in power from 1983, was committed not to radical reform but to change through the mechanisms of tripartitism and consensus. One of the main mechanisms was a prices and incomes accord with the unions, which did rather reinstate the primacy of the older political contestants. Feminists drew attention to the marginality of women in the accord and debated whether it was inevitable or inherent. Given that it was an attempt by Labor to persuade the unions to exercise wage restraint, women's near exclusion is no surprise. The accord was seen as a pact between men. There is a strong resonance here with social contract mythology, and particularly its fraternal dimension, as identified by Carole Pateman.[21] As the main strategy for maintaining living standards in Australia since the early part of the century has been through the protection of jobs through tariff barriers, the arbitration system and the family wage, we could argue a long history of a fraternal contract in welfare creating women's 'dependence'. Fraternalism has a particular meaning in Australia where male 'mateship' amounts almost to a religious cult. The emotionalism concerning the return of the surviving diggers to Anzac Cove on the seventy-fifth anniversary of Gallipoli reminds us that the national identity, and the myths that legitimate the Australian state, celebrate masculine separatism and treat women as 'other'.

Femocrats have debated whether women would be better off with or without the accord. They have also had to adapt themselves to the discourses of corporatism and managerial efficiency, which have become smoothly conjoined with the philosophy of 'mateship'. While gains have been made through partnership with the ALP, the price has at times been high. Anna Yeatman argues that femocrats have colluded in the rolling back of the welfare state and been rather too ready to endorse the official discourse of 'Laborism'.[22] This locates 'people' as workers, and 'workers' as 'men'. Instead of citizens with 'rights' there are 'disadvantaged groups', mostly women, who fall outside of the contract. For them a 'social justice strategy' is offered, which effectively entrenches them in a position of disadvantage.

Yeatman also criticizes the women's movement for failing to challenge the government's use of feminist rhetoric to enforce child maintenance payments from non-custodial parents, mostly fathers, thus reprivatizing parenting arrangements. Others might see this as constructing competing masculine interests: those of individual fathers in dodging liability versus the collective interests of the fraternity. Given the history of child desertion in Australia, it is not immediately obvious that feminists should oppose the legislation. Many argued that in the context of budget constraints it was a positive move that will significantly improve the situation of single mothers. Others have suggested that it reinforces traditional heterosexual dependent relations and scares off men from donating sperm to single women who want children.

Yeatman stresses that politics is pre-eminently a set of debates and struggles over meaning. And she finds femocrats, whether they work in the bureaucracy, in academia or in women's services, rather wanting in their capacity to engage at this level. Certainly it is true that little informed social policy debate takes place in Australia. While sophisticated critiques of degendering have been applied to the public sphere,[23] the implications for policy development are rarely spelt out. Because of the pragmatism towards the state it has not been the subject of intellectual debate in the way it has in Britain, and many feminists would endorse Allen's view that it is not a priority.[24]

In Scandinavia the state is seen as 'an instrument of popular will', which is used to control the private forces of market and family.[25] Norwegians and Swedes use the words 'society' and 'state' interchangeably, and notions of community, rights and entitlements, and distributive justice have been important in women's claims for equality. In feminist engagements with the state in Scandinavia the emphasis has been less on 'class' or 'bureaucracy' than on 'power', and particularly on sexual power hierarchy. This perhaps reflects the relatively high level of representation of women within the elective bodies on the one hand, and an extensive welfare state on the other. Such gains, it has become clear, do not necessarily imply a major shift in gender relations. As Hernes points out,[26] women's increased political power in Sweden has to be balanced against shifts in the centre of the power to the administrative arena. This relates to the significance of corporate structures, where decision-making takes place with little input from women. In some accounts power is represented as a possession while in others there is a sense of power as shifting. There is also some doubt about the extent of women's integration into Scandinavian labour markets. The development of the welfare state has seen a partnership between state and family which compromises women's labour force participation. Women's 'interests' have been centrally constructed in relation to welfare rather than to jobs (which have been the emphasis in Australia). Ongoing gender inequalities can thus be linked to differences in labour market participation, which in turn affects representation in the corporate system.

The Marxist, liberal and social democratic perspectives within which feminists have operated in these countries have not come to grips with the gendered nature of the state. The state is described as masculine or patriarchal but these words have only an adjectival force. Berte Siim comments, typically, that 'state policies can be said to reflect male dominance to the extent they have incorporated the dominant male assumptions and have been governed mainly by male interests and, therefore, have not permitted any real threat to male supremacy.'[27] The American radical feminist Catherine Mackinnon has attempted to theorize the fundamentally patriarchal nature of the state, emphasizing the ways in which the law incorporates a male standpoint and institutionalizes masculine interests.[28] Here too, the 'maleness' of the state is simply a reflection of the maleness of everything else in patriarchal society. She does not add much to our conceptualizations of either 'maleness' or 'the state'. More than this, she backs into a political corner, since it is not at all clear how the patriarchal state might be effectively challenged or from what quarters. She paints women as both total victims of this all-encompassing system and yet able to use the state in a variety of ways for their own ends.[29] 'Men' and 'women' are taken for granted here as unified categories.

Feminist theories of the state have frequently assumed unitary interests between men, between sections of capital and between women. Debates among feminist political scientists focus on the questions of subjective versus objective interests, and interests versus needs.[30] Some writers, like Halsaa,[31] argue that there is an objective basis to women's interests in the reproductive work that only women are able to do. Others raise questions about who is to define women's needs and act on behalf of them; while those concerned with subjective needs have stressed the necessity for participation or 'being among' those creating the alternatives. We believe that the notion of objective versus subjective interests fails to capture the diverse, shifting and conflicting nature of the experiences and representations which form the human subject. While complexity is acknowledged, the framework here is still that of representation rather than articulation. The issue needs to be shifted, from how women's interests can be most accurately represented, to the processes whereby they are constituted.

The state should be seen as erratic and disconnected rather than contradictory. It is not an object or an actor so much as a series of arenas or, in Yeatman's words, a 'plurality of discursive forums'.[32] The current collection of practices and discourses which construct 'the state' are an historical product, not structurally 'given'. What intentionality there is comes from the success with which various groupings are able to articulate their interests and hegemonize their claims: it is always likely to be partial and temporary. If we take this view we do not have to puzzle about why the state acts so contradictorily or, on occasion, fails to act at all. We do not have to conclude in advance that it will act uniformly to maintain capitalist or patriarchal relations, or that this is its 'purpose'. The outcomes of particular policies will depend not purely on the limits placed by 'structures' but on the range of discursive struggles which define and constitute the state and specific interests, from one moment to the next.

More recent socialist and feminist work has recognized that there are many varieties of state, spatially and historically. The state is now regarded as too diverse, divided and contradictory to evoke as an entity. Each has its own combination of institutions, apparatuses and arenas, which have their own histories, contradictions, relations and connections, internally and externally. Work on the welfare state has recognized the need to shift our analyses to particular institutions and their specific histories, rather than assuming any unity or integration of its parts.[33] Local, regional and national as well as historical and cultural specificities have to be acknowledged. To argue that the welfare state supports the traditional patriarchal family is no longer useful, if it ever was. As Alison Smith suggests in her discussion of women's refuges,[34] the legal agencies cannot be perceived as simply shoring up some 'archetypal conception of family relations but instead should be seen as contributing to their changing forms'.

Work is being done on the ways in which gender inequalities are embedded in the state and vice versa. Nancy Fraser,[35] for example, has pointed to the divisions in the US welfare system between work-oriented social insurance programmes (masculine) and the 'unearned' public assistance schemes which cater predominantly for women. Franzway, Court and Connell emphasize the practices that construct the state rather than taking its structures as given.[36] Unlike Mackinnon, they establish a dynamic relationship between gender and the state. The state does not simply reflect gender inequalities but, through its practices, plays an important role in constituting them; simultaneously, gender practices become institutionalized in historically specific state forms. It is a two-way street.

This emphasis on practice and discourse is characteristic of newly emerging feminist and post-Marxist accounts of the state. There is a move away from abstract theorizing and from any belief in the fixed or coherent character of state structures. At first sight this might look like a retreat to pluralism. But post-structuralist theorists share the view that analyses of power should proceed from a micro-level. Much traditional social science tends towards the empirical and the behaviourist, while post-structuralist thinking is concerned with fragmentation and multiplicity of meaning. It emphasizes the importance of language and discourse, not just in describing the world but in constituting social reality. Neither social reality nor the natural world has fixed, intrinsic meanings which language reflects or expresses. Instead there has been an emphasis on the relational, historical and precarious character of 'reality'. Language is also the place where our 'identities' are constructed. Subjectivity is produced in a whole range of discursive practices, the meanings of which are a constant site of struggle over power. It is neither unified nor fixed but a site of disunity and conflict. Post-structuralists regard the 'real world' and the notion of 'interests' as anything but clear-cut. Their concern is therefore with the discursive fields in which social reality and individual and group identities and interests are constituted. Power is regarded as immanent in all social relationships rather than based on deeper economic or sexual divisions. Meaning arises out of the play of differences in language rather than being already given in reality; and meanings are not fixed or static but dynamic and contextual. In post-structuralist accounts of the state, 'discourse' and 'subjectivity' rather than structures and interests become the key terms.

## DISCOURSE AND SUBJECTIVITY

In Foucault's work, discourses are much more than ways of constituting knowledge. They include the social practices, and the forms of subjectivity and power relations that inhere in such knowledges. The most powerful discourses have firm institutional locations – in law, medicine, social welfare and so on – though these too must be seen as sites of contest. Laclau and Mouffe suggest that the distinction between the discursive and the non-discursive is unnecessary:[37] that if we look closely at the 'non-discursive' complexes, such as institutions, productive organizations or techniques, we will always find that they are given meaning through discursive structures.

Laclau and Mouffe's analysis draws together in a systematic way many of the themes that we have already posed. It also raises some major questions for feminist strategy. We shall therefore discuss their position in some detail before concluding with a discussion of the implications for feminism.

First, their work marks a complete break with any essentialist conceptions of social structure or relations. While not denying that the 'real' world has an objective existence, Laclau and Mouffe insist that it can only be known through discourse.[38] They reject totalizing theories of society, stressing that the social constitutes itself as a *symbolic* order. 'Symbolic' is used here in place of ideology to mark the intended break with the base–superstructure model, and it is meant to include material practices. The social formation is not a totality governed by an organizing principle, the determination of the economic in the last instance. The mode of production itself is a conceptual and social construct dependent, for example, on legal discourse. Relations of production therefore do not have any explanatory priority. Society is not a closed system.

The 'relative autonomy' of the state from the economy is thus rendered meaningless, while 'its' relation to civil society becomes more complex. As Laclau and Mouffe put it, the state 'is not a homogeneous medium, separated from civil society by a ditch, but an uneven set of branches and functions, only relatively integrated by the hegemonic practices which take place within it'.[39]

The emphasis on the symbolic order implies that the social can never be permanently fixed and will always be subject to contested meanings: 'Society never manages fully to be society, because everything in it is penetrated by its limits which prevent it from constituting itself as an objective reality.'[40] Given the impossibility of permanently 'fixing' meaning, one might ask how meaning is possible at all. Laclau and Mouffe stress the 'articulatory practices' which temporarily arrest the flow of differences to construct privileged sites or nodal points which partially fix meaning. 'Man' is one such nodal point which underlies the 'humanization' of a number of social practices since the eighteenth century. In the case of 'woman', they add slightly patronizingly, there is an ensemble of practices and discourses that mutually reinforce and act on each other, making it possible to speak of a sex/gender system. 'Men' and 'women' and their 'interests' rest not on biological difference, reproductive relations or the sexual division of labour, but on the discursive practices that produce them.

Classes do not arise automatically out of the mode of production and are given no presumed primacy in political struggles. Members of classes (and by implication, genders and other interest groups) do not simply know their material interests but have to form conceptions of them. Any connections among groups have to be constructed, articulated and maintained; they are not pre-given. Groups make these connections using the discursive frameworks available to the time and culture.

'Interests', then, are precarious historical products which are always subjected to processes of dissolution and redefinition. They are not self-constituted identities but rather 'differences' in the Saussurian sense, whose only identity is established relationally. Subjects cannot be the origin of social relations but rather are subject positions in discursive structures. And *every* social practice is articulatory: it cannot simply be the expression of something already acquired but involves a continuous process of constructing new differences.

Laclau and Mouffe are concerned to establish links between struggles. They are aware that such struggles all have a partial character and, left to themselves, can be articulated to a variety of discourses, including those of the right. Here the establishment of nodal points is very important. These may be compared with Lacan's *'points de capiton'*, or with the points at which a loose cover is held on to an armchair.[41] They are the privileged points or signifiers which, at least partially, fix meaning. Without such reference points communication would be impossible, for meaning would be constantly sliding away. The sense of permanence and fixity that they evoke is, however, an illusion. While nodal points are always necessary, they do in fact shift. Laclau and Mouffe castigate the British left for treating one set of nodal points as if it were absolute, and thus limiting their capacity for action and analysis, handing over to the right the capacity to fix meanings.

What, then, are the discursive conditions under which collective action against *all* forms of inequality and subordination might emerge? Their own nodal points would be established in a programme for radical democracy. This recognizes a plurality of antagonisms, based not on 'objective' interests but on a plurality of subject positions. While each should be given maximum autonomy, it should be in an overall context of a 'democratic equivalence' between group demands: that is, not only a respect for the rights of others but a willingness to modify their subjectivities in the process. For example, the class subjectivity of white male workers is overdetermined by both racial and sexual attitudes which must be contested; and workers' control could be established so as to ignore ecology or the demands of other groups affected by production decisions. It is precisely because the identity of each social movement can never be acquired once and for all that we can expect modifications. Given that so much depends on the extension of democracy, the 'against the state' discourse, which has informed radical political practice in Britain, is rejected here, and we believe rightly so, in favour of the consolidation and democratic reform of the constitutive principles of the liberal state.

## FEMINIST STRATEGIES

We are not arguing that 'the state' as a category ought to be abandoned, but for a recognition that, far from being a unified structure, it is a by-product of political struggles. If we accept that power resides in all social relations this opens up the possibility of a multiplicity of forms of resistance. Interests are also constructed discursively and constituted in their intersection with the state arenas. Notions of women's interests have been crucial in the different discourses around state activity. A focus on interests provides a way of avoiding some of the traps of analysing the state as a given entity. The critique of a category of unified subject opens the way to recognition of a plurality of antagonisms constituted on the basis of different subject positions.

From the discussion so far, we may draw out three key issues for feminist strategies in the 1990s: our relation to the categories man/ woman, our relation to differences among women, and our relation to a wider democratic politics. It seems clear that feminism can no longer ground itself in an essentialist conception of 'woman' or on an understanding of a 'gender identity' or 'interest' shared by all women. The tendency of white, middle-class women to treat their own experience as normative has already been widely criticized.[42] Yet many feminists would still be reluctant to let go of some core of common identity which unites women across class, ethnic and racial boundaries. While we reject such notions of 'identity' we do believe that, along with continuing inequalities at every level, women have in common a discursive marginality. 'Woman' is only knowable in so far as she is similar to, different from or complementary to 'man': phallocentric discourse makes women and their interests virtually unrepresentable except in relation to a masculine norm.[43] In the face of this, the assertion of the feminine may be an important political tactic. This is not a return to essentialism so much as a technique of empowerment: in Braidotti's words, 'essentialism with a difference'.[44] This is an act of self-legitimation which, she suggests, 'opens up the field of possible "becoming", providing the foundation for a new alliance among women, a symbolic bond among woman *qua* female sexed beings'.[45]

If 'women's interests' are constructed rather than pre-given, so are men's. If we have to let go of the authentic female subject, then we can let go too of the male subject. Patriarchal discourse need not be seen as homogeneous and uniformly repressive, and women do not need to be portrayed as victims. This opens up possibilities of exposing differences between men and, where appropriate, creating alliances. The interests of men as 'fathers', for example, do not always coincide with their interests as 'brothers' or 'mates', and each in turn will shift and change each time they are articulated.[46] We might note in passing that men, as men, are now beginning to associate formally against what they see as the unfair advantages of women. The association for 'weekend fathers' in Sweden is just one of many organizations that aim to influence judicial procedures surrounding custody and divorce. 'Fathers' rights' have even extended to rights over the unborn foetus. As Carol Smart warns,[47] in the face of these developments, feminists need to rethink their relation to the whole discourse of 'rights' and remember that discourses should be evaluated not in the abstract but always in a social context.

The political demands of 'women' on the state presuppose a coherent set of interests outside the political and bureaucratic arenas which can be met, rather than recognizing that these interests are actively constructed in the process of responding to some demands and not others. It is in the process of engagement with the arenas of the state that interests are constructed. Through creating a framework of meanings, through the use of particular languages or discourses, certain possibilities for change emerge. Interests are produced by conscious and unwitting practices by the actors themselves in the processes of engagement. Feminists who engage with the state do so within a set of parameters that are discursively constituted and will formulate their interests accordingly. Interests are constituted and constrained by the discursively available possibilities for representation and action in any particular situation. These will also be a result of 'past struggles in which the "interests" of certain forms of interest representation have been constituted in the constraints and pressures on discursive availability'.[48]

If we include a perspective of heterogeneity of women and of feminist response, no one policy will be a gain for all women. Take the example of pornography. There is no one feminist position but a variety of demands for government regulation or latitude. The absence of a coherent feminist position mirrors the lack of coherence, interest or clarity within the state arenas. Each and every instance of policy-making reflects a different configuration of power relations and networks. Policy and its implementation will depend not only on how strongly these different interests are articulated but on how they mesh with the demands of other groups. 'Women's interests' will here be articulated in a variety of competing ways. In Britain a new group, Women Against Pornography and Censorship, has cleverly sought to occupy the discursive field, by arguing that the sexual exploitation of women is a civil liberties issue, and that pornography itself is a form of censorship in so far as it establishes a particular representation of women as normative. Drawing on community support for legislation against sex and race discrimination, the group locates pornography both as a form of sex discrimination and as an incitement to sexual hatred and violence in analogous terms to racial hatred and violence.[49] This is calculated to draw support from across the discursive board, including the right. It is also intended to pull the rug from under their feminist opponents, who situate pornography in more complex terms in relation to representation and fantasy.

A feminist orientation to the politics of difference means that we each recognize that any standpoint we take is necessarily partial and based on the way in which we are positioned in relation to class, race, educational background and any number of other factors. Our subjectivity will have been formed within a multiplicity of discourses, many of them conflicting and contradictory.[50] While this may be threatening, it also allows change and flexibility. Rather than seeking a politics based on 'unity', we can move towards one based on respect for the differences of others, and on alliances with them.

This brings us back to the 'radical democracy' project, which we endorse with some reservations. Precisely because subjectivity can never be acquired once and for all, and is constructed as part of a chain of differences, it should be possible for all who are committed to the project to construct their identities and interests in ways that are respectful of others. It makes obvious sense for feminists to ally themselves with those committed to working collectively to end all forms of inequality and subordination. Nevertheless we consider that this seriously underplays gender inequality. While acknowledging surface sexism, it takes no account of the problem of phallocentrism in discourse, and neither does it take any serious account of sexual difference. It assumes one sex only, and that sex is male. The class subjectivity of white male workers remains a reference point, even as it is acknowledged that this group must reconsider its standpoint. Laclau and Mouffe are very low key about 'socialism', but they obviously regard the socialization of production as a necessary (if not sufficient) condition of radical democracy.[51] Given that no other 'necessary' conditions are laid down, it is not clear why this one is privileged. Feminists could justifiably see this as (male) socialist hegemony back in a more sophisticated form. This being said, such a project offers interesting possibilities for feminism in the nineties.

Rethinking the state, we conclude, requires a shift away from seeing the state as a coherent, if contradictory, unity. Instead we see it as a diverse set of discursive arenas which play a crucial role in organizing relations of power. Rather than abandoning the state as an analytic or political category, it is important to analyse the strategic possibilities available at any one time. Women's interests and thereby feminist politics are constructed in the process of interaction with specific institutions and sites. The policies that ensue depend not just on the constraints of structures but on the discursive struggles which define and constitute particular interests and the state at any one time.

NOTES

1  K. Jones and A. Jonasdottir, *The Political Interests of Gender* (Sage, London, 1988).
2  W. Hollway, 'Gender Difference and the Production of Subjectivity', in

J. Henriques, W. Hollway, C. Urwin, C. Venn and V. Walkerdine, *Changing the Subject* (Methuen, London, 1984).

3  Especially his *History of Sexuality*, volume 1 (Vintage Books, New York, 1981); 'On Governmentality', *Ideology and Consciousness*, 6 (1979); 'Truth and Power', in C. Gordon (ed.), *Power/Knowledge: Selected Interviews and Other Writings 1972–1977: Michel Foucault* (Harvester Press, Brighton, 1980); and see M. Morris and P. Patton (eds), *Michel Foucault: Power, Truth, Strategy* (Feral Publications, Sydney, 1979).

4  E. Laclau and C. Mouffe, *Hegemony and Socialist Strategy* (Verso, London, 1985).

5  M. Frye, *The Politics of Reality* (The Crossing Press, Trumansberg, N.Y., 1983).

6  J. Allen, 'Does Feminism Need a Theory of the State?', in S. Watson (ed.), *Playing the State* (Verso, London, 1990).

7  Foucault, *History of Sexuality*, volume 1.

8  Foucault, 'On Governmentality', p. 20.

9  Ibid.

10  C. Pateman, *The Sexual Contract* (Polity Press, London, 1988).

11  Ibid., p. 74.

12  E. Wilson, *Women and the Welfare State* (Tavistock, London, 1977).

13  M. McIntosh, 'The State and the Oppression of Women', in A. Kuhn and A. Wolpe (eds), *Feminism and Materialism* (Routledge, London, 1978). Other accounts tended to be more descriptive, e.g. H. Land, 'Who Still Cares for the Family?', *Journal of Social Policy*, 7 (1978).

14  McIntosh, 'The State and the Oppression of Women', p. 259.

15  Z. Eisenstein, *Capitalist Patriarchy and the Case for Socialist Feminism* (Monthly Review Press, New York, 1978).

16  B. Siim, 'Towards a Feminist Rethinking of the Welfare State', in Jones and Jonasdottir, *Political Interests of Gender*, p. 171.

17  London/Edinburgh Return Group, *In and Against the State* (Pluto Press, London, 1979).

18  S. Goss, 'Women's Initiatives in Local Government', in M. Boddy and C. Fudge (eds), *Local Socialism* (Macmillan, London, 1984).

19  L. Loach, 'Feminists Abroad', *New Statesman and Society*, 2 March 1990.

20  L. McFerren, 'Interpretations of a Frontline State: Australian Women's Refuges and the State', in Watson, *Playing the State*.

21  Pateman, *The Sexual Contract*.

22  A. Yeatman, *Bureaucrats, Technocrats, Femocrats: Essays on the Contemporary Australian State* (Allen and Unwin, Sydney, 1990).

23  C. Pateman and E. Gross (eds), *Feminist Challenges* (Allen and Unwin, Sydney, 1987); B. Sullivan, 'Sex Equality and The Australian Body Politic', in Watson, *Playing the State*.

24  Allen, 'Does Feminism Need a Theory of the State?'

25  H. Hernes, 'Women and the Welfare State: The Transition from Private to

Public Dependence', in A. Showstack Sasson (ed.), *Women and the State* (Hutchinson, London, 1987), p. 156.

26  H. Hernes, *Welfare State and Woman Power: Essays in State Feminism* (Norwegian University Press, Oslo, 1987), p. 151.

27  Siim, 'Towards a Feminist Rethinking of the Welfare State', p. 178.

28  C.A. Mackinnon, 'Feminism, Marxism, Method and the State: Toward a Feminist Jurisprudence', *Signs*, 8 (1983).

29  See C. Smart, *Feminism and the Power of Law* (Routledge, London, 1989).

30  A. Jonasdottir, 'On the Concept of Interest, Women's Interests, and the Limitations of Interest Theory', in Jones and Jonasdottir, *Political Interests of Gender*; D. Dahlerup, 'Overcoming the Barriers: An Approach to the Study of how Women's Issues are Kept from the Political Agenda', in J.H. Stiehm (ed.), *Women's Views of the Political World of Men* (Transitional Publishers, New York, 1984).

31  B. Halsaa, 'Har kuïnnor gemensamma intressen?', discussed in H. Skjeie, *The Feminisation of Power: Norway's Political Experiment (1986–)* (Institute for Social Research, Oslo, 1988), p. 48.

32  Yeatman, *Bureaucrats, Technocrats, Femocrats*, p. 170.

33  S. Shaver, 'Gender, Class and the Welfare State: The Case of Income Security', *Feminist Review*, 32 (1989).

34  A. Smith, 'Women's Refuges: The Only Resort? Feminism, Domestic Violence and the State', in D. Barry and P. Botsman (eds), 'Public/Private', *Local Consumption*, series 6, Sydney (1985).

35  N. Fraser, 'Women, Welfare and the Politics of Need Interpretation', *Thesis Eleven*, 17 (1987).

36  S. Franzway, D. Court and R.W. Connell, *Staking a Claim: Feminism, Bureaucracy and the State* (Paladin, London, 1989).

37  Laclau and Mouffe, *Hegemony and Socialist Strategy*, p. 107.

38  Ibid.

39  Ibid., p. 180.

40  Ibid., p. 127.

41  Ibid., pp. 112–14.

42  e.g. M. Barrett and M. McIntosh, 'Ethnocentrism and Socialist Feminism', *Feminist Review*, 20 (1985).

43  See especially L. Irigaray, *This Sex Which Is Not One* (Cornell University Press, Ithaca, N.Y., 1985); E. Grosz, *Sexual Subversions* (Allen and Unwin, Sydney, 1989).

44  R. Braidotti, 'The Politics of Ontological Difference', in T. Brennan (ed.), *Between Feminism and Psychoanalysis* (Routledge, London, 1989).

45  Ibid., p. 102.

46  R. Pringle and S. Watson, 'Fathers, Brothers, Mates: The Fraternal State in Australia', in Watson, *Playing the State*, pp. 229–43.

47  Smart, *Feminism and the Power of Law*.

48  S. Clegg, *Frameworks of Power* (Sage, London, 1988), p. 181.

49  Women Against Pornography and Censorship, 'Questions and Answers'

(Women Against Pornography and Censorship, London, April 1989); C. Itzin, 'Pornography: Is the New Campaign Against Pornography and Censorship a Contradiction?', *Observer*, 16 April 1989.

50 R. Pringle, *Secretaries Talk: Sexuality, Power and Work* (Verso, London, 1989).

51 Laclau and Mouffe, *Hegemony and Socialist Strategy*.

# 5

# Feminist Encounters:
## Locating the Politics of Experience

## Chandra Talpade Mohanty

Feminist and anti-racist struggles in the 1990s face some of the same urgent questions encountered in the 1970s. After two decades of engagement in feminist political activism and scholarship in a variety of socio-political and geographical locations, questions of difference (sex, race, class, nation), experience and history remain at the centre of feminist analysis. Only, at least in the US academy, feminists no longer have to contend as they did in the 1970s with phallocentric denials of the legitimacy of gender as a category of analysis. Instead, the crucial questions in the 1990s concern the construction, examination and, most significantly, the institutionalization of difference *within* feminist discourses. It is this institutionalization of difference that concerns me here. Specifically, I ask the following question: how does the politics of location in the contemporary USA determine and produce experience and difference as analytical and political categories in feminist 'cross-cultural' work? By the term 'politics of location' I refer to the historical, geographical, cultural, psychic and imaginative boundaries which provide the ground for political definition and self-definition for contemporary US feminists.[1]

Since the 1970s, there have been key paradigm shifts in western feminist theory. These shifts can be traced to political, historical, methodological and philosophical developments in our understanding of questions of power, struggle and social transformation. Feminists have drawn on decolonization movements around the world, on movements for racial equality, on peasant struggles and gay and lesbian movements, as well as on the methodologies of Marxism, psychoanalysis, deconstruction and post-structuralism to situate our thinking in the 1990s. While these developments have often led to progressive, indeed radical analyses of sexual difference, the focus on questions of subjectivity and identity which is a hallmark of contemporary feminist theory has also had some problematic effects in the area of race and Third World/post-colonial studies. One problematic effect of the post-modern critique of essentialist notions of identity has been the dissolution of the category of race – however, this is often accomplished at the expense of a recognition of racism. Another effect has been the generation of discourses of diversity and pluralism which are grounded in an apolitical, often individualized identity politics.[2] Here, questions of *historical interconnection* are transformed into questions of discrete and separate histories (or even herstories) and into questions of identity politics.[3] While I cannot deal with such effects in detail here, I work through them in a limited way by suggesting the importance of analysing and theorizing difference in the context of feminist cross-cultural work. Through this theorization of experience, I suggest that historicizing and locating political agency is a necessary alternative to formulations of the 'universality' of gendered oppression and struggles. This universality of gender oppression is problematic, based as it is on the assumption that the categories of race and class have to be invisible for gender to be visible. In the 1990s, the challenges posed by black and Third World feminists can point the way towards a more precise, transformative feminist politics. Thus, the juncture of feminist and anti-racist/Third World/post-colonial studies is of great significance, materially as well as methodologically.[4]

Feminist analyses which attempt to cross national, racial and ethnic boundaries produce and reproduce difference in particular ways. This codification of difference occurs through the naturalization of analytic categories which are supposed to have cross-cultural validity. I attempt an analysis of two recent feminist texts which address the turn of the century directly. Both texts also foreground analytic categories which address questions of cross-cultural, cross-national differences among women. Robin Morgan's 'Planetary Feminism: The Politics of the 21st Century' and Bernice Johnson Reagon's 'Coalition Politics: Turning the Century' are both *movement* texts and are written for diverse mass audiences. Morgan's essay forms the introduction to her 1984 book, *Sisterhood is Global: The International Women's Movement Anthology*, while Reagon's piece was first given as a talk at the West Coast Women's Music Festival in 1981, and has since been published in Barbara Smith's 1983 anthology, *Home Girls: A Black Feminist Anthology*.[5] Both essays construct contesting notions of experience, difference and struggle within and across cultural boundaries. I stage an encounter between these texts because they represent for me, despite their differences from each other, an alternative presence – a thought, an idea, a record of activism and struggle – which can help me both locate and position myself in relation to 'history'. Through this presence, and with these texts, I can hope to approach the end of the century and not be overwhelmed.

The status of 'female' or 'woman/women's' experience has always been a central concern in feminist discourse. After all, it is on the basis of shared experience that feminists of different political persuasions have argued for unity or identity among women. Teresa de Lauretis, in fact, gives this question a sort of foundational status: 'The relation of experience to discourse, finally, is what is at issue in the definition of feminism.'[6] Feminist discourses, critical and liberatory in intent, are not thereby exempt from inscription in their internal power relations. Thus, the recent definition, classification and assimilation of categories of experientially based notions of 'woman' (or analogously, in some analyses, 'lesbian') to forge political unity require our attention and careful analysis. Gender is *produced* as well as uncovered in feminist discourse, and definitions of experience, with attendant notions of unity and difference, form the very basis of this production. For instance, gender inscribed within a purely male/female framework reinforces what Monique Wittig has called the heterosexual contract.[7] Here difference is constructed along male/female lines, and it is being female (as opposed to male) which is at the centre of the analysis. Identity is seen as either male or female. A similar definition of experience can also be used to craft lesbian identity. Katie King's analysis indicates this:

> The construction of political identity in terms of lesbianism as a magical sign forms the pattern into which the feminist taxonomic identities of recent years attempt to assimilate themselves ... Identifying with lesbianism falsely implies that one knows all about heterosexism and homophobia magically through identity or association. The 'experience' of lesbianism is offered as salvation from the individual practice of heterosexism and homophobia and the source of intuitive institutional and structural understanding of them. The power of lesbianism as a privileged signifier makes analysis of heterosexism and homophobia difficult since it obscures the need for counter-intuitive challenges to ideology.[8]

King's analysis calls into question the authority and presence of 'experience' in constructing lesbian identity. She criticizes feminist analyses in which difference is inscribed simply within a lesbian/heterosexual framework, with 'experience' functioning as an unexamined, catch-all category. This is similar to the female/male framework Wittig calls attention to, for although the terms of the equation are different, the status and definition of 'experience' are the same. The politics of being 'woman' or 'lesbian' are deduced from the *experience* of being woman or lesbian. Being female is thus seen as *naturally* related to being feminist, where the experience of being female transforms us into feminists through osmosis. Feminism is not defined as a highly contested political terrain; it is the mere effect of being female.[9] This is what one might call the feminist osmosis thesis: females are feminists by association and identification with the experiences which constitute us as female.

The problem is, however, we cannot avoid the challenge of *theorizing* experience. For most of us would not want to ignore the range and scope of the feminist political arena, one characterized quite succinctly by de Lauretis: 'feminism defines itself as a political instance, not merely a sexual politics but a politics of everyday life, which later . . . enters the public sphere of expression and creative practice, displacing aesthetic hierarchies and generic categories, and . . . thus establishes the semiotic ground for a different production of reference and meaning.'[10] It is this recognition that leads me to an analysis of the status of experience and difference, and the relation of this to political praxis in Robin Morgan's and Bernice Reagon's texts.

### 'A PLACE ON THE MAP IS ALSO A PLACE IN HISTORY'[11]

The last decade has witnessed the publication of numerous feminist writings on what is generally referred to as an international women's movement, and we have its concrete embodiment in *Sisterhood is Global*, a text which in fact describes itself as '*The* International Women's Movement Anthology'. There is considerable difference between international feminist networks organized around specific issues like sex-tourism and multinational exploitation of women's work, and the notion of *an* international women's movement which, as I attempt to demonstrate, implicitly *assumes* global or universal sisterhood. But it is best to begin by recognizing the significance and value of the publication of an anthology such as this. The value of documenting the indigenous histories of women's struggles is unquestionable. Morgan states that the book took twelve years in conception and development, five years in actual work, and innumerable hours in networking and fundraising.

It is obvious that without Morgan's vision and perseverance this anthology would not have been published. The range of writing represented is
truly impressive. At a time when most of the globe seems to be taken
over by religious fundamentalism and big business, and the colonization
of space takes precedence over survival concerns, an anthology that
documents women's organized resistances has significant value in helping us envision a better future. In fact, it is because I recognize the value
and importance of this anthology that I am concerned about the political
implications of Morgan's framework for cross-cultural comparison.
Thus my comments and criticisms are intended to encourage a greater
internal self-consciousness within feminist politics and writing, not to
lay blame or induce guilt.

   Universal sisterhood is produced in Morgan's text through specific
assumptions about women as a cross-culturally singular, homogeneous
group with the same interests, perspectives and goals and similar experiences. Morgan's definitions of 'women's experience' and history lead to
a particular self-presentation of western women, a specific codification
of differences among women, and eventually to what I consider to be
problematic suggestions for political strategy.[12] Since feminist discourse
is productive of analytic categories and strategic decisions which have
material effects, the construction of the category of universal sisterhood
in a text which is widely read deserves attention. In addition, *Sisterhood
is Global* is still the only text which proclaims itself as the anthology of
*the* international women's movement. It has had world-wide distribution, and Robin Morgan herself has earned the respect of feminists
everywhere. And since authority is always charged with responsibility,
the discursive production and dissemination of notions of universal
sisterhood is a significant political event which perhaps solicits its own
analysis.

   Morgan's explicit intent is 'to further the dialogue between and
solidarity of women everywhere' (p. 8). This is a valid and admirable
project to the extent that one is willing to assume, if not the reality, then
at least the possibility, of universal sisterhood on the basis of shared
good will. But the moment we attempt to articulate the operation of
contemporary imperialism with the notion of an international women's
movement based on global sisterhood, the awkward political implications of Morgan's task become clear. Her particular notion of universal
sisterhood seems predicated on the erasure of the history and effects of
contemporary imperialism. Robin Morgan seems to situate *all* women
(including herself) outside contemporary world history, leading to what
I see as her ultimate suggestion that transcendence rather than engage-

ment is the model for future social change. And this, I think, is a model which can have dangerous implications for women who do not and cannot speak from a location of white, western, middle-class privilege. A place on the map (New York City) is, after all, also a locatable place in history.

What is the relation between experience and politics in Robin Morgan's text? In 'Planetary Feminism' the category of 'women's experience' is constructed within two parameters: woman as victim, and woman as truth-teller. Morgan suggests that it is not mystical or biological commonalities which characterize women across cultures and histories, but rather a common condition and world view:

> The quality of feminist political philosophy (in all its myriad forms) makes possible a totally new way of viewing international affairs, one less concerned with diplomatic postures and abstractions, but focused instead on concrete, *unifying* realities of priority importance to the survival and betterment of living beings. For example, the historical, cross-cultural opposition women express to war and our healthy skepticism of certain technological advances (by which most men seem overly impressed at first and disillusioned at last) are only two instances of shared attitudes among women which seem basic to a common world view. Nor is there anything mystical or biologically deterministic about this commonality. It is the result of a *common condition* which, despite variations in degree, is experienced by all human beings who are born female. (p. 4)

This may be convincing up to a point, but the political analysis that underlies this characterization of the commonality among women is shaky at best. At various points in the essay, this 'common condition' that women share is referred to as the suffering inflicted by a universal 'patriarchal mentality' (p. 1), women's opposition to male power and androcentrism, and the experience of rape, battery, labour and childbirth. For Morgan, the magnitude of suffering experienced by most of the women in the world leads to their potential power as a world political force, a force constituted in opposition to Big Brother in the US, Western and Eastern Europe, Moscow, China, Africa, the Middle East and Latin America. The assertion that women constitute a potential world political force is suggestive; however, Big Brother is *not exactly the same* even in, say, the US and Latin America. Despite the similarity of power interests and location, the two contexts present significant differences in the manifestations of power and hence of the possibility of struggles against it. I part company with Morgan when she seems to believe that Big Brother is the same the world over because 'he' simply represents male interests, notwithstanding particular imperial histories or the role of monopoly capital in different countries.

In Morgan's analysis, women are unified by their shared perspective (for example, opposition to war), shared goals (betterment of human beings) and shared experience of oppression. Here the homogeneity of women as a group is produced not on the basis of biological essentials (Morgan offers a rich, layered critique of biological materialism), but rather through the psychologization of complex and contradictory historical and cultural realities. This leads in turn to the assumption of women as a unified group on the basis of secondary sociological universals. What binds women together is an ahistorical notion of the sameness of their oppression and, consequently, the sameness of their struggles. Therefore in Morgan's text cross-cultural comparisons are based on the assumption of the singularity and homogeneity of women as a *group*. This homogeneity of women as a group, is, in turn, predicated on a definition of the *experience of oppression* where difference can only be understood as male/female. Morgan assumes universal sisterhood on the basis of women's shared opposition to androcentrism, an opposition which, according to her, grows directly out of women's shared status as its victims. The analytic elision between the *experience* of oppression and the *opposition* to it illustrates an aspect of what I referred to earlier as the feminist osmosis thesis: being female and being feminist are one and the same, we are *all* oppressed and hence we *all* resist. Politics and ideology as self-conscious struggles and choices necessarily get written out of such an analysis.

Assumptions pertaining to the relation of experience to history are evident in Morgan's discussion of another aspect of women's experience: woman as truth-teller. According to her, women speak of the 'real' unsullied by 'rhetoric' or 'diplomatic abstractions'. They, as opposed to men (also a coherent singular group in this analytic economy), are authentic human beings whose 'freedom of choice' has been taken away from them: 'Our emphasis is on the individual voice of a woman speaking not as an official representative of her country, but rather as a truth-teller, with an emphasis on reality as opposed to rhetoric' (p. xvi). In addition, Morgan asserts that women social scientists are 'freer of androcentric bias' and 'more likely to elicit more trust and . . . more honest responses from female respondents of their studies' (p. xvii). There is an argument to be made for women interviewing women, but I do not think this is it. The assumptions underlying these statements indicate to me that Morgan thinks women have some kind of privileged access to the 'real', the 'truth', and can elicit 'trust' from other women purely on the basis of their being not-male. There is a problematic conflation here of the biological and the psychological with the discursive and the ideological. 'Women' are collapsed into the 'suppressed feminine' and men into the dominant ideology.

These oppositions are possible only because Morgan implicitly erases from her account the possibility that women might have *acted*, that they were anything but pure victims. For Morgan, history is a male construction; what women need is herstory, separate and outside of his-story. The writing of history (the discursive and the representational) is confused with women as historical actors. The fact that women are representationally absent from his-story does not mean that they are/were not significant social actors in history. However, Morgan's focus on herstory as separate and outside history not only hands over all of world history to the boys, but potentially suggests that women have been universally duped, not allowed to 'tell the truth', and robbed of all *agency*. The implication of this is that women as a group seem to have forfeited any kind of material referentiality.

What, then, does this analysis suggest about the status of experience in this text? In Morgan's account, women have a sort of cross-cultural coherence as distinct from men. The status or position of women is assumed to be self-evident. However, this focus on the position of women whereby women are seen as a coherent group in *all* contexts, regardless of class or ethnicity, structures the world in ultimately Manichaean terms, where women are always seen in opposition to men, patriarchy is always essentially the invariable phenomenon of male domination, and the religious, legal, economic and familial systems are implicitly assumed to be constructed by men. Here, men and women are seen as whole groups with *already constituted* experiences as groups, and questions of history, conflict and difference are formulated from what can only be this privileged location of knowledge.

I am bothered, then, by the fact that Morgan can see contemporary imperialism only in terms of a 'patriarchal mentality' which is enforced by men as a *group*. Women across class, race and national boundaries are participants to the extent that we are 'caught up in political webs not of our making which we are powerless to unravel' (p. 25). Since women as a unified group are seen as unimplicated in the process of history and contemporary imperialism, the logical strategic response for Morgan appears to be political transcendence: 'To fight back in solidarity, however, as a real political force requires that women transcend the patriarchal barriers of class and race, and furthermore, transcend even the solutions the Big Brothers propose to the problems they themselves created' (p. 18). Morgan's emphasis on women's transcendence is evident in her discussions of (1) women's deep opposition to nationalism as practised in patriarchal society, and (2) women's involvement in peace and disarmament movements across the world, because, in her opinion, they desire peace (as opposed to men who cause war). Thus, the concrete reality of women's involvement in peace movements is substituted by an abstract 'desire' for peace which is supposed to transcend race, class and national conflicts among women. Tangible responsibility and credit for organizing peace movements is replaced by an essentialist and psychological unifying desire. The problem is that in this case women are not seen as political agents; they are merely allowed to be well intentioned. Although Morgan does offer some specific suggestions for political strategy which require resisting 'the system', her fundamental suggestion is that women transcend the left, the right, and the centre, the law of the father, God, and the system. Since women have been analytically constituted outside real politics or history, progress for them can only be seen in terms of transcendence.

The *experience* of struggle is thus defined as both personal and ahistorical. In other words, the political is *limited to* the personal and all conflicts among and within women are flattened. If sisterhood itself is defined on the basis of personal intentions, attitudes or desires, conflict is also automatically constructed on only the psychological level. Experience is thus written in as simultaneously individual (that is, located in the individual body/psyche of wom*a*n) and general (located in women as a preconstituted collective). There seem to be two problems with this definition. First, experience is seen as being immediately accessible, understood and named. The complex relationships between behaviour and its representation are either ignored or made irrelevant; experience is collapsed into discourse and vice versa. Second, since experience has a fundamentally psychological status, questions of history and collectivity are formulated on the level of attitude and intention. In effect, the sociality of collective struggles is understood in terms of something like individual–group relations, relations which are common-sensically seen as detached from history. If the assumption of the *sameness* of experience is what ties woman (individual) to women (group), regardless of class, race, nation and sexualities, the notion of experience is anchored firmly in the notion of the individual self, a determined and specifiable constituent of European modernity. However, this notion of the individual needs to be self-consciously historicized if as feminists we wish to go beyond the limited bourgeois ideology of individualism, especially as we attempt to understand what cross-cultural sisterhood might be made to mean.

Towards the end of 'Planetary Feminism' Morgan talks about feminist diplomacy:

> What if feminist diplomacy turned out to be simply another form of the feminist aphorism 'the personal is political'? Danda writes here of her own feminist epiphany, Amanda of her moments of despair, La Silenciada of personally bearing witness to the death of a revolution's ideals. Tinne confides her fears, Nawal addresses us in a voice direct from prison, Hilkla tells us about her family and childhood; Ama Ata confesses the anguish of the woman artist, Stella shares her mourning with us, Mahnaz communicates her grief and her hope, Nell her daring balance of irony and lyricism, Paola the story of her origins and girlhood. Manjula isn't afraid to speak of pain, Corrine traces her own political evolution alongside that of her movement. Maria de Lourdes declares the personal and the political inseparable. Motlalepula still remembers the burning of a particular maroon dress, Ingrid and Renate invite us into their private correspondence, Marielouise opens herself in a poem, Elena appeals personally to us for help, Gwendoline testifies about her private life as a public figure . . .
> And do we not, after all, recognize one another? (pp. 35–6)

It is this passage more than any other that encapsulates Morgan's individualized and essentially equalizing notion of universal sisterhood, and its corresponding political implications. The lyricism, the use of first names (the one and only time this is done), and the insistence that we must easily 'recognize one another' indicate what is left unsaid: we must identify with *all* women. But it is difficult to imagine such a generalized identification predicated on the commonality of women's interests and goals across very real divisive class and ethnic lines – especially, for example, in the context of the mass proletarianization of Third World women by corporate capital based in the US, Europe and Japan.

Universal sisterhood, defined as the transcendence of the 'male' world, thus ends up being a middle-class, psychologized notion which effectively erases material and ideological power differences within and among groups of women, especially between First and Third World women (and, paradoxically, removes us all as actors from history and politics). It is in this erasure of difference as inequality and dependence that the privilege of Morgan's political 'location' might be visible. Ultimately in this reductive utopian vision, men *participate* in politics while

women can only hope to *transcend* them. Morgan's notion of universal
sisterhood *does* construct a unity. However, for me, the real challenge
arises in being able to craft a notion of political unity without relying on
the logic of appropriation and incorporation and, just as significantly, a
denial of *agency*. For me the unity of women is best understood not as
*given*, on the basis of a natural/psychological commonality; it is something that has to be worked for, struggled towards – *in history*. What we
need to do is articulate ways in which the historical forms of oppression
relate to the category 'women', and not to try to deduce one from the
other. In other words, it is Morgan's formulation of the relation of
synchronous, alternative histories (herstories) to a diachronic, dominant
historical narrative (History) that is problematic. One of the tasks of
feminist analysis is uncovering alternative, non-identical histories which
challenge and disrupt the spatial and temporal location of a hegemonic
history. However, sometimes attempts to uncover and locate alternative
histories code these very histories as either totally dependent on and
determined by a dominant narrative, or as isolated and autonomous
narratives, untouched in their essence by the dominant figurations. In
these rewritings, what is lost is the recognition that it is the very
co-implication of histories with History which helps us situate and
understand oppositional agency. In Morgan's text, it is the move to
characterize alternative herstories as separate and different from history
that results in a denial of feminist agency. And it is this potential
repositioning of the relation of oppositional histories/spaces to a dominant historical narrative that I find valuable in Bernice Reagon's discussion of coalition politics.


'IT AIN'T HOME NO MORE': RETHINKING UNITY

While Morgan uses the notion of sisterhood to construct a cross-cultural
unity of women and speaks of 'planetary feminism as the politics of the
21st century', Bernice Johnson Reagon uses *coalition* as the basis to talk
about the cross-cultural commonality of struggles, identifying *survival*,
rather than *shared oppression*, as the ground for coalition. She begins
with this valuable political reminder: 'You don't go into coalition because you *like* it. The only reason you would consider trying to team up
with somebody who could possibly kill you, is because that's the only
way you can figure you can stay alive' (p. 357).
    The governing metaphor Reagon uses to speak of coalition, difference

and struggle is that of a 'barred room'. However, whereas Morgan's barred room might be owned and controlled by the Big Brothers in different countries, Reagon's internal critique of the contemporary left focuses on the barred rooms constructed by oppositional political movements such as feminist, civil rights, gay and lesbian, and chicano political organizations. She maintains that these barred rooms may provide a 'nurturing space' for a little while, but they ultimately provide an illusion of community based on isolation and the freezing of difference. Thus, while sameness of experience, oppression, culture, etc. may be adequate to construct this space, the moment we 'get ready to clean house' this very sameness in community is exposed as having been built on a debilitating ossification of difference.

Reagon is concerned with differences *within* political struggles, and the negative effects, in the long run, of a nurturing, 'nationalist' perspective: 'At a certain stage nationalism is crucial to a people if you are going to ever impact as a group in your own interest. Nationalism at another point becomes reactionary because it is totally inadequate for surviving in the world with many peoples' (p. 358). This is similar to Gramsci's analysis of oppositional political strategy in terms of the difference between wars of manoeuvre (separation and consolidation) and wars of position (re-entry into the mainstream in order to challenge it on its own terms). Reagon's insistence on breaking out of barred rooms and struggling for coalition is a recognition of the importance – indeed the inevitable necessity – of wars of position. It is based, I think, on a recognition of the need to resist the imperatives of an expansionist US state, and of imperial History. It is also, however, a recognition of the limits of identity politics. For once you open the door and let others in, 'the room don't feel like the room no more. And it ain't home no more' (p. 359).

The relation of coalition to home is a central metaphor for Reagon. She speaks of coalition as opposed, by definition, to home.[13] In fact, the confusion of home with coalition is what concerns her as an urgent problem, and it is here that the status of experience in her text becomes clear. She criticizes the idea of enforcing 'women-only' or 'woman-identified' space by using an 'in-house' definition of woman. What concerns her is not a sameness which allows us to identify with each other as women, but the exclusions particular normative definitions of 'woman' enforce. It is the exercise of violence in creating a legitimate *inside* and an illegitimate *outside* in the name of identity that is significant to her – or, in other words, the exercise of violence when unity or

coalition is confused with home and used to enforce a premature sisterhood or solidarity. According to her this 'comes from taking a word like
"women" and using it as a code' (p. 360). The experience of being
woman can create an illusory unity, for it is not the experience of being
woman, but the meanings attached to gender, race, class and age at
various historical moments that is of strategic significance.

Thus, by calling into question the term 'woman' as the automatic
basis of unity, Bernice Reagon would want to splinter the notion of
experience suggested by Robin Morgan. Her critique of nationalist and
culturalist positions, which after an initial necessary period of consolidation work in harmful and exclusionary ways, provides us with a fundamentally political analytic space for an understanding of experience.
By always insisting on an analysis of the operations and effects of power
in our attempts to create alternative communities, Reagon foregrounds
our *strategic* locations and positionings. Instead of separating experience
and politics and basing the latter on the former, she emphasizes the
politics that always define and inform experience (in particular, in left,
anti-racist and feminist communities). By examining the differences and
potential divisions *within* political subjects as well as collectives, Reagon
offers an implicit critique of totalizing theories of history and social
change. She underscores the significance of the traditions of political
struggle, what she calls an 'old-age perspective' – and this is, I would
add, a global perspective. What is significant, however, is that the global
is forged on the basis of memories and counter-narratives, not on an
ahistorical universalism. For Reagon, global, old-age perspectives are
founded on humility, the gradual chipping away of our assumed, often
ethnocentric centres of self/other definitions.

Thus, her particular location and political priorities lead her to
emphasize a politics of engagement (a war of position), and to interrogate totalizing notions of difference and the identification of exclusive
spaces as 'homes'. Perhaps it is partly also her insistence on the urgency
and difficult nature of political struggle that leads Reagon to talk about
difference in terms of racism, while Morgan often formulates difference
in terms of cultural pluralism. This is Bernice Reagon's way of 'throwing yourself into the next century':

> Most of us think that the space we live in is the most important space
> there is, and that the condition we find ourselves in is the condition that
> must be changed or else. That is only partially the case. If you analyze the
> situation properly, you will know that there might be a few things you
> can do in your personal, individual interest so that you can experience and

enjoy change. But most of the things that you do, if you do them right, are for people who live long after you are forgotten. That will happen if you give it away . . . The only way you can take yourself seriously is if you can throw yourself into the next period beyond your little meager human-body-mouth-talking all the time. (p. 365)

We take ourselves seriously only when we go 'beyond' ourselves, valuing not just the plurality of the differences among us but also the massive presence of the Difference that our recent planetary history has installed. This 'Difference' is what we see only through the lenses of our present moment, our present struggles.

I have looked at two recent feminist texts and argued that feminist discourse must be self-conscious in its production of notions of experience and difference. The rationale for staging an encounter between the two texts, written by a white and black activist respectively, was not to identify 'good' and 'bad' feminist texts. Instead, I was interested in foregrounding questions of cross-cultural analysis which permeate 'movement' or popular (not just academic) feminist texts, and in indicating the significance of a politics of location in the US of the 1980s and the 1990s. Instead of privileging a certain limited version of identity politics, it is the current *intersection* of anti-racist, anti-imperialist and gay and lesbian struggles which we need to understand to map the ground for feminist political strategy and critical analysis.[14] A reading of these texts also opens up for me a temporality of *struggle*, which disrupts and challenges the logic of linearity, development and progress which are the hallmarks of European modernity.

But why focus on a temporality of struggle? And how do I define *my* place on the map? For me, the notion of a temporality of struggle defies and subverts the logic of European modernity and the 'law of identical temporality'. It suggests an insistent, simultaneous, non-synchronous process characterized by multiple locations, rather than a search for origins and endings which, as Adrienne Rich says, 'seems a way of stopping time in its tracks'.[15] The year 2000 is the end of the Christian millennium, and Christianity is certainly an indelible part of post-colonial history. But we cannot afford to forget those alternative, resistant spaces occupied by oppositional histories and memories. By not insisting on *a* history or *a* geography but focusing on a temporality of struggle, I create the historical ground from which I can define myself in the USA of the 1990s, a place from which I can speak to the future – not the end of an era but the promise of many.

The USA of the 1990s: a geopolitical power seemingly unbounded in its effects, peopled with 'natives' struggling for land and legal rights, and 'immigrants' with their own histories and memories. Alicia Dujovne Ortiz writes about Buenos Aires as 'the very image of expansiveness'.[16] This is also how I visualize the USA of the 1990s. Ortiz writes of Buenos Aires:

> A city without doors. Or rather, a port city, a gateway which never closes. I have always been astonished by those great cities of the world which have such precise boundaries that one can say exactly where they end. Buenos Aires has no end. One wants to ring it with a beltway, as if to point an index finger, trembling with uncertainty, and say: 'You end there. Up to this point you are you. Beyond that, God alone knows!' . . . a city that is impossible to limit with the eye or the mind. So, what does it mean to say that one is a native of Buenos Aires? To belong to Buenos Aires, to be *Porteno* – to come from this Port? What does this mean? What or who can we hang onto? Usually we cling to history or geography. In this case, what are we to do? Here geography is merely an abstract line that marks the separation of the earth and sky.[17]

If the logic of imperialism and the logic of modernity share a notion of time, they also share a notion of space as territory. In the North America of the 1990s geography seems more and more like 'an abstract line that marks the separation of the earth and sky'. Witness the contemporary struggle for control over oil in the name of 'democracy and freedom' in Saudi Arabia. Even the boundaries between space and outer space are not binding any more. In this expansive and expanding continent, how does one locate oneself? And what does location as I have inherited it have to do with self-conscious, strategic location as I choose it now?

A National Public Radio news broadcast announces that all immigrants to the United States now have to undergo mandatory AIDS testing. I am reminded very sharply of my immigrant status in this country, of my plastic identification card which is proof of my legitimate location in the US. But location, for feminists, necessarily implies self- as well as collective definition, since meanings of the self are inextricably bound up with our understanding of collectives as social agents. For me, a comparative reading of Morgan's and Reagon's documents of activism precipitates the recognition that experience of the self, which is often discontinuous and fragmented, must be historicized before it can be generalized into a collective vision. In other words, experience must be historically interpreted and theorized if it is to become the basis of feminist solidarity and struggle, and it is at this moment that an understanding of the politics of location proves crucial.

In this country I am, for instance, subject to a number of legal/ political definitions: 'post-colonial', 'immigrant', 'Third World'. These definitions, while in no way comprehensive, do trace an analytic and political space from which I can insist on a temporality of struggle. Movement *between* cultures, languages and complex configurations of meaning and power have always been the territory of the colonized. It is this *process*, what Caren Kaplan in her discussion of the reading and writing of home/exile has called 'a continual reterritorialization, with the proviso that one moves on',[18] that I am calling a temporality of struggle. It is this process, this reterritorialization through struggle, that allows me a paradoxical continuity of self, mapping and transforming my political location. It suggests a particular notion of political agency, since my location forces and enables specific modes of reading and knowing the dominant. The struggles I choose to engage in are then an intensification of these modes of knowing – an engagement on a different level of knowledge. There is, quite simply, no transcendental location possible in the USA of the 1990s.

I have argued for a politics of engagement rather than a politics of transcendence, for the present and the future. I *know* – in my own non-synchronous temporality – that by the year 2000 apartheid will be discussed as a nightmarish chapter in black South Africa's history, the resistance to and victory over the efforts of the US government and multinational mining conglomerates to relocate the Navajo and Hopi reservations from Big Mountain, Arizona, will be written into elementary-school textbooks, and the Palestinian homeland will no longer be referred to as the 'Middle East question' – it will be a reality. But that is my preferred history: what I hope and struggle for, I garner as *my* knowledge, create it as the place from where I seek to know. After all, it is the way in which I understand, define and engage in feminist, anti-imperialist and anti-racist collectives and movements that anchors my belief in the future and in the efficacy of struggles for social change.

NOTES

This essay is a slightly revised, updated version of an essay published in the journal *Copyright*, 1, Fall 1987, pp. 30–44. I develop the arguments raised here, especially the question of political agency in greater detail in my book in

progress on western feminist theory, Third World feminisms, and the problems
of cross-cultural enquiry.

1   I am indebted to Adrienne Rich's essay, 'Notes Toward a Politics of
    Location (1984)', for the notion of the 'politics of location' (in her *Blood,
    Bread, and Poetry: Selected Prose 1979–1985* [W.W. Norton & Company,
    New York, 1986], pp. 210–31). In a number of essays in this collection,
    Rich writes eloquently and provocatively about the politics of her own
    location as a white, Jewish, lesbian feminist in North America. See espe-
    cially 'North American Tunnel Vision (1983)', and 'Blood, Bread and Poetry:
    The Location of the Poet (1984)'.
        While I attempt to modify and extend Rich's notion, I share her sense of
    urgency as she asks feminists to re-examine the politics of our location in
    North America:

    > A natural extension of all this seemed to me the need to examine not only
    > racial and ethnic identity, but location in the United States of North America.
    > As a feminist in the United States it seemed necessary to examine how we
    > participate in mainstream North American cultural chauvinism, the sometimes
    > unconscious belief that white North Americans possess a superior right to
    > judge, select, and ransack other cultures, that we are more 'advanced' than
    > other peoples of this hemisphere ... It was not enough to say 'As a woman I
    > have no country; as a woman my country is the whole world.' Magnificent as
    > that vision may be, we can't explode into breadth without a conscious grasp
    > on the particular and concrete meaning of our location here and now, in the
    > United States of America. ('North American Tunnel Vision', p. 162)

2   I address one version of this, the management of race and cultural pluralism
    in the US academy, in some depth in my essay 'On Race and Voice:
    Challenges for Liberal Education in the 1990s', *Cultural Critique*, 14
    (1989–90), pp. 179–208.
3   Two recent essays develop the point I am trying to suggest here. Jenny
    Bourne identifies the problems with most forms of contemporary identity
    politics which equalize notions of oppression, thereby writing out of the
    picture any analysis of structural exploitation or domination. See her 'Jew-
    ish Feminism and Identity Politics', *Race and Class*, XXIX (1987), pp.
    1–24.
        In a similar vein, S.P. Mohanty uses the opposition between 'History'
    and 'histories' to criticize an implicit assumption in contemporary cultural
    theory that pluralism is an adequate substitute for political analyses of
    dependent relationships and larger historical configurations. For Mohanty,
    the ultimate target is the cultural and historical *relativism* which he iden-
    tifies as the unexamined philosophical 'dogma' underlying political celebra-
    tions of pure difference. This is how he characterizes the initial issues
    involved:

    > Plurality [is] thus a political ideal as much as it [is] a methodological slogan.
    > But ... a nagging question [remains]: How do we negotiate between my

history and yours? How would it be possible for us to recover our commonality, not the humanist myth of our shared human attributes which are
meant to distinguish us all from animals, but, more significantly, the imbrica-
tion of our various pasts and presents, the ineluctable relationships of shared
and contested meanings, values, material resources? It is necessary to assert
our dense particularities, our lived and imagined differences. But could we
afford to leave unexamined the question of how our differences are intertwined
and indeed hierarchically organized? Could we, in other words, really afford
to have *entirely* different histories, to see ourselves as living – and having lived
– in entirely heterogeneous and discrete spaces?

See his 'Us and Them: On the Philosophical Bases of Political Criticism',
*The Yale Journal Of Criticism*, 2 (1989), pp. 1–31; p. 13.

4  For instance, some of the questions which arise in feminist analyses and
politics which are situated at the juncture of studies of race, colonialism and
Third World political economy pertain to the systemic production, constitution, operation and reproduction of the institutional manifestations of
power. How does power operate in the constitution of gendered and racial
subjects? How do we talk about contemporary political praxis, collective
consciousness and collective struggle in the context of an analysis of power?
Other questions concern the discursive codification of sexual politics and
the corresponding feminist political strategies these codifications engender.
Why is sexual politics defined around particular issues? One might examine
the cultural and historical processes and conditions under which sexuality
is constructed during conditions of war. One might also ask under what
historical conditions sexuality is defined as sexual violence, and investigate
the emergence of gay and lesbian sexual identities. The discursive organization of these questions is significant because they help to chart and shape
collective resistance. Some of these questions are addressed by contributors
in a collection of essays I have co-edited with Ann Russo and Lourdes
Torres, entitled *Third World Women and the Politics of Feminism* (Indiana
University Press, Bloomington, Ind., and Indianapolis, 1991).

5  Robin Morgan, 'Planetary Feminism: The Politics of the 21st Century', in
her *Sisterhood is Global: The International Women's Movement Anthology*
(Anchor Press/Doubleday, New York, 1984), pp. 1–37; I also refer to the
'Prefatory Note and Methodology' section (pp. xiii–xxiii) of *Sisterhood is
Global* in this essay. Bernice Johnson Reagon, 'Coalition Politics: Turning
the Century', in Barbara Smith (ed.), *Home Girls: A Black Feminist Anthology* (Kitchen Table, Women of Color Press, New York, 1983), pp. 356–68.

6  Teresa de Lauretis, 'Feminist Studies/Critical Studies: Issues, Terms and
Contexts', in de Lauretis (ed.), *Feminist Studies/Critical Studies* (Indiana
University Press, Bloomington, Ind., 1986), pp. 1–19; p. 5.

7  Monique Wittig develops this idea in 'The Straight Mind', *Feminist Issues*, 1
(1980), pp. 103–10; p. 103.

8  Katie King, 'The Situation of Lesbianism as Feminism's Magical Sign:

Contests for Meaning and the US Women's Movement, 1968–1972', *Communication*, 9 (1986), pp. 65–91; p. 85.

9 Linda Gordon discusses this relation of female to feminist in her 'What's New in Women's History', in de Lauretis, *Feminist Studies/Critical Studies*, pp. 20–31.

10 de Lauretis, 'Feminist Studies/Critical Studies: Issues, Terms and Contexts', p. 10.

11 Rich, 'Notes Toward a Politics of Location', p. 212.

12 Elsewhere I have attempted a detailed analysis of some recent western feminist social science texts about the Third World. Focusing on works which have appeared in an influential series published by Zed Press of London, I examine this discursive construction of women in the Third World and the resultant western feminist self-representations. See 'Under Western Eyes: Feminist Scholarship and Colonial Discourses', *Feminist Review*, 30 (1988), pp. 61–88.

13 For an extensive discussion of the appeal and contradictions of notions of home and identity in contemporary feminist politics, see Biddy Martin and Chandra Talpade Mohanty, 'Feminist Politics: What's Home Got to Do With It?', in de Lauretis, *Feminist Studies/Critical Studies*, pp. 191–212.

14 For a rich and informative account of contemporary racial politics in the U.S., see Michael Omi and Howard Winant, *Racial Formation in the United States: From the 1960s to the 1980s* (Routledge and Kegan Paul, New York and London, 1986). Surprisingly, this text erases gender and gay politics altogether, leading me to wonder how we can talk about the 'racial state' without addressing questions of gender and sexual politics. A good companion text which in fact emphasizes such questions is G. Anzaldua and C. Moraga (eds), *This Bridge Called My Back: Writings By Radical Women of Color* (Kitchen Table, Women of Color Press, New York, 1983). Another, more contemporary text which continues some of the discussions in *This Bridge*, also edited by Gloria Anzaldua, is entitled *Making Face, Making Soul, Haciendo Caras, Creative and Critical Perspectives by Women of Color* (Aunt Lute, San Francisco, 1990).

15 Rich, 'Notes Toward a Politics of Location', p. 227.

16 Alicia Dujovne Ortiz, '*Buenos Aires* (an excerpt)', *Discourse*, 8 (1986–7), pp. 73–83; p. 76.

17 Ibid., p. 76.

18 Caren Kaplan, 'The Poetics of Displacement in *Buenos Aires*', *Discourse*, 8 (1986–7), pp. 94–102; p. 98.

# 6

# Sexual Practice and Changing Lesbian Identities

## Biddy Martin

A few weeks before writing this I had the opportunity to see an exhibit entitled 'Perversity and Diversity' on the campus of the University of Rochester. The show was curated by lesbian and gay students and housed in a small exhibit area in front of the Arts Library, accessible through underground hallways. The glass wall separating the exhibition space from the hallway outside was covered with blocks of white paper, on each of which the words 'lesbian', 'gay', 'queer', 'dyke', 'faggot', 'muffdiver', 'bulldyke' were printed one under the other. These words announced the exhibit to passers-by. As one of the visitors to the exhibit pointed out, they also shielded those who were inside the exhibit from the view of those who passed by in the halls. I was interested in the relation between this display of labels and the exhibit behind it. The labels had an ambiguous quality; some of the words could be, and were, read as forms of what has come to be called 'hate speech', but were also presented and read as terms that have been successfully appropriated and redeployed by gay men and lesbians. The emphasis on appropriation, and the relationship of the wall of words to the exhibit behind it, seemed to suggest that the appropriate response to 'hate speech' is not necessarily more regulation and control of speech, but a proliferation of it, and an effort to change the conditions that privilege some forms of speech over others. This seems particularly important now, at a moment when rightwingers like Jesse Helms have had so much success in efforts to censor our speech, at a moment when AIDS education or miseducation has accounted for so many deaths, because the people most affected are denied not only access and resources but, as Cindy Patton argues so emphatically in *Inventing AIDS*,[1] equal discursive power in the struggle to define the meanings of AIDS.

The exhibit itself featured primarily reproductions of the graphic art that has been so central to the last five years of AIDS and 'queer' activism. The students had displayed ACT-UP posters, T-shirts, badges and placards of their own making. The T-shirt that displayed a photograph of two women having oral sex and sported the caption 'Power Breakfast' had unfortunately been stolen before I got to see the exhibit. To avoid the loss of other precious objects, the curators had removed some of the sex toys and accoutrements that had been hanging on the wall, including a harness and dildo and some of the condoms.

Visitors to the exhibit were encouraged to write their responses to what they had seen on sheets of paper that had been provided for that purpose. The sheets of paper were collected at the end of each day in a thick, book-like record that then became part of the exhibit. The visitors had chosen to write all over one of the walls, however, not only in response to the exhibit, but in response to one another. By the time I saw the show, the walls were covered not only with this graffiti-like exchange, but with tacked-up, typed statements, and even with papers written about the exhibit for courses. The commentaries and conversations among exhibit visitors, some of which were ongoing, became the most compelling part of the exhibit, despite the predictability of much of the virulently homophobic scribbling/writing, and the sometimes painfully defensive and self-justifying responses of self-identified lesbians and gay men. Two things were particularly striking to me: the comments of people who found the 'Power Breakfast' T-Shirt, in particular, or the exhibit as a whole 'unnecessarily violent and aggressive', and the comments of those who seemed most offended by the exhibit's at least implicit claim to being art. Those who experienced the mere presence of the exhibit as an aggressive assault made me think again about the emotional investments in discursive and consequent psychic foreclosures on sexual representation. These foreclosures may have felt so stunning because of what the exhibit seemed to represent and to confirm about one ironic effect of AIDS, namely an opening up of public discussions of sexuality, even in the face of renewed repressions.

The visitors who were offended by the implicit claim to art demonstrated one of the more subtle ways in which the closet operates to safeguard what Eve Sedgwick has characterized as 'the ambient heterosexual population'.[2] Some of the comments seemed to imply that their authors would have found the content inoffensive or less offensive had it not sullied, by attempting to associate itself with, the realm of universal good taste or aesthetics. I couldn't help thinking about the Irish-American woman who was interviewed during the St Patrick's Day Parade in New York, who claimed that 'we grant them their sexual preference, but they don't belong in a parade of this kind', which I took to mean that we're acceptable as long as we don't demand a visible place among normal folk. Such incidents are helpful reminders of the high stakes in symbolic orders. We are not always confronted with direct, coercive efforts to control what we do in bed, but we are constantly threatened with erasure from discursive fields where the naturalization of sexual and gender norms works to obliterate actual pluralities.

Like so much activism over the past five years, cultural interventions such as the Rochester exhibit suggest that we go beyond the demand for a right to privacy, which is still denied us, beyond even the demand for circumscribed social spaces in the form of bars, businesses and pro-grammes, to a demand for broad public discussion. The effort to open up the public realm to a discussion and appreciation of sexual diversity and variation challenges the epistemological and political terms in which homosexuality and other 'perversions' have been closeted for the benefit of 'the ambient heterosexual population', or what Cindy Patton, in *Inventing AIDS*, calls a repressive administrative state. According to Patton, 'the closet and its occupant the homosexual are merely a trope of the administrative state, the product of a convenient repressive ideology with a mobile class of bodies which can readily, easily, and publicly be humiliated, taunted, beaten, arrested, electro-shocked, driven to madness, murdered, made into the spectacle of AIDS' (p. 129).

The exhibit had, at the very least, obviously incited a great deal of interest and debate on the Rochester campus, and this seemed important at a moment when conservative scholars have stepped up their campaigns against what they call 'left-wing politically correct repression' in order to eradicate any serious discussion of sexuality, gender, race or class at the university. But it is also significant in the context of ongoing feminist discussions of sexuality, in which powerfully visible feminists continue to make insidious arguments about women's sexuality that close off, rather than open up, curiosity about our desires, fantasies, practices and pleasures.

The exhibit's explicit, if marginal, focus on sexual practices made it possible to implicate the audience in a way that documenting the history of an apparently coherent, bounded group cannot. The visitors to the exhibit wittingly and unwittingly contributed to the production of meanings, as well as to the thoroughly political project of drawing the line between acceptable and unacceptable sex and sexual representation.[3] It is significant in this regard that the exhibit was entitled 'Perversity and Diversity', and that neither gender nor sexual identity were offered up as organizing principles, making the exhibit a materialization of two important claims in gay and lesbian studies: that sexuality and gender are distinct analytic and political categories; and that the gender of sexual objects is a historically recent and arbitrary basis on which to map sexuality on to bodies, to define a person's identity and to organize significant aspects of social life. These claims prompt us to imagine how identities and social relations might be remapped as a consequence of upheavals in the categories with which we think about sex.

It is also worth noting that the exhibit celebrated the centrality of art activism in oppositional political responses to AIDS. Cindy Patton is just one cultural critic who has stressed the importance of art activism in response to the silencing tactics of government AIDS policies: 'AIDS activists know that silence equals death, but we also know that this cannot be said, it must be performed . . . The insight that "silence equals death" has spawned an international agitprop activism that circulates around the meanings elided in the legitimated discourses of science, media, public politics' (p. 131). Art activism provides a means of imagining and representing subjects rendered unintelligible by the hegemony of certain discursive formations. Douglas Crimp and Adam Rolston characterize AIDS art activism as a form of politicized post-modernism, one that defies traditional conceptions of authorship and originality with its emphasis on appropriation and collective production. The graphic art that has been used so effectively by ACT-UP is, as Crimp and Rolston put it, 'grounded in the accumulated knowledge and political analysis of the AIDS crisis produced collectively by the entire movement'.[4] As Crimp and others stress, this graphic art has played a significant role in organizing efforts and in efforts to define positions: 'AIDS activist graphics enunciate AIDS politics to and for all of us in the movement. They suggest slogans (SILENCE = DEATH becomes "We'll never be silent again"), target opponents (the *New York Times*, President Reagan, Cardinal O'Connor), define positions ("All people with AIDS are innocent"), propose actions ("Boycott Burroughs Wellcome")' (p. 20).

A recent lecture by Susie 'Sexpert' Bright, editor of the lesbian porn magazine *On Our Backs*, provided another interesting occasion to reflect on changing lesbian identities. There was something extraordinary about the direct manner in which Bright talked about sex, sexual practices and body parts, without assuming a clinical, antiseptic or sensationalist tone. She managed to speak about sex in the form of serious, but not unduly weighty, and always humorous talk. What she conveyed, but also produced, was genuine curiosity about her own and our sexual fantasies, practices and pleasures, and her performance made it apparent how rare this kind of curiosity is, and how scarce the discursive and social space in which curiosity might be opened up.

Susie Bright spoke about the deployment of rigid sexual categories, not only by the right but also within our own communities, where investments in the stability, internal coherence and uniqueness of lesbian identity have not only obscured sexual differences but generated an active resistance to knowing what we fantasize, desire, do and think. As psychoanalysis teaches us, ignorance is never about a simple lack of knowledge, but always about an active resistance. One of the most stunning aspects of Bright's talk was her emphasis on her own efforts to notice those active resistances in herself and to distinguish them from simple indifference. At various points in her lecture and in her generous responses to questions, Bright showed how investments in sexual identity categories become stumbling blocks in current discussions of sexual practices and pleasures.

While I listened to Bright, I was reminded of a passage in a German novel written in 1901 that could have been part, and probably is part, of any number of contemporary lesbian novels or conversations. In this novel, published under the pseudonym Aimée Duc and entitled *Are They Women*, a group of women who identify themselves in the newly available medical terms of 'the third sex' are engaged in a heated discussion of a certain Elisa Fritz, once one of them, but now married to a man.[5] The participants in the discussion work to re-establish the boundaries around the only apparently non-contradictory category of 'the third sex' by supposing that Fritz had never really been one of them, that her claims to have been part of 'the third sex' were fraudulent. The difficulty in sustaining the neat division between real and unreal members, between the inside and outside of the category, emerges when one of the women reminds Fritz's most vociferous critic that she herself had once been married. In response to this reminder, Minotschka can manage only the ultimately weak assertion that 'that was different.' A number of scholars have demonstrated that the construction of homosexuality and lesbianism, in particular, as a 'third sex' leaves conventional assumptions of gender polarity and normal heterosexuality intact by containing difference in a third, static category. It is perhaps harder to see how contemporary efforts to define the essence of lesbian identity or subjectivity succeed in normalizing gender divisions and reproducing the only apparent self-evidence of heterosexuality.

A conversation that Jan Clausen, once self-identified and known to others as a lesbian writer, sets up as a preface to her now 'infamous' article in the gay and lesbian journal *Outlook* on her involvement with a man could almost have been lifted from Aimée Duc's novel.[6] Clausen's fictionalized account puts us in the position of overhearing a conversation among a group of lesbians in present-day Brooklyn about a former 'lesbian spokesperson' now involved with a man. Predictably enough, one of the unnamed conversants suggests that this spokesperson may have been straight all along. In the exchange that ensues, this suspicion of fraudulent membership in the group is contested, but the terms in which the discussion proceeds are more interesting and entertaining than the outcome. In an effort at what we hope is irony, Clausen has her imaginary figures try to interpret what this former 'spokesperson's' clothes, her new purse and her longstanding habit of shaving her legs tell them about whether she might be authentically lesbian or heterosexual. One of the women wonders whether her white middle-class privilege tempted her back into heterosexuality. The effort to decide whether her lesbian past or her apparently heterosexual present is the more authentic remains inconclusive. Near the end of the dialogue, one of the participants 'confesses' that she 'almost slept with a guy last year when Lilith dumped me'. The text registers in bold face what it calls an awkward pause, then sets forth with the weak assurance that 'that isn't the same thing at all.'

I find Clausen's particular use of this prefatory scene to set up and authorize her homogenizations and criticisms of 'the lesbian community' problematic. Her critiques smack of an increasingly popular kind of vanguardism that rewrites the lesbianisms and feminisms of the seventies as one naive, repressive and ultimately boring lump. But I want to pursue the conversation that Clausen uses to open her essay because it has important resonances. A friend of mine recently referred to these efforts at boundary control as 'purification rituals', and they do seem to involve efforts to rid the category 'lesbian' of anything messy, anything like its inevitable internal differences or our own irreducible heterogeneities. On a more compassionate note, I would suggest that they are also ritualistic efforts to deal with what is experienced as loss, and exhibit all the forms of denial that accompany unresolved losses. Surely the perceived need for uniformity, authenticity and firm, separate foundations in a world outside of heterosexuality operates as a defence against the continued marginalization, denial and prohibition of women's love and desire for other women. The question is whether the perceived need for uniformity, complete autonomy and authenticity is the best way to challenge heterosexism and misogyny, or an effective strategy to defend against annihilation. The amount of work required to keep the category intact exposes its ultimate instability and its lack of fixed foundations. Both of the fictional conversations I have described lead from an effort to externalize difference to the at least halting recognition of internal contradictions, from efforts to contest the authenticity of a (former) lesbian involved with a man to worries that such ambiguities also operate within those who remain safely in the category. But the introduction of irreducible internal differences is foreclosed by concluding assurances that what happened at an earlier point to a current member of the group 'was different'. These passages show the importance of the temporal dimension in efforts to establish a position or identity. For lesbians involved in the project of stabilizing a lesbian position in the present, a potentially contradictory past must be defused by being rendered 'different'. This reverses homophobic efforts to destabilize a lesbian's self-definition as a lesbian in the present by suggesting that she will grow out of it, that the future will be 'different'.

Whatever the intent of these efforts to render lesbianism internally coherent and stable, discipline and control are the effects. Unruly sexual fantasies, desires, pleasures and practices, but also more complex analyses of social realities, are sacrificed to investments in identity. Over the past several years, lesbians' involvement in AIDS activism and AIDS education have converged with the courageous work of sex radicals to challenge the rigid constructions of identity and to open up curiosity about those fantasies and practices that cut across identity categories. Against lesbian-feminist constructions of lesbians' fundamental difference from gay men, lesbian activists, writers and theorists are busy asking questions about the potentially positive impact of gay male sexuality and sexual representation on lesbian sex, about lesbians' fantasies of being gay men, and about their sexual enactments of those fantasies. In her lecture at Cornell, Susie Bright announced that lesbians' anxieties about penetration and its potentially heterosexual or male implications are now old news. And in her advice columns in *On Our Backs*, Bright has suggested that some practices once associated with or claimed by lesbian sadomasochists are now common practice among lesbians. For self-respecting lesbian sadomasochists, the ante has been upped considerably in terms of what it might take to be a s/m lesbian.

In her essay on bisexuality, entitled 'Drawing the Line', Greta Christina suggests a similar shift.

Over the last several years, the lesbian community has expanded its boundaries and definitions dramatically. Remember how it used to be? You weren't a 'real' lesbian if you: used dildos, slept around, wore heels

and make-up, did S/M, dug Miami Vice, weren't in a long-term relationship and didn't want to be, liked porn, fucked strangers, or thought
Mick Jagger was cool and Holly Near was a geek. Along with our great
increases in self-acceptance (and the somewhat meager increases in acceptance by straight society) has come greater flexibility, a rejoicing in diversity
that wasn't around 15 years ago.[7]

Her humour notwithstanding, Christina, too, participates in the too-
common homogenization of a more complicated past, but she points
to important ways in which the politicization of bisexuality and the
appropriation of the term 'queer' open up new alignments or realign-
ments across categories of gender and sexual identity. These new alignments co-exist and contend with other constructions of lesbian identity,
including those that emphasize the gender specificity of lesbians' experiences and oppression and the differences between lesbians and gay men.
Contests over the meanings of lesbianism are not new, but perhaps the
irreducibly complex and contested status of identity has itself been made
more visible, and tolerable, at least momentarily.

According to Eve Sedgwick, both heterosexist and antihomophobic
definitions of homosexuality have been caught in a 'conceptually intractable' set of contradictions for over a hundred years, contradictions that
remain available for manipulation in the service of power/knowledge.[8]
The first major contradiction in 'common-sense' conceptions of homosexuality is that between what Sedgwick calls 'universalizing' and
'minoritizing' views.

> Most moderately to well-educated Western people in this century seem
> to share a similar understanding of homosexual definition, independent
> of whether they themselves are gay or straight, homophobic or anti-
> homophobic . . . [That understanding] holds the minoritizing view that
> there is a distinct population of persons who 'really are' gay; at the same
> time, it holds the universalizing views that sexual desire is an unpredict-
> ably powerful solvent of stable identities; that apparently heterosexual
> persons and object choices are strongly marked by same-sex influences
> and desires, and vice versa for apparently homosexual ones; and that at
> least male heterosexual identity and modern masculinist culture may re-
> quire for their maintenance the scapegoating crystallization of a same-sex
> male desire that is widespread and in the first place internal. (p. 85)

Sedgwick has offered the clearest, most elegant formulations for the
contradictory tropes most salient in western cultures over the past
hundred years for relating same-sex desire to gender. The trope of
'gender inversion' figures the lesbian as virile and the male homosexual

as effeminate. According to Sedgwick, 'one vital impulse of this trope is the preservation of an essential *heterosexuality* within desire itself, through a particular reading of the homosexuality of persons: desire, in this view, by definition subsists in the current that runs between one male self and one female self, in whatever sex of bodies these selves may be manifested' (p. 87). The trope of gender inversion co-exists with the contradictory trope of 'gender separatism', which figures same-sex desire as the ultimate expression of a person's identification with her or his own gender. Sedgwick credits Adrienne Rich's construction of lesbianism as woman identification with having challenged the very old but still common virilization of lesbians, a virilization that exposes the profound extent to which lesbianism has been constructed on analogy with male sexuality.

Sedgwick argues that the woman-identified-woman and Rich's lesbian continuum challenge the distinction drawn by inversion models between desire and identification. She also suggests that gender-identification models tend to adopt a universalist view of the hetero/homo divide. But as so many critics have shown, the collapse of sexuality and gender, and of identification and desire in the woman-identified-woman, seem to have erased desire in favour of identification.

The renewed emphasis on sex, on alignments with gay men and on sexual practices such as butch–femme roles does not represent a simple return from woman identification to minoritizing models of gender inversion. The now much maligned lesbianisms and feminisms of the seventies have helped make it possible for lesbian activists, writers and theorists to engage 'phallic' fantasies, desires and sexualities without fear of the charge of imitation. Lesbians' ongoing sexual, textual and theoretical explorations suggest that there might be something to gain again from prying 'the phallic' loose from its identification with men and 'the feminine' from its conflation with woman.

In her deconstruction of feminist identity politics and its foundationalist premises, Judith Butler displaces the opposition between the tropes of gender inversion and gender identification by arguing for the disaggregation of sex, gender, sexual identity and desires.[9] Butler challenges feminists to cease reproducing the assumption of just two neatly divided genders, but goes further to challenge the foundationalist assumption that two discrete (biological) sexes underlie the social construction of gender. In one of her best-known formulations, Butler argues that 'sex will be shown to have been gender all along' (*GT*, p. 8).

Feminists' construction of 'sex/gender systems' as the object of analysis too easily reproduces what Butler calls 'expressive models of gender'.

Expressive models of gender do the work of normalization and control
by assuming 'an abiding substance or gendered self' that grounds the
unity of sex, gender and desire. On this model, any dissonance in
features, acts or desires can be referred back to a gendered core, to
which they then become merely secondary and 'accidental' (*GT*, p. 24).
What remains unchallenged is the very notion of essential gendered
identities. Over against feminists' use of an expressive model of gender,
Butler suggests a performative model. The assumption of two neatly
divided genders, as of just two discrete sexes, is constituted retrospec-
tively on the basis of repeated performances of culturally sanctioned acts
of gender, according to Butler, who offers a model of signification over
the foundationalisms of identity politics:

> The deconstruction of identity is not the deconstruction of politics;
> rather, it establishes as political the very terms through which identity is
> articulated. This kind of critique brings into question the foundationalist
> frame in which feminism as an identity politics has been articulated. The
> internal paradox of this foundationalism is that it presumes, fixes, and
> constrains the very 'subjects' that it hopes to represent and liberate. (*GT*,
> p. 148)

In a recent essay, Butler argues explicitly that a lesbian identity that
becomes normative 'turn[s] against the sexuality that the category pur-
ports to describe'.[10] In her challenge to any assumption of 'expressive or
causal lines between sex, gender, gender presentation, sexual practice,
fantasy, and sexuality', Butler reminds her readers that 'part of what
constitutes sexuality is precisely that which does not appear and that
which, to some degree, can never appear.'[11]

Following the axioms of post-structuralist theories of language and
representation, Butler understands identity as the sedimentation of
meanings, or the after-effect of repeated signifying practices. To understand identity as signifying practice is 'to understand culturally intellig-
ible subjects as the resulting effect of a rule-bound discourse that inserts
itself in the pervasive and mundane signifying acts of linguistic life'.
Butler continues:

> Abstractly considered, language refers to an open system of signs by
> which intelligibility is insistently created and contested. As historically
> specific organizations of language, discourses present themselves in the
> plural, coexisting within temporal frames and instituting unpredictable
> and inadvertent convergences from which specific modalities of discursive
> possibilities are engendered. (*GT*, p. 145)

Clearly, then, the 'subject of feminism' cannot be thought as a stable, unified or internally coherent woman, or lesbian, without arresting and obscuring the plurality of discursive domains, the 'unpredictable and inadvertent convergences', in which subjects are constituted. Butler moves from this emphasis on the plurality and heterogeneity of discursive fields to the suggestion that resistance and subversion can only emerge, but do indeed emerge, 'within the practices of repetitive signifying', not from claims to independent and discrete identities.

> If the rules governing signification not only restrict, but enable the assertion of alternative domains of cultural intelligibility, i.e., new possibilities for gender that contest the rigid codes of hierarchical binarisms, then it is only within the practices of repetitive signifying that a subversion of identity becomes possible. (*GT*, p. 145)

It is important to note that Butler's understanding of signification and subversion allows for the at least 'provisional semantic stabilization' of the category homosexual. Butler emphasizes over and over that she is not interested in difference *qua* difference, or in 'celebrating each and every new possibility *qua* possibility', but in 'redescribing those possibilities that already exist, but which exist within cultural domains designated as culturally unintelligible and impossible' (*GT*, pp. 148–9).

Homosexual practices, such as drag and butch–femme roles, become privileged sites for the redescription of 'possibilities that already exist'. Butler redescribes these practices/performances as reconfigurations of sex and gender that expose the fraudulence of all claims to authentic gender identity. Remember that for Butler acts or practices cannot be said to be expressions of an underlying or interior gender core or self; the illusion of underlying core is produced by the gendered performances that are then taken to be its manifestation or expression. Drag cannot be said to be an imitation of femininity any more than butch–femme roles can be said to be an imitation of heterosexuality, since for Butler all performances of gender and its relation to sex are imitations of fantasized ideals, hence masquerades, never copies of originals or of simple biological foundations. Heterosexuality is itself masquerade without an original, or, as Butler suggests about homosexuality in a recent essay, necessary drag.[12] Heterosexuality, like the gender divisions on which it relies, is constituted through repetitive signifying practices that strive, but necessarily fail, to replicate fantasized ideals of masculinity, femininity and normal sexuality. In the process, heterosexuality must ward off the excesses that emerge in the intervals of repeated performances, excesses that it may then hypostatize in an Other, the homosexual. Why else would it have to define itself in terms of what it is not, homosexuality? Butler stresses the 'compulsion to repeat' that is so fundamental to the project of naturalization, or the project of 'produc[ing] the *effect* of its own originality'. Butler continues:

> Logically, this notion of an 'origin' is suspect, for how can something operate as an origin if there are no secondary consequences which retrospectively confirm the originality of that origin? The origin requires its derivations in order to affirm itself as an origin, for origins only make sense to the extent that they are differentiated from that which they produce as derivations. Hence, if it were not for the notion of the homosexual *as* copy, there would be no construct of heterosexuality *as* origin.[13]

Butler's readings of drag and butch–femme roles show how a model of signification might displace the debates over whether gay and lesbian sexual practices constitute imitations or the real thing:

> The performance of drag plays upon the distinction between the anatomy of the performer and the gender that is being performed. But we are actually in the presence of three contingent dimensions of significant corporeality: anatomical sex, gender identity, and gender performance. If the anatomy of the performer is already distinct from the gender of the performer, and both of those are distinct from the gender of the performance, then the performance suggests a dissonance not only between sex and performance, but sex and gender, and gender and performance. As much as drag creates a unified picture of 'woman,' it also reveals the distinctness of those aspects of gendered experience which are falsely naturalized as a unity through the regulatory fiction of heterosexual coherence. (*GT*, p. 137)

Butler is careful to emphasize that drag represents not a parody of an original, but a parody '*of* the very notion of an original' (*GT*, p. 138). Butler refuses, quite rightly I think, to legislate what would count as a subversive performance and writes explicitly of the importance of context. Only a more contextualized reading of specific performances, one that attends to questions of institutional constraint, could begin to answer the question that she is so often asked about when particular performances of gender might be subversive, or what it might mean to call them subversive.[14]

Butler's argument underscores the importance of rendering visible the complexities that already exist, but are rendered unthinkable, invisible

or impossible by discursive/institutional orderings with deep investments in defining viable subjects. Her readings of butch–femme roles are a
model of this project:

> Within lesbian contexts, the 'identification' with masculinity that appears
> as butch identity is not a simple assimilation of lesbianism back into the
> terms of heterosexuality. As one lesbian femme explained, she likes her
> boys to be girls, meaning that 'being a girl' contextualizes and resignifies
> 'masculinity' in a butch identity. As a result, that masculinity, if that it can
> be called, is always brought into relief against a culturally intelligible
> 'female body.' It is precisely this dissonant juxtaposition and the sexual
> tensions that its transgression generates that constitute the object of desire.
> In other words, the object (and clearly, there is not just one) of lesbian-
> femme desire is neither some decontextualized female body nor a discrete
> yet superimposed masculine identity, but the destabilization of both terms
> as they come into erotic interplay. (*GT*, p. 123)

Butler's reading emphasizes 'the erotic significance of these identities as
internally dissonant and complex in their resignification of the hegemonic categories by which they are enabled'. She goes on to stress that 'the
structuring presence of heterosexual constructs within gay and lesbian
sexuality does not mean that those constructs *determine* gay and lesbian
sexuality' (*GT*, p. 123). It is to conceive of the only apparent divide
between them as arbitrary and unstable; it is to imagine heterosexuality
and homosexuality in a relation of co-implication. Susie Sexpert is
excellent on the subject of imitation and co-implication. During her
several years of working against lesbians' fears that penetration and the
use of dildos might be imitative or even symptomatic of heterosexual
desire, Susie Bright suggested over and over that 'penetration is as
heterosexual as kissing', but she also went further to suggest that lesbians take credit for what they have offered all the heterosexuals who
now benefit from the multiple pleasures that lesbians discovered in that
mobile phallus, the dildo. Bright recently explained that she regretted
having stressed the distinctions between penises and dildos, and now
encourages lesbians/women to develop our phallic fantasies, including
the fantasies that get materialized in butches' habit of 'packing dildos'
when they leave the privacy of their homes.
  Lesbianism, for Bright, for Butler and for many others, cannot be
posited as an absolutely separate identity with separate foundations and
internal homogeneity without being complicit with the repressive, even
deathly operations of normalization and exclusion, even of lesbians'
own fantasies, pleasures and practices. The project, not only for Butler,

but for Butler understood here as a particular theoretical articulation of what others have written, practised and courageously defended, is to counter the government's rigid deployment of identity categories with practices of resignification and intervention. The work of resignification and redescription avoids the trap of celebrating instability for its own sake. As Sedgwick notes, the conceptual relations in which sexual definition has been caught have always been inherently unstable, and, moreover, 'an understanding of their irresolvable instability has been continually available, and has continually lent discursive authority, to antigay as well as to gay cultural forces of this century' (p. 10). Sedgwick goes on to make what I consider to be a crucial point:

> Rather than embrace an idealist faith in the necessarily, immanently self-corrosive efficacy of the contradictions inherent to these definitional binarisms, I will suggest instead that contests for discursive power can be specified as competitions for the material or rhetorical leverage required to set the terms of, and to profit in some way from, the operations of such an incoherence of definition. (p. 11)

Of course, lesbianism and male homosexuality are not only implicated in the hegemonic terms of heterosexuality, and caught in the irreducibly complex web of sexual definition, they are implicated in a range of intersecting discursive fields. Or to put it in a different vernacular, sexuality has no meaning outside of the cultural contexts in which it appears. I emphasize this here in order to call attention to some of the problems I see in the new focus on sexuality as a distinct analytic and political category, to the danger that sexuality is in the process of being centred in ways that make it not only autonomous, but independent of other variables.

Jackie Goldsby suggests as much in a recent article in *Outlook*, entitled 'What it Means to be Colored Me'.[15] Goldsby poses important questions about celebrations of sexuality among lesbians and gay men. Goldsby focuses on Susie Bright's celebration (at the 1989 Lesbian/Gay Film Festival) of one particular pornographic scene of 'a blond-haired Eve-type wedged in the forked trunk of a tree', with 'her Black fuck-buddy's long, overly long tongue flick[ing] and dart[ing] across Eve's precious torso'. Goldsby's description of the scene stresses the 'larger-than-life white dildo' that the black woman uses to 'ram Eve to a fascistic orgasm'. In her critique, Goldsby suggests that Bright's 'reading [of the scene] was no more than a dismissal of porn's racial politics: stereotypical images exist, but at least it shows you (who?) images of inter- and intraracial sex'. And Goldsby goes on to suggest some of the questions that matter to her, including: 'How has Black sexuality been historically constructed so that its representation in porn is *never* not racist, if the presumed gaze is either male and/or white? What modes of narrative and production would upend that power dynamic?' (p. 15). Goldsby calls attention to the ways in which networks of power continue to organize sexual differences. It seems crucial to sustain a non-censorious curiosity about the complex relations between power and sexuality even as we open up the space for curiosity and honest exploration of fantasies, desires and practices. In the field of representations, there is no disclosure without concomitant closures, erasures and silences. What gets occluded even as the supposedly repressed or disallowed enjoys a new celebration?

When Butler calls for the subversive proliferation of gender configurations 'outside the frame of masculinist domination and compulsory heterosexuality' (*GT*, p. 141), her formulation obscures for me what I take to be one of her most important points, namely that gender is never performed in isolation from its complex configuration with, or implication in, other discursive fields, that it is never not racialized, for example. I quote Butler again:

> The very injunction to be a given gender takes place through discursive routes: to be a good mother, to be a heterosexually desirable object, to be a fit worker, in sum, to signify a multiplicity of guarantees in response to a variety of different demands at once. The coexistence or convergence of such discursive injunctions produces the possibility of a complex configuration and redeployment. (*GT*, p. 145)

If these injunctions to be a given gender take place through discursive routes (and Butler might have included in the list, not only to be a fit worker, to be a good mother, but to be a good loyal white southerner, for example, or to be a good Irish Catholic), then the emphasis on 'proliferating gender configurations' can obscure the fact that complex configurations necessarily already exist. To emphasize future possibilities outside masculinist domination and compulsory heterosexuality can have the effect of homogenizing the present and/or past. Such homogenizations, as Butler shows, are crucial to hegemonic culture.

For Joan Nestle, whose writings are collected in *A Restricted Country* (1987), butch–femme roles in the fifties were not 'phony heterosexual replicas', but 'complex erotic statements' that signalled erotic choices.[16] Nestle began a long time ago to critique the normativity of lesbian-feminism's 'woman-identified-woman' and what it renders unintelligible. What it rendered unfeminist was not only the lesbian erotic culture built in the 1950s, but those sexual practices that seemed to disturb any assumption of homogeneity and conflict-free community among lesbians as women. By effacing troubling lesbian desires and practices, the woman-identified-woman also rendered important political alignments unthinkable. For Nestle, the problem is not 'identity formation' in the abstract; she is interested in the specificities of particular identity formations and the precise interests they have served. Nestle's writings recontextualize lesbian erotic and cultural practices in a way that illuminates their implication in a range of intersecting discursive and social fields and injunctions.

Nestle makes it explicit that she is at pains to expose the erasure of class specificities in the construction of the woman-identified-woman of 1970s feminism. She stresses the ways in which definitions of appropriate objects of study mask or camouflage class and sex biases in the university, where fascination with romantic female friendships or the butch–femme relationships among upper-class expatriate Americans in Paris has not only obscured, but implicitly delegitimated, other versions of lesbian history. Nestle provokes feminist researchers to recover the shared histories of queers and prostitutes; she not only stresses the forms of legal harassment, moral condemnation and marginalization they share, she makes those two categories internal to one another by offering preliminary sources on the prevalence of lesbians as prostitutes (for men), and lesbians as customers of prostitutes. This, of course, is a far cry from the ways in which lesbianism has been set off from prostitution, as its escape, in some lesbian-feminist work.

In Nestle's work, lesbian sexual and cultural practices are implicated not only in heterosexuality, but in discursive constructions of class as they intersect with constructions of sex and gender. Her work not only challenges the conflation of woman with lesbian, it fractures the category lesbian by reinscribing lesbianism in the terms of concrete sexual practices that cut across categories. Nestle opens up unthought or submerged possibilities by way of her curiosity about what people desire and what they do. She challenges what she sees as struggles throughout the seventies for respectability, the respectability offered those willing to operate as a metaphor or allegory for what was defined as the larger struggle of women. Nestle uses sex to bring that magical sign back down to the messy social and discursive spaces in which its meanings are contested:

I wince when a gay activist says we are more than our sexuality, or when lesbian culture celebrants downplay lust and desire, seduction and fulfillment. If we are the people who call down history from its heights in marble assembly halls, if we put desire into history, if we document how a collective erotic imagination questions and modifies monolithic societal structures like gender, if we change the notion of woman as self-chosen victim by our public stances and private styles, then surely no apologies are due. Being a sexual people is our gift to the world. (p. 10)

Calling down history from marble assembly halls, putting desire into history, questioning monolithic structures like gender, refusing to be cast as victims – these are the interventions that Nestle's sexual people perform. Nestle puts the body, its construction, its desires back into history so that the only apparent basis of equality in disembodiment will cease to obscure the difference it makes where our bodies are located, where they get located by others, and what we do with them. This is not about a return to bodily essences or to natural libidos, but about attention to the discursive, social, intersubjective locations in which bodies, bodily boundaries and social divisions are given meaning and force.

Nestle enjoins lesbians not to leave gay men 'holding the sexual bag'. 'It is tempting', she writes, 'for some Lesbians to see themselves as the clean sex deviant, to disassociate themselves from public sexual activity, multiple partners, and intergenerational sex.' She continues:

> Lesbian purity, a public image that drapes us in the cloak of monogamous long-term relationships, discreet at-home gatherings, and a basic urge to re-create the family helps no one. By allowing ourselves to be portrayed as the good deviant, the respectable deviant, we lose more than we will ever gain. We lose the complexity of our lives, and we lose what for me has been a lifelong lesson: you do not betray your comrades when the scapegoating begins. (p. 123)

Nestle restores queerness to lesbianism in order to locate it again in the sexual orderings that its equation with gender (identification) has obscured. Nestle writes about choices and modes of survival, about erotic and social competences, about concrete struggles and pleasures, and about political alignments among lesbians, gay men, sex workers (including prostitutes and porn writers) and other sexual minorities that have been effaced by the emphasis on lesbianism as gender identification.

Nestle revives the city and city streets as the material location for gay and lesbian experience, and in so doing recovers a significant piece of gay and lesbian history; but Nestle's construction of sexual experiences on the Lower East Side of New York also invokes, in order to rework, the longstanding identification of homosexuality with the city, and the city with moral decay and sexual degeneracy. In the essay entitled 'I Am', Nestle uses the city streets to build a polemic against the construction of lesbianism as nature:

> I am of the people who have no mythologies, no goddesses powerful and hidden, to call on. I am of the people who have no memories of other lands beneath their feet other than the cement slabs of city streets. I have no secret languages, no deeper words than the words I have learned in this world . . . My mother is not spirit but memory. She cannot be called forth by candles or by chants. She is now sights and sounds . . . I have no rituals to call up lost worlds of power . . . I stand knowing in my bones this city of tired workers. I have enough to cherish in just the courage of these days and nights. This is my land, my ancient totems, this tenacious grip on life. (pp. 14–15)

Nestle's use of the city and the unmanageability in its streets of the boundaries between supposedly distinct categories of people makes visible associations between lesbians and prostitutes, lesbians and heterosexual women like her mother, whose sexual adventuring and desires 'had made her homeless'. Nestle introduces us to a world in which lesbians are prostitutes who sleep with men, lesbians are customers of prostitutes, a world in which a mother offers her daughter an identification with her desire, rather than with her mothering. Nestle's focus on sexual practices robs lesbianism of any ontological claim to an outside not only of heterosexuality, but of other discursive/institutional structures as well.

I want to pursue what Nestle means when she writes that 'being a sexual people is our gift to the world', and I want to focus, as I think she does, on how sex signifies and how crucial its meanings are to social orderings, how urgent its normalization is, how invested sexual boundaries and patterns of access are.

Butch–femme relationships, as I experienced them', writes Nestle, 'were complex erotic statements, not phony heterosexual replicas.'

> They were filled with deeply Lesbian language of stance, dress, gesture, loving, courage, and autonomy. None of the butch women I was with, and this included a passing woman, ever presented themselves to me as men; they did announce themselves as tabooed women who were willing to identify their passion for other women by wearing clothes that symbolized the taking of responsibility. Part of this responsibility was sexual

expertise. The butch–femme couple embarrassed other Lesbians for it speaks of what some wanted to keep hidden: the clearly sexual implications of the two women together. (pp. 100–1)

In Nestle's account, butch–femme roles, and the codes through which they were announced, are not figured as expressions of some underlying gender core or identification, or as imitations of heterosexual gender complementarities, but as the thoroughly performative construction of a public erotic culture in defiance of the injunction to be normal heterosexual women. Butch–femme roles were about the both public and private construction of sexual, not gender, differences between women. In their research on lesbian bar culture in Buffalo, New York, in the forties, fifties and sixties, Madeline Davis and Elizabeth Kennedy also suggest that butch–femme roles were a crucial part of constructing an erotic culture and of signalling a thoroughly political defiance of gender and sexual conventions.[17] Davis and Kennedy suggest, as Nestle's own work does, that butches and obviously butch–femme couples did the work of making sexual differences publicly visible. Kennedy and Davis also suggest that butch–femme roles involved the construction of erotic differences that allowed for the circulation of desires that then destabilized, even sometimes reversed, but did not eradicate differences in erotic positionality.

Nestle's sex fiction shows both the importance and the fluidity of different erotic positions by relating instances in which butches and femmes change roles, when 'the wanting to be taken becomes the desire to take', or when even stone butches 'roll over'. In her piece entitled 'Change of Life', the narrator-femme remembers the joke among young femmes in the bars in the 1950s that femmes become butches at forty, and she proceeds to describe one instance of her own change of life. 'I would move on her, waiting for her to beg me to enter, and when I did, when I knew what this woman wanted, and when I undertook to give it to her as best I could as deep as I could for as long as I could, I would be answering all the desires I had ever had when I was on my back under the women who moved me' (p. 131).

Nestle also makes butch–femme positions both operative and fluid because of her care, in every case, to render something of the tenderness of the butch's desire to take, and something of the power of the femme's desire to be taken. Nestle uses the specifics of butch–femme dynamics to construct an erotic culture in which erotic differences are clearly irreducible to conventional distinctions between masculine and feminine positions. In their work, too, Kennedy and Davis stress the ways in

which butch–femme roles draw on, but reconfigure, conventional
distinctions between male and female sexuality, by emphasizing, for
example, that the butch's desire is organized around the femme's pleasure, even to the point of refusing the reciprocation of her touch. And
they, too, emphasize the femme's power to orchestrate, demand and
educate. Nestle's 'Esther's Story' provides a striking example of the
complexities and fluidities of butch–femme exchanges. Esther is described as a passing woman, a woman who passed as a man, a taxi
driver, and a tough stone butch, 'whose hands tremble with respect and
need'.

> She was tough, a passing woman whose lover was a prostitute. Sea Colony
> talk. We all knew stories about each other, but like huge ice floes, we
> could occupy the same ocean without touching. This night we touched
> ... We sat in silence for a while, with Esther's cigarette a sharp red circle
> moving in the car's darkness. She put out the light and turned toward me.
> I leaned into her, fearing her knowledge, her toughness – and then I
> realized her hands were trembling. Through my blouse, I could feel her
> hands like butterflies shaking with respect and need. Younger lovers had
> been harder, more toughened to the joy of touch, but my passing woman
> trembled with her gentleness. (p. 41)

In 'A Different Place', Nestle shows yet other ways in which butch–
femme exchanges destabilize the relation between what Butler describes
as 'some decontextualized female body and a discrete yet superimposed
masculine identity'. 'A Different Place' begins with a description of Jay.

> Jay lays back in the tub, the hot water soaking her tired muscles. It had
> been a long day on the job, a day that seemed to consist of moving a
> hundred two-by-fours made of steel ... She loved construction work,
> loved to see the houses change shape under the guidance of her hands,
> loved to solve a problem of angles first with her mind and then with her
> tools. But she was still glad when quitting time came, particularly today.
> Her girlfriend from New York was spending the night, was, in fact,
> waiting for her in the bedroom. (p. 134)

The next sentence, which begins a new paragraph, reads: 'She spread her
legs, letting the hot water push against her, watched it circle her breasts
– all breasts and muscle. Not a bad combination' (p. 134). I like the
move from the end of the first paragraph, which describes Jay in terms
that signal 'masculinity', to the opening sentence of the second paragraph, that opens the legs not of the girlfriend, but of Jay. In a descrip-

tion just a page later of anal penetration, Nestle again renders something of the power of the femme's passion and her aggressive need: 'Carol's moans became louder. Her whole body was pointed at Jay's finger, and now femme hunger was in control. She was thrusting her ass back and forth onto Jay's finger with her own rhythm.' And the account concludes with Jay 'watching and wondering at the strength of a woman's want' (p. 137).

I like these passages because they challenge any effort to make sex, gender identity, desire, sexual practice and sexual role continuous with one another. For Butler, such moments represent a 'logic of inversion' that shows the impossibility of 'capturing' causal links. 'That which is excluded for a given gender presentation to "succeed," may be precisely what is played out sexually, that is, an "inverted" relation, as it were, between gender and gender presentation, and gender presentation and sexuality.'[18] Butler elaborates on butch–femme inversions:

> For a butch can present herself as capable, forceful, and all-providing, and a stone butch may well seek to constitute her lover as the exclusive site of erotic attention and pleasure. And yet, this 'providing' butch who seems *at first* to replicate a certain husband-like role, can find herself caught in a logic of inversion whereby that 'providingness' turns to a self-sacrifice, which implicates her in the most ancient trap of feminine self-abnegation... On the other hand, the femme... may well eroticize a certain dependency only to learn that the very power to orchestrate that dependency exposes her own incontrovertible power, at which point she inverts into a butch or becomes caught up in the spectre of that inversion, or perhaps delights in it.[19]

For Nestle, questions of sexual dependence and submission are also crossed over by other dynamics, and her writings displace only apparent oppositions between giving and taking by implicating sexual exchanges in other experiences. 'The Gift of Taking', for example, reinscribes the meanings of submission in the terms of a very powerful gift that the narrator's submission brings, the at least momentary suspension of her hatred of her own body. 'My submission in this room with this woman is my source of strength, of wisdom. It informs all my abilities in the other world, but here I can give it time to breathe its own air, to break the surface, and show its own face.' The narrator continues: 'and now yearning for penetration by this woman's hand, her erotic acceptance that will free me from the crime of being a big-assed woman. I know this woman, my friend, will bring my body to light, will make use of it and hear it, will strain it to its fullest, and she will help me through her demands and her pleasure to forget self-hatred' (pp. 127–8).

Nestle's other explicit sex fiction highlights the links between sexual taboos and socially imposed boundaries and routes of access. 'Mara's Room' is one of the most effective at exposing the ways in which bodily boundaries both signify and sustain social separations. The story Nestle tells in 'Mara's Room' is from what she describes as 'the Lower East Side days, New York University graduate school days'. Mara was a married woman whom the narrator tells us she had long desired. They sit across a table from each other, now 'a little older'. The narration continues: 'My old want of her was back. I had never dared to cross the line between our worlds; husband and child stood as sentinels on the border' (p. 72). Later, it is Mara who pushes against those borders. 'Later in the darkness. Mara pushed at me hard, opening my thighs. "Let me in." I was frozen by the collision of our worlds. I spread my legs slowly, but her rush came too quickly.' The narrator explains her numbness by writing that she 'was frozen because for me you were a real woman, not a place of secret explosions. You came in dazzling waves of freedom, you came on shores never to be visited again, and I knew even before your body slid back into its full weight that I had lost you again' (p. 73).

The next sentence, which opens the next paragraph, brings the confirmation of that sense of loss.

> When the revelation had passed, you lay beside me. Carrying my history on my lips, I bent my head between your legs to taste, to soothe, to speak to you in the language of my love, but it was too much. You pushed my head away. The secret glory had burst and the curtains again descended, long heavy drapes of custom and fear. There could be no acknowledged touch outside the frenzy of deliverance. The next morning, a kiss was not allowed. (p. 73)

Mara refuses oral sex after 'the frenzy of deliverance' was over and discursive boundaries re-established. After that, Joan's touch threatened to transgress the boundaries set by 'custom and fear', boundaries lying in wait for that moment of frenzy to end. Restored to her senses, the borders around her heterosexualized woman's body become impermeable again to this woman, whose entry is barred once again by the 'husband and child [standing] as sentinels on the border'. Fear and custom foreclose on the potential to open up what is falsely naturalized and bounded as heterosexuality to the excesses, contradictions, granulations that threaten its self-evidence and coherence. In this passage, Nestle manages to show both how tenacious and how permeable the borders are, and how crucial it is to relegate their potential destabilization to an outside, an outsider, and/or to momentary frenzies. By the next day, lesbianism is once more safely lodged in an Other, in 'the lesbian'.

For anyone familiar with Lorde's *Zami*, Nestle's accounts of butch–femme culture and the fifties bar scene call up Lorde's reinscriptions of some of the very same bars.[20] Like Nestle's, Lorde's reconstructions of the fifties demonstrate the importance of bar culture to the formation of lesbian and gay community. However, Lorde's reconstructed memories of the bars introduce race and racism into the variables that made up that emerging culture. *Zami* offers a range of different angles on lesbian bar culture, a number of different representations that show the significance of the shifting positions from which the narrator experiences the bars and butch–femme culture.[21]

On at least two occasions in *Zami*, Lorde suggests that 'lesbians were probably the only Black and white women in New York City in the fifties who were making any real attempt to communicate with each other' (p. 179). But these attempts at communication are traversed by structures of racism and homophobia. And for the narrator of *Zami*, the roles that were available in fifties bar culture were what Katie King has called 'color-coded':

> The Black women I usually saw around the Bag were into heavy roles, and it frightened me. This was partly the fear of my own Blackness mirrored, and partly the realities of the masquerade. Their need for power and control seemed a much-too-open piece of myself, dressed in enemy clothing. They were tough in a way I felt I could never be. Even if they were not, their self-protective instincts warned them to appear that way. By white america's racist distortions of beauty, Black women playing 'femme' had very little chance at the Bag. There was constant competition among butches to have the most 'gorgeous femme' on their arm. And 'gorgeous' was defined by a white male world's standards. (p. 224)

In her reading of Lorde's reconstructions of butch–femme culture, Katie King makes the important argument that Lorde also 'pulls away' from turning racism into absolute essence and determinant when she describes a black lesbian party outside the bars where butch–femme codes operate very differently. King characterizes Lorde's description of the party as 'a happy conflation of good food and sex and sensual descriptions of the physical codes of black butches and femmes –

touches, smells, textures – [that] make up and break up the negative contours of role-playing, dissolving the powers of butch/femme codes to represent essentially white/black domination.[22] The short passage that follows supports King's characterization:

> Femmes wore their hair in tightly curled pageboy bobs, or piled high on their heads in sculptured bunches of curls, or in feather cuts framing their faces. That sweetly clean fragrance of beauty-parlor that hung over all Black women's gatherings in the fifties was present here also, adding its identifiable smell of hot comb and hair pomade to the other aromas in the room.
>   Butches wore their hair cut shorter, in a D.A. shaped to a point in the back, or a short pageboy, or sometimes in a tightly curled poodle that predated the natural afro. But this was a rarity. (p. 242)

Lorde's refusal to allow any single difference or hierarchy to become absolute determinant or essence finds its clearest formulation when she writes that 'it was a while before we came to realize that our place was the very house of difference' (p. 226).

There are a number of passages in *Zami* for which Nestle's reconfigurations of butch–femme roles offer an at least implicit critique, passages in which Lorde makes a polemic that follows the logic of some seventies lesbian-feminisms: 'For some of us', Lorde writes at one point, 'role-playing reflected all the depreciating attitudes toward women which we loathed in straight society. It was a rejection of these roles that had drawn us into the life in the first place' (p. 221).

I offer Lorde's various reinscriptions of butch–femme cultures not in order to suggest that Lorde's constructions of butch–femme culture should be substituted for Nestle's or Nestle's for Lorde's as the more correct, but in order to stress the complexities that emerge when Nestle's and Lorde's accounts are read together, when their mappings of sexual roles are superimposed. King's celebration of Lorde's several configurations of roles and encounters underlines the importance of those complexities:

> How to return to this scene, how to enter into the relations of power and visibility and collusion and rejection and attraction/repulsion and lust and loving is Lorde's event – an event not possible except in piling historical moment on top of historical moment. This is not one instance of time-space particularity, nor is it the utopian construction of a transhistorical myth, but instead the layerings of instance, of political meanings con-

strained in particularity, lacquered over so finely that they are inseparable and mutually constructing while distinct.[23]

Such layerings of instance in Lorde, Nestle, Goldsby and Bright demonstrate that we confront not just the restricting frame of masculinist domination and compulsory heterosexuality, rather a much more complex set of social performances and regulations, in which gender is never stable or unified.

For all the importance of the newly militant politics of sexuality, there is a danger of reproducing some of the problems that emerged from feminists' exclusive focus on gender. Ironically, in some cases, gender itself seems to be one of the excluded terms in the articulation of a new politics of sexuality. In my reading of the popular gay press, of journals such as *Outlook*, I have been surprised and disturbed to see how often a new politics of sexuality has been formulated against feminism, rather than in a more complex relation to it, how often 'the lesbian-feminist community' has been cast as the repressive mother who stands in the way of sex and alignments with men. This is not to say that certain lesbian-feminist constructions of lesbian identity have not proved rigid and disabling, but to define a politics of sexuality as if gender were no longer a significant social marker or as if feminist analysis and politics had not been critical to current developments seems willfully blind. Furthermore, to write the history of current positions as a straight line from the lesbian-feminism of the seventies to the sexual radicalism of the late eighties and nineties simplifies the past twenty years of feminist and lesbian politics beyond recognition, and completely erases the anti-racist politics that are inextricably bound up with shifts in constructions of gender and sexuality among feminists.

To 'put desire back into history', as Nestle challenges us to do, means refusing to abstract it out of the complex relations through which sexuality is constructed and enacted. I have used Nestle and Lorde to suggest that practices like butch–femme roles are completely saturated with issues that exceed what is narrowly conceived to be sexuality. It is not only for women of colour that such roles are thoroughly racialized. All my experience growing up as a white woman in the south tells me that there were/are no questions of desire that are not also always questions about race, about familial-racial loyalties or transgressions, about class- and race-appropriate femininities, masculinities, erotic positions and roles. These connections are insistently obscured by constructions of supposedly unified, natural genders and heterosexual complementarities. Reagan–Bush AIDS policies, their politics on crime, drugs and jobs have shown consistently that constructions of 'normal families' and morality serve not only to pathologize homosexuals and other sexual minorities, but to eradicate the achievements of the women's movement, specifically with regard to abortion, and to pathologize people of colour and the poor, in an effort to make them responsible for social and economic problems that the government has no interest in solving. I emphasize these issues at a moment when Lesbian and Gay Studies is being institutionalized at some universities in the United States, in the hope that it will not go the route of making something called 'sexuality' central without concern for what is relegated to the margins or out of sight in such centering moves.

NOTES

1  Cindy Patton, *Inventing AIDS* (Routledge, New York, 1990), p. 129. Subsequent page references are cited in the text.
2  Eve Sedgwick, *Epistemology of the Closet* (University of California Press, Berkeley, Cal., 1990).
3  In this sense, the exhibit recalls the exhibition of sexually explicit lesbian images by the Canadian collective Kiss and Tell, called 'Drawing the Line', and described in *Outlook*, 10 (1990), pp. 6–11.
4  Douglas Crimp and Adam Rolston, *AIDSDemoGraphics* (Bay Press, Seattle, 1990), p. 20. Subsequent page references are cited in the text.
5  Aimée Duc, *Sind es Frauen? Roman über das dritte Geschlecht* (Amazonen Frauenverlag, Berlin, 1976).
6  Jan Clausen, 'My Interesting Condition', in *Outlook*, 7 (1990), pp. 10–24.
7  Greta Christina, 'Drawing the Line', *On Our Backs*, 6 (1990), pp. 14–15, 35.
8  Sedgwick, *The Epistemology of the Closet*, p. 1. Subsequent page references are cited in the text.
9  Judith Butler, *Gender Trouble: Feminism and the Subversion of Identity* (Routledge, New York, 1989). Subsequent page references are cited in the text as *GT*.
10  Judith Butler, 'Imitation and Gender Insubordination', in Diana Fuss (ed.), *Inside Out: Lesbian Theories/Gay Theories* (Routledge, New York, in preparation).
11  Ibid.
12  Butler develops this line of argument in 'Imitation and Gender Insubordination'.
13  Ibid.
14  I prefer to shift the focus away from the question of subversive gender performances to what I take to be the more important focus in Butler's work on rendering visible already existing complexities.

15  Jackie Goldsby, 'What it Means to be Colored Me', *Outlook*, 9 (1990), pp. 8–17. Subsequent page references are cited in the text.

16  Joan Nestle, *A Restricted Country* (Firebrand Press, Ithaca, N.Y., 1987), p. 100. Subsequent page references are cited in the text.

17  Madeline Davis and Elizabeth Lapovsky Kennedy, 'Oral History and the Study of Sexuality in the Lesbian Community: Buffalo, New York, 1940–1960', in Martin Bauml Duberman, Martha Vicinus and George Chauncey, Jr. (eds), *Hidden from History: Reclaiming the Gay and Lesbian Past* (New American Library, New York, 1989), pp. 426–40.

18  Butler, 'Imitation and Gender Insubordination'.

19  Ibid.

20  Audre Lorde, *Zami: A New Spelling of My Name* (The Crossing Press, Trumansburg, N.Y., 1982). Subsequent page references are cited in the text.

21  Katie King provides a subtle reading of Lorde's treatment of butch–femme roles in 'Audre Lorde's Lacquered Layerings: The Lesbian Bar as a Site of Literary Production', *Cultural Studies*, 2 (1988), pp. 321–42.

22  Ibid., p. 328.

23  Ibid., p. 325.

# 7

# Power, Bodies and Difference

## Moira Gatens

Over the last two decades the diversification of feminist theories has rendered the rather convenient tripartite division into Marxist feminism, liberal feminism and radical feminism virtually useless. These divisions no longer capture the salient features of the multiple ways in which current feminist theories interact with dominant socio-political theories.[1] Most noticeably, feminist theories today no longer feel compelled to carry their allegiances 'on their sleeves' (*Marxist* feminism, *liberal* feminism) in order to signal their authority to speak. In this sense, both Marxism and liberalism provided, and sometimes still provide, a legitimizing or patronymic function. Radical feminism distinguished itself from other forms of feminist theory by avowing its independence from so-called patriarchal theories. It alone claimed to be 'unmarked' by the name of the father.

The reluctance of contemporary feminisms to identify themselves with a theory-patronym may be seen as an indication of the profound suspicion and distrust which many feminists display towards dominant socio-political theories. Many contemporary feminist theorists no longer have faith in the utility of existing socio-political theories to explain or clarify the socio-political status of women. This 'loss of faith' in what has variously been named malestream, phallocentric or simply masculinist theories signals that many feminists no longer believe that these theories are marred by only a superficial sex-blindness, or sexism. The problem is now located at a much more fundamental level. It cannot be simply a matter of removing superficial biases from socio-political theories, since the bias is now understood as intrinsic to the structure of the theories in question.[2] For example, feminist philosophers have argued convincingly that reason is not something from which women have been simply excluded. Rather, rationality itself has been defined against the feminine and traditional female roles.[3] Likewise, it has been demonstrated that women's exclusion from the political body is not a contingent feature of their history but a consequence of the dominant conception of political society. Women have been constructed as 'naturally deficient in a specifically *political* capacity, the capacity to create and maintain political right'.[4] These studies have shown that the application of dominant theories of social and political life to the situation of women inevitably involves the devaluation of women and all that women have been associated with historically. The reason is that these theories harbour fundamental, not superficial, biases against women.

This analysis may be seen to imply that many contemporary feminist approaches to theory are themselves forms or varieties of radical feminism. This would be a rather simplistic description, since many recent developments in contemporary feminist theory explicitly stress the necessity to engage with dominant or 'malestream' theories of social and political life – an attitude not easily identified with radical feminism. Such engagement is active and critical. These feminist theorists do not go to Marxism or liberalism hoping for 'the answer' or 'the solution' to 'the woman question' but, more probably, will approach dominant theories, and their implicit biases, as themselves part of the problem. For this reason it seems appropriate to name these contemporary feminist approaches to dominant socio-political theories 'deconstructive'.

For the purposes of this essay the term 'deconstructive' will not be used in the strict Derridean sense. Rather, it will be used to identify feminist approaches which eschew viewing theories such as Marxism, liberalism, existentialism, psychoanalysis and so on as essentially sex-neutral discourses through which an understanding of women's situation may be 'truly' grasped. Deconstructive feminism is concerned to investigate the elemental make-up of these theories and to expose their latent discursive commitments. For example, much political theory typically treats the family as a natural rather than a social phenomenon. A deconstructive approach highlights what is at stake in opposing the family, understood as natural, to the public sphere, understood as a social construct. It is this assumption which allows political theorists to mask the specifically political features of the relations between the sexes by treating these relations as natural.[5]

A feature common to most, if not all, dominant socio-political theories is a commitment to the dualisms central to western thought: nature and culture, body and mind, passion and reason. In the realm of social and political theory, these dualisms often translate as distinctions between reproduction and production, the family and the state, the individual and the social. As many feminists have argued, the left-hand side of these dualisms is more intimately connected with women and femininity and the right-hand side with men and masculinity. It is also important to note that it is only the right-hand side of these distinctions which is deemed to fall within the realm of history. Only culture, the mind and reason, social production, the state and society are understood as having a dynamic and developmental character. The body and its passions, reproduction, the family and the individual are often conceived as timeless and unvarying aspects of nature. This way of conceptualizing human existence is deeply complicit in claims such as 'women have no history'[6] and 'reproduction involves the mere repetition of life.'[7]

It is this deep interrogation of the discursive commitments of socio-political theories that marks off current forms of feminist theory from their predecessors. It distinguishes what has been termed deconstructive feminist theory from any feminist theory which theorizes women's existence by attempting to extend the terms of 'malestream' theories; for example, Marxist feminism, liberal feminism, existentialist feminism and so on. Yet deconstructive feminism is also distinct from radical feminism in that it does not take woman's essence or biology as somehow enabling her to produce, *ex nihilo*, pure or non-patriarchal theory. On the contrary, deconstructive feminisms view such claims with extreme scepticism. Michèle le Doeuff, for example, claims that:

> [w]hether we like it or not, we are within philosophy, surrounded by masculine-feminine divisions that philosophy has helped to articulate and refine. The problem is to know whether we want to remain there and be dominated by them, or whether we can take up a critical position in relation to them, a position which will necessarily evolve through deciphering the basic philosophical assumptions latent in discourse about women. The worst metaphysical positions are those which one adopts unconsciously whilst believing or claiming that one is speaking from a position outside philosophy.[8]

The last sentence of this passage may serve as a caution to those who believe that it is possible to create feminist theories which owe nothing to the culture from which they emanate. To acknowledge this is not, however, to take up a nihilistic or resigned attitude to the possibility of working towards alternatives to existing socio-political theories, where this might involve critically engaging with their 'latent assumptions'. Suppressed or marginalized philosophies – for example, those of Spinoza[9] or Nietzsche – also may be of use to feminist theorists in that they may emphasize features of existence which have been obscured or elided by traditional discourses.

It is obviously impossible to present a fair or extensive treatment of the great variety in contemporary feminist theories in the space of a single essay. Indeed, it is not possible even to present a fair outline of what have been named deconstructive feminisms. Rather, this chapter will attempt to offer an outline of what I take to be some of the most important conceptual shifts between feminist theories of the 1970s on the one hand, and contemporary deconstructive feminisms on the other. This contrast will be achieved by concentrating on shifts in the use of three key terms: *power, the body* and *difference*. These terms are used by both deconstructive and other feminist theorists; nevertheless it will be argued that they are used in quite different and incompatible ways. Inevitably, in an essay of this sort, there will be many generalizations. The aim is not to belittle feminisms of the 1970s but rather to show that deconstructive feminisms have developed in a historical context, where previous feminist research plays an integral and indispensable role in the articulation of contemporary feminist concerns. This is simply to say that if previous feminists had not attempted to use dominant theories to explicate women's socio-political status, the difficulties inherent in that project would not have come to light. Deconstructive feminisms assume and respond to these difficulties.

## POWER

Both liberal and Marxist political theories have tended to conceptualize power as something which an individual, or a group, either does or does not have. Power is conceived as something which is intimately connected with authority, domination or exploitation. In liberal political theory the role of the state is conceived in terms of the exercise of legitimate power over its subjects to ensure the peaceable and equitable opportunity of exchange. Power is thought to reside in, and radiate out from, sovereignty.

Marxist political theory, of course, takes a quite different view of the matter. Power is not thought to be the exercise of the legitimate authority of the sovereign. Rather, the state is conceived as being in the service of the ruling class and the exercise of power in society is the exercise of the power of one class over another. In this sense, power is held by one group which uses this power in order to dominate and exploit another group which lacks power. However, both philosophies assume that power is principally manifested in the regulation and control of politico-economic relations. It is in relation to these that power assumes material forms, although Marxists would also claim that power is exercised by ideological means. Louis Althusser formulated the difference between these two distinct forms of state power in terms of repressive state apparatuses, which include the police, judiciary, army and so on; and ideological state apparatuses, which include schools, religion, the family and so forth.[10]

When feminist theorists seek to make use of these socio-political theories, the kinds of problem that they address tend to centre on the manner in which the power of the state operates in relation to women. Liberal feminists conceive the problem of women's confinement to the private sphere as central to their low socio-political status. Equality, wealth and opportunity are located in the public sphere. Hence the issue of providing women with access to power becomes the issue of providing them with equal access to the public sphere. The state is obliged to provide women with the same opportunities it provides for men. Thus, the struggle for liberal feminists tends to involve equality of opportunity in education and the workplace, equality under the law and so on. These demands inevitably spill over into related demands for child-care or maternity leave. However, since these demands must be put in terms that are sex-neutral, maternity leave must be matched by paternity leave and equal opportunity must be phrased in terms which include men.

The fundamental premiss of liberal philosophy to provide equal access to power can be articulated only in terms that are sexually neutral. What this involves, for women, is the difficulty, if not impossibility, of occupying the public sphere on genuinely equal terms with men. Put simply, given that the public sphere has historically been an almost exclusively male sphere, it has developed in a manner which assumes that its occupants have a male body. Specifically, it is a sphere that does not concern itself with reproduction but with production. It does not concern itself with (private) domestic labour but with (social) wage-labour. This is to say that liberal society assumes that its citizens continue to be what they were historically, namely male heads of households who have at their disposal the services of an unpaid domestic worker/mother/wife.

In this sense, the (traditionally male) public sphere of liberal society can be understood as one which defines itself in opposition to the (traditionally female) private sphere. The status of women in liberal theory and society presents feminists with a series of paradoxes.[11] Equality in this context can involve only the abstract opportunity to become equal to men. It is the male body, and its historically and culturally determined powers and capacities, that is taken as the norm or the standard of the liberal 'individual'. Women can achieve this standard provided that they either elide their own corporeal specificity or are able to juggle both their traditional role in the private sphere and their newfound 'equality'. This situation fails to take account of the specific powers and capacities that women have developed in their historical and cultural context, a point which will be treated in the following section.

Marxism also tends to concentrate on a rather narrow use of power, one in which economic relations are taken to be the origin of all power relations. The effect of this, in the context of studying women's socio-political status, is that those forms of power which are specific to women's existence can only be perceived in their relation to the economic structure of society. It is tempting to suggest that women would first have to become genuine members of liberal society in order to lend credence to the relevance of the Marxist critique to their situation. This is particularly pertinent to those varieties of Marxism which take the structure of society to be determined by its economic base. It was the economism of much Marxist theory which placed the so-called domestic labour debate high on the agenda for Marxist feminists of the 1970s. This highlights the way in which theories can determine which questions are 'central', irrespective of the specificity of the object being studied. It is an example of how the deep biases in socio-political theories can obscure features of women's existence that may be crucial to an understanding of their situation, while emphasizing instead issues that appear prominent not because of women's situation but because of the underlying commitments of the theory in question.[12]

The difficulties involved in offering a Marxist analysis of women under patriarchal capitalism are obviously tied to the fact that, in Marxist terms, women cannot be seen to constitute a class. Consequently, Marxist feminist theory found it difficult to offer an account of the operations of power in the lives of women. The theory, like the culture, could conceive women, *qua women*, only on the model of appendages to men. Capital extracts surplus-value from wage-labour, the price of which assumes the subsistence of not only the wage-labourer but also his household. Those women who do perform wage-labour were conceived as unsexed labour, while those women who do not perform wage-labour have only an indirect connection to capital and social relations. Power, as it operates in the lives of women, was largely conceived on the model of the power of ideology. Hence it is not surprising that many Marxist feminists welcomed the addition of psychoanalytic theory in order to explain the way in which the ideology of masculinity and femininity constructs men and women as appropriate patriarchal subjects in capitalist society. Moreover, in that many Marxist feminists took (traditional) women's work to involve the reproduction of labour-power, psychoanalysis offered a theoretical perspective from which to examine the way in which *appropriate* kinds of labourer are produced.

The most prominent exponent of the utility of psychoanalytic theory to Marxist feminism was Juliet Mitchell, in her extremely influential book *Psychoanalysis and Feminism*.[13] Mitchell claimed that Marxism offers an account of class and capital whereas psychoanalysis offers an account of sex and patriarchy. Significantly, these two theories were understood as concerned respectively with the economic infrastructure and the ideological superstructure. Men's exploitation centres on the state and class society whereas women's specific oppression centres on ideology and patriarchal society. Mitchell, following Althusser, thus managed to achieve the reduction of psychic life to the domain of ideology. This is an important consequence, primarily because it was often used to 'justify' the postponement of women's struggles or, more benignly, to tie the outcome of women's struggles to that of the class struggle.

This view of the operation of power and oppression in women's lives involved an unconvincing analysis of how gender operates in society, as well as of the way in which sexual difference intersects with power and domination. Kate Millett, for example, argued that '[s]ince patriarchy's biological foundations appear to be so very insecure, one has some cause to admire the strength of a "socialisation" which can continue a universal condition "on faith alone", as it were, or through an acquired value system exclusively.'[14] This passage reveals the way in which Millett understood biology as referring to the sexed body (male or female) and ideology as referring to the masculine or feminine subject. Such an understanding fails to note the ways in which values are embedded in social practices that take the body as their target. The biology/ideology distinction treats 'value system[s]' in an idealist manner and so obscures the ways in which social values are embedded in bodies, not simply 'minds', a point to which I will return. Both the liberal and the Marxist analyses of society suffer from similar problems in relation to the study of women's socio-political status. The implicit theory of power held by both approaches is narrowly economic, which is inadequate in the context of women's historically tentative relation to the public sphere and wage-labour. This view of power is arguably suitable to an analysis of some aspects of men's socio-political lives, but inadequate when applied to women, or indeed in relation to other issues such as racial oppression.

Part of the problem here is the inability of both liberal and Marxist theory to address the issue of corporeal specificity in any terms other than those of biological 'facts' or ideology. Neither theory is able to think difference outside of the body/mind, fact/value or science/ideology distinctions. For example, these are precisely the terms in which the sex/gender distinction is couched. Sex concerns the body, facts and science (biology), whereas gender concerns the mind, values and ideology (conditioning).[15] Both theories are committed to a form of humanism which assumes a fundamental universality across history and across cultures in relation to the needs, capacities and 'nature' of the human being or the human body. This is, in part, an effect of assuming that bodies and their needs are a timeless part of nature. This puts the emphasis on the way in which the biologically given human being becomes a socially produced masculine or feminine subject. Since masculinity and femininity are conceived as psychological traits, their genesis and reproduction must be located at the level of the mind, values or ideology.

This approach to the issues of sexual difference, power and domination is not able to consider the ways in which power differentially *constitutes* particular kinds of body and empowers them to perform particular kinds of task, thus constructing specific kinds of subject. Put differently, one could argue that gender is a material effect of the way in which power takes hold of the body rather than an ideological effect of the way power 'conditions' the mind. To make this kind of claim would involve using quite a different notion of power and the body than that used in dominant socio-political theories.

Perhaps the most prominent exponent of this alternative account of power is Michel Foucault. He stresses that dominant accounts of power tend to conceive power on the model of repression, where power is reduced to that which says 'No'.[16] Foucault's work has concentrated on the body–power relation and on the discourses and practices which he takes to involve productive operations of power. This is not to say that he disavows the existence, or indeed the importance, of state power or repressive state practices. Rather, it is to say that his work seeks to emphasize the less spectacular but more insidious forms of power. Moreover, these non-repressive forms of power cannot be adequately captured by the notion of ideology. He summarizes his reservations concerning the utility of the term ideology in three points:

[first], like it or not, it always stands in virtual opposition to something else which is supposed to count as truth. Now I believe that the problem does not consist in drawing the line between that in a discourse which falls under the category of scientificity or truth, and that which comes under some other category, but in seeing historically how effects of truth are produced within discourses which in themselves are neither true nor false. The second drawback is that the concept of ideology refers, I think necessarily, to something of the order of a subject. Thirdly, ideology stands in a secondary position relative to something which functions as its infrastructure, as its material, economic determinant.[17]

Foucault's reservations about the concept of ideology overlap in an interesting way with the reservations which have been expressed here concerning the utility of Marxist and liberal socio-political theories to the situation of women. First, the science/ideology distinction has been relied upon in understanding women's oppression as linked to a patriarchal value-system which constructs gendered subjects, while the 'truth' of the sex of woman is to be determined by the scientific discourse of biology. Second, the notion that gender is a social addition to the human subject is coherent only on the condition that human subjects pre-exist their social contexts. Finally, the limitation in viewing patriarchy as operating primarily by ideological means is that it assumes that the determinant infrastructure of society is economic. For these reasons, the Foucauldian approach to the micro-politics of power is particularly appropriate to an investigation of the ways in which power and domination operate in relation to sexual difference.

One of the main benefits of Foucault's approach is that its emphasis on the body allows one to consider not simply how discourses and practices create ideologically appropriate subjects but also how these practices construct certain sorts of body with particular kinds of power and capacity; that is, how bodies are turned into individuals of various kinds.[18] In short, it allows an analysis of the productiveness of power as well as its repressive functions. From this perspective one might also begin to appreciate how it may well make sense to speak of the body as having a history.

THE BODY

There is probably no simple explanation for the recent proliferation of writings concerning the body. Clearly, Foucault's work has been influential in making the body a favoured subject for analysis in contemporary philosophy, sociology and anthropology. However, the impact of feminist theory on the social sciences has no less a claim to credit for bringing the body into the limelight. The difficulties encountered by primarily middle-class women, who have had the greatest access to 'equality' in the public sphere, may well have served as a catalyst for feminist reflections on the body.

One response to the differential powers and capacities of women and men in the context of public life is to claim that women just are biologically disadvantaged relative to men. From this perspective it seems crucial to call for the further erosion of the reproductive differences between the sexes by way of advances in medical science. On this view, social reform can only achieve so much, leaving the rectification of the remaining determinations of women's situation to the increase in control over nature; that is, biology. Simone de Beauvoir retains the doubtful privilege of being the clearest exponent of this view. In the 1970s, Shulamith Firestone's *The Dialectic of Sex* was influential in perpetuating the view that science could fulfil a liberatory role for women.[19] Both theorists assumed that the specificity of the reproductive body must be overcome if sexual equality is to be realized.

An alternative response to questions of corporeal specificity is to claim that women should not aspire to be 'like men'. Interestingly, this response comes from both feminists and anti-feminists alike.[20] Recent feminist research suggests that the history of western thought shows a deep hatred and fear of the body.[21] This somatophobia is understood by some feminists to be specifically masculine and intimately related to gynophobia and misogyny.[22] In response to this negative attitude towards the body and women, some feminists advocate the affirmation and celebration of women's bodies and their capacity to recreate and nurture. In its strongest form this view argues that the specific capacities and powers of women's bodies imply an essential difference between men and women, where women may be presented as essentially peace-loving, 'biophilic' or caring, and men as essentially aggressive, 'necrophilic' or selfish.[23] These theorists argue that there is an essential sexual difference which should be retained, not eroded by scientific intervention.

These two responses to women's corporeal specificity are often taken to exhaust what has been termed the 'sexual equality versus sexual difference debate'. Yet both responses are caught up within the same paradigm. Both understand the body as a given biological entity which either has or does not have certain ahistorical characteristics and capacities. To this extent, the sexual difference versus sexual equality debate is located within a framework which assumes a body/mind, nature/culture dualism. The different responses are both in answer to the question of which should be given priority: the mind or the body, nature or culture.

An alternative view of the body and power might refuse this dualistic manner of articulating the issue of sexual difference. Specifically, to claim a history for the body involves taking seriously the ways in which diet, environment and the typical activities of a body may vary historically and create its capacities, its desires and its actual material form.[24] The body of a woman confined to the role of wife/mother/domestic worker, for example, is invested with particular desires, capacities and forms that have little in common with the body of a female Olympic athlete. In this case biological commonality fails to account for the specificity of these two bodies. Indeed, the female Olympic athlete may have more in common with a male Olympic athlete than with a wife/ mother. This commonality is not simply at the level of interests or desires but at the level of the actual form and capacities of the body. By drawing attention to the context in which bodies move and recreate themselves, we also draw attention to the complex dialectic between bodies and their environments. If the body is granted a history then traditional associations between the female body and the domestic sphere and the male body and the public sphere can be acknowledged as historical realities, which have historical effects, without resorting to biological essentialism. The present capacities of female bodies are, by and large, very different to the present capacities of male bodies. It is important to create the means of articulating the historical realities of sexual difference without thereby reifying these differences. Rather, what is required is an account of the ways in which the typical spheres of movement of men and women and their respective activities construct and recreate particular kinds of body to perform particular kinds of task. This sort of analysis is necessary if the historical effects of the ways in which power constructs bodies are to be understood and challenged.[25]

This would involve not simply a study of how men and women become masculine and feminine subjects but how bodies become marked as male and female. Again, Foucault made this point well, arguing that what is needed is:

an analysis in which the biological and the historical are not consecutive to one another, as in the evolutionism of the first sociologists, but are bound together in an increasingly complex fashion in accordance with the development of the modern technologies of power that take life as their objective. Hence, I do not envisage a 'history of mentalities' that would take account of bodies only through the manner in which they have been perceived and given meaning and value; but a 'history of bodies' and the manner in which what is most material and most vital in them has been invested.[26]

Foucault's studies tend to concentrate on the history of the construction of male bodies and are not forthcoming on the question of sexual difference.[27] However, a critical use of psychoanalytic theory, in particular the theory of the body image, in conjunction with Foucault's analysis of power can provide some very useful insights in this context.

The works of Jacques Lacan, Maurice Merleau-Ponty and Paul Schilder offer an account of the body image which posits that a body is not properly a human body, that is, a human subject or individual, unless it has an image of itself as a discrete entity, or as a *gestalt*.[28] It is this orientation of one's body in space, and in relation to other bodies, that provides a perspective on the world and that is assumed in the constitution of the signifying subject. Lacan, in particular, presents the emergence of this *gestalt* as, in some sense, genetic. His famous 'Mirror Stage' paper, for example, offers ethological evidence for the identificatory effect produced by images and movements of others of the same species and even images and movements which merely *simulate* those of the species in question.[29] Lacan takes this 'homeomorphic identification' to be at the origin of an organism's orientation toward its own species. It would seem that it is this genetic basis to his account of the mirror stage that allows him, even while stressing the cultural specificity of body images, to assert the 'natural' dominance of the penis in the shaping of the *gestalt*.[30]

Foucault's historically dynamic account of the manner in which the micro-political operations of power produce socially appropriate bodies offers an alternative to Lacan's ethological account. Using Foucault's approach, the imaginary body can be posited as an effect of socially and historically specific practices: an effect, that is, not of genetics but of relations of power. It would be beside the point to insist that, none the less, this imaginary body is in fact the anatomical body overlaid by culture, since the anatomical body is itself a theoretical object for the discourse of anatomy which is produced by human beings in culture. There is a regress involved in positing the anatomical body as the touchstone for cultural bodies since it is a particular culture which chooses to represent bodies anatomically. Another culture might take the clan totem as the essence or truth of particular bodies. The human body is always a signified body and as such cannot be understood as a 'neutral object' upon which science may construct 'true' discourses. The *human* body and its history presuppose each other.

This conception of the imaginary body may provide the framework in which we can give an account of how power, domination and sexual difference intersect in the lived experience of men and women. Gender itself may be understood on this model not as the effect of ideology or cultural values but as the way in which power takes hold of and constructs bodies in particular ways. Significantly, the sexed body can no longer be conceived as the unproblematic biological and factual base upon which gender is inscribed, but must itself be recognized as constructed by discourses and practices that take the body both as their target and as their vehicle of expression. Power is not then reducible to what is imposed, from above, on naturally differentiated male and female bodies, but is also constitutive of those bodies, in so far as they are constituted as male and female.

Shifting the analysis of the operations of power to this micro-level of bodies and their powers and capacities has an interesting effect when one turns to a consideration of the political body. If we understand the masculinity or maleness of the political body and the public sphere as an *arbitrary* historical fact about the genesis of states, then sexual equality should be achievable provided we ensure that women have equal access to the political body and the public sphere. However, the relation between the public sphere and male bodies is not an arbitrary one. The political body was conceived historically as the organization of many bodies into one body which would itself enhance and intensify the powers and capacities of specifically male bodies.[31]

Female embodiment as it is currently lived is itself a barrier to women's 'equal' participation in socio-political life. Suppose our body politic were one which was created for the enhancement and intensification of women's historical and present capacities. The primary aim of such a body politic might be to foster conditions for the healthy reproduction of its members. If this were the case, then presumably some men would now be demanding that medical science provide ways for them to overcome their 'natural' or biological disadvantages, by inventing, for example, means by which they could lactate. This may seem a far-fetched suggestion, but it nevertheless makes the point that a biological disadvantage can be posited as such only in a cultural context.

### DIFFERENCE

The crux of the issue of difference as it is understood here is that difference does not have to do with biological 'facts' so much as with the manner in which culture marks bodies and creates specific conditions in which they live and recreate themselves. It is beside the point to 'grant' equal access to women and others excluded from the traditional body politic, since this amounts to 'granting' access to the body politic and the public sphere in terms of an individual's ability to emulate those powers and capacities that have, in a context of male/masculine privilege, been deemed valuable by that sphere. The present and future enhancement of the powers and capacities of women must take account of the ways in which their bodies are presently constituted.

Clearly, the sketch of power and bodies that has been offered here is not one which would lend itself to an understanding of sexual difference in terms of essentialism or biologism. The female body cannot provide the ontological foundation required by those who assert an essential sexual difference. On the contrary, it is the construction of biological discourse as being able to provide this status that is in need of analysis. The cluster of terms 'the female body', 'femininity' and 'woman' need to be analysed in terms of their historical and discursive associations. If discourses cannot be deemed as 'outside', or apart from, power relations then their analysis becomes crucial to an analysis of power. This is why language, signifying practices and discourses have become central stakes in feminist struggles.

Writing itself is a political issue and a political practice for many contemporary feminists. For this reason it is inappropriate to reduce the project of *écriture féminine* to an essentialist strategy. The 'difference' which this form of writing seeks to promote is a difference rooted not in biology but rather in discourse – including biological discourses. It is unhelpful to quibble over whether this writing is an attempt to 'write the female body' or to 'write femininity', since it is no longer clear what this distinction amounts to.[32] What is clear is that discourses, such as Lacanian psychoanalysis, and social practices, such as marriage, construct female and male bodies in ways that constitute and validate the power relations between men and women.

The account of female sexuality offered by Lacanian psychoanalysis constructs female bodies as lacking or castrated and male bodies as full or phallic. This construction tells of a power relation where the actual understanding of sexual difference implies a passive/active relation.

Writing of a sexuality that is not simply the inverse or the complement
of male sexuality presents a discursive challenge to the traditional
psychoanalytic understanding of sexual difference, where difference is
exhausted by phallic presence or absence. Irigaray's writing of the 'two
lips' of feminine morphology is an active engagement with the construction of what here has been called the imaginary body. It is not an
attempt to construct a 'true' theory of sexual difference, starting from
the foundation of female biology. Rather, it is a challenge to the traditional construction of feminine morphology where the bodies of women
are seen as receptacles for masculine completeness. At the same time as
Irigaray's writing offers a challenge to traditional conceptions of
women, it introduces the possibility of *dialogue* between men and
women in place of the monological pronouncements made by men over
the mute body of the (female) hysteric.[33]

Legal practices and discourses surrounding marriage also assume this
conception of sexual difference by allotting conjugal rights to the
(active) male over the body of the (passive) female. Significantly, the
act which is taken to consummate marriage is legally defined as an
act performed by a man on a woman. Needless to say, these legal,
psychoanalytic and social understandings of the female body have been
articulated from the perspective of male writers, who take it upon
themselves to represent women, femaleness and femininity. From this
perspective, it is not surprising that women are represented as pale
shadows and incomplete complements to the more excellent type: 'man'.
The project of *écriture féminine* involves challenging the masculine
monopoly on the construction of femininity, the female body and
woman. It also involves a rejection of the notion that there can be *a*
theory of woman, for this would be to accept that woman *is* some (*one*)
thing.

The works of Luce Irigaray, Hélène Cixous and Adrienne Rich are
each in their own ways involved in investigating the manner in which
women's bodies are constructed and lived in culture.[34] Each could be
seen to be writing from an embodied perspective about the female
body, femininity and women. Yet none of these writers claims to
*represent* (all) women or the multiplicity of women's experiences. This
would be for them to take up a masculine attitude in relation to other
women. Significantly, all three writers critically address the dualisms
which have dominated western thought. Addressing constructions of the
feminine in history necessarily involves addressing those terms which
have been associated with femininity: the body, emotion and so on.
When Irigaray, for example, writes of the 'repression of the feminine',

she is also alluding to the repression of the body and passion in western thought. To attempt to 'write' the repressed side of these dualisms is not, necessarily, to be working for the reversal of the traditional values associated with each but rather to unbalance or disarrange the discourses in which these dualisms operate. It is to create new conditions for the articulation of difference.

To understand 'difference feminism' as the obverse of 'equality feminism' would be to miss entirely the point of this essay. Difference, as it has been presented here, is not concerned with privileging an essentially biological difference between the sexes. Rather, it is concerned with the mechanisms by which bodies are recognized as different only in so far as they are constructed as possessing or lacking some socially privileged quality or qualities. What is crucial in our current context is the thorough interrogation of the means by which bodies become invested with differences which are then taken to be fundamental ontological differences. Differences as well as commonality must be respected among those who have historically been excluded from speech/writing and are now struggling for expression. If bodies and their powers and capacities are invested in multiple ways, then accordingly their struggles will be multiple.

The conception of difference offered here is not one which seeks to construct a dualistic theory of an essential sexual difference. Rather, it entertains a multiplicity of differences. To insist on sexual difference as *the* fundamental and eternally immutable difference would be to take for granted the intricate and pervasive ways in which patriarchal culture has made that difference its insignia.

### NOTES

1 An excellent collection of essays which offers an overview of feminist perspectives on political theory from Plato to Habermas is M.L. Shanley and C. Pateman (eds), *Feminist Interpretations and Political Theory* (Polity Press, Cambridge, 1991).

2 See M. Gatens, *Feminism and Philosophy: Perspectives on Difference and Equality* (Polity Press, Cambridge, 1991), for a detailed defence of this view.

3 See G. Lloyd, *The Man of Reason: 'Male' and 'Female' in Western Philosophy* (Methuen, London, 1984); J. Grimshaw, *Feminist Philosophers: Women's Perspectives on Philosophical Traditions* (Wheatsheaf Books, Brighton, 1986), esp. ch. 2; M. Le Doeuff, *The Philosophical Imaginary* (Athlone, London, 1989).

4 C. Pateman, *The Sexual Contract* (Polity Press, Cambridge, 1989), p. 96.

5 S. Moller Okin's critique of John Rawls's influential *A Theory of Justice* provides a good example of this approach. See her 'John Rawls: Justice as Fairness – For Whom?', in Shanley and Pateman, *Feminist Interpretations and Political Theory*, pp. 181–98.

6 For example, Andrea Dworkin has stated 'I think that the situation of women is basically ahistorical.' Cited in Pateman, *The Sexual Contract*, p. 236, note 24.

7 S. de Beauvoir, *The Second Sex* (Penguin, Harmondsworth, 1975), p. 96.

8 M. le Doeuff, 'Women and Philosophy', *Radical Philosophy*, 17 (1977), pp. 2–11; p. 2.

9 I have used a Spinozistic approach in 'Towards a Feminist Philosophy of the Body', in B. Caine, E. Gross and M. de Lepervanche (eds), *Crossing Boundaries* (Allen and Unwin, Sydney, 1988), pp. 59–70. More recently, G. Lloyd has used Spinoza's monist theory of existence to appraise the sex/gender distinction critically in 'Woman as Other: Sex, Gender and Subjectivity', *Australian Feminist Studies*, 10 (1989), pp. 13–22.

10 See L. Althusser, 'Ideology and Ideological State Apparatuses', in his *Lenin and Philosophy and Other Essays* (New Left Books, London, 1977), pp. 121–73.

11 I have argued against the possibility of including women in liberal society, *on an equal footing with men*, in *Feminism and Philosophy*, esp. ch. 2.

12 See C. di Stefano, 'Masculine Marx', in Shanley and Pateman, *Feminist Interpretations and Political Theory*, pp. 146–63.

13 J. Mitchell, *Psychoanalysis and Feminism* (Penguin, Harmondsworth, 1974).

14 K. Millett, *Sexual Politics* (Granada, London, 1972), p. 31.

15 For a discussion of the difficulties involved in the sex/gender distinction see M. Gatens, 'A Critique of the Sex/Gender Distinction', in J. Allen and P. Patton (eds), *Beyond Marxism?* (Intervention Publications, Sydney, 1983), pp. 142–61, reprinted in S. Gunew (ed.), *A Reader in Feminist Knowledge* (Routledge, London, 1991), pp. 139–57.

16 See, for example, M. Foucault, *The History of Sexuality* (Allen Lane, London, 1978), part 2, chs 1, 2; part 4, ch. 2.

17 M. Foucault, *Power/Knowledge*, ed. C. Gordon (Harvester Press, Sussex, 1980), p. 118.

18 Ibid., p. 98.

19 S. Firestone, *The Dialectic of Sex* (Bantam Books, New York, 1970).

20 For an example of the former, see M. Daly, *Gyn/Ecology: The Metaethics of Radical Feminism* (Beacon Press, Boston, Mass., 1978); and for one of the latter, see C. McMillan, *Women, Reason and Nature* (Basil Blackwell, Oxford, 1982).

21 See E. Spelman, 'Woman as Body: Ancient and Contemporary Views', *Feminist Studies*, 8 (1982), pp. 109–31.

22 See Daly, *Gyn/Ecology*, pp. 109–12.

23 Ibid., pp. 61–2.

24  See M. Foucault, 'Nietzsche, Genealogy, History', in his *Language, Counter-Memory, Practice*, ed. D. Bouchard (Cornell University Press, Ithaca, N.Y., 1977), pp. 139–64.
25  See C. Gallagher and T. Laqueur (eds), *The Making of the Modern Body* (University of California Press, Berkeley, Cal., 1987).
26  Foucault, *History of Sexuality*, p. 152.
27  For a sympathetic feminist reading of Foucault's work, see J. Sawicki, 'Foucault and Feminism: Toward a Politics of Difference', in Shanley and Pateman, *Feminist Interpretations and Political Theory*, pp. 217–31.
28  See J. Lacan, 'Some Reflections on the Ego', *International Journal of Psychoanalysis*, 34 (1953), pp. 11–17; Lacan, 'The Mirror Stage' in *Ecrits* (Tavistock, London, 1977), pp. 1–7; M. Merleau-Ponty, 'The Child and his Relation to Others', in Merleau-Ponty, *The Primacy of Perception* (Northwestern University Press, Evanston, Ill., 1964), pp. 96–155; P. Schilder, *The Image and Appearance of the Human Body* (International University Press, New York, 1978).
29  Lacan writes:

> it is a necessary condition for the maturation of the gonad of the female pigeon that it should see another member of its species, of either sex; so sufficient in itself is this condition that the desired effect may be obtained merely by placing the individual within reach of the field of reflection of a mirror. Similarly, in the case of the migratory locust, the transition within a generation from the solitary to the gregarious form can be obtained by exposing the individual, at a certain stage, to the exclusively visual action of a similar image, provided it is animated by movements of a style sufficiently close to that characteristic of the species. ('Mirror Stage', p. 3)

30  Lacan, 'Some Reflections', p. 13.
31  For a recent feminist account of the aims of the masculine political body, see Pateman, *Sexual Contract*, ch. 4; Gatens, 'Representation in/and the Body Politic', in R. Diprose and R. Ferrel (eds), *Cartographies: The Mapping of Bodies and Spaces* (Allen and Unwin, Sydney, 1991), pp. 79–87.
32  See, for example, Toril Moi's arguments in *Sexual/Textual Politics* (Methuen, London, 1985), pp. 102–26, which misunderstand the conception of difference being employed by Cixous.
33  See, for example, the writings of Freud and Breuer on hysteria and femininity in volume 2 of *The Standard Edition of the Complete Psychological Works of Freud*, ed. J. Strachey (Hogarth Press, London, 1974).
34  See L. Irigaray, *This Sex Which is Not One* (Cornell University Press, Ithaca, N.Y., 1985) and *Speculum of the Other Woman* (Cornell University Press, Ithaca, N.Y., 1985); H. Cixous, 'Castration or Decapitation?', *Signs*, 7 (1981), pp. 41–55; A. Rich, *Blood, Bread and Poetry* (Virago, London, 1987).

# 8

# Painting, Feminism, History

## *Griselda Pollock*

In the painting 'The Painter and his Model' (1917), Henri Matisse represents an artist at work in the privileged space of modern art, the studio. Not a documentary image of Matisse's actual working space on the Quai St Michel in Paris, it symbolically represents the ideological conditions in which modern art was created – by *the* painter in *the* studio. The painter, Matisse, is a man, as is *the painter* he symbolizes. More often the man/artist is clothed, while the model, prototypically a woman, is naked, and often supine in some gracelessly uncomfortable posture. Matisse's reversal juxtaposes a caucasian flesh-coloured and possibly nude artist to the crumpled mess of faceless costume in the armchair in the corner, his female model. Masculine nudity, associated with Apollonian intelligence and creativity, signifies a mastering and active body, and strips the artist of any specific social or historical signs other than the white masculinity with which he is clothed because he is the artist. The body is not anatomically sexed; cultural connotations provide its gender through the assimilation of the term artist to man.

The painting is a palimpsest of three orders of space which define modern western art-making. It is a social space shaped in the concrete social and economic relations in one particular studio in Paris in 1917 in which a white bourgeois man paid a probably working-class woman to work for him. Then it is a representation of the symbolic space of art, the studio, and it makes a statement about the basic components of art-making – the artist, the model and the site of their one-way transaction, the canvas. Finally it presents to us the space of representation, that canvas, upon which is painted a fictive body which has been invented by the combination of the painter's look and gesture. A social and a sexual hierarchy are pictured: the artist is canonically male (signalling the fusion of Culture with masculinity); *his* material is female

**Plate 1** Henri Matisse, *The Painter and His Model*, 1917, Musée National d'Art Moderne, Paris © Succession H Matisse/DACS 1992.

**Plate 2**   Brassai, *Henri Matisse in his Studio*. Photograph London, Victoria and Albert Museum.

(the assimilation of nature, matter and femininity). By its formal disposition of man/artist: woman/model, the painting articulates the symbolic value and symbolic gender in western modernism's discourse of the 'body of the painter'.

This essay examines the problematic for women created by this regime, and I shall argue that the complex relations between painting (art), feminism and history can be rhetorically tracked in the contradictory placements and significations of two bodies: the 'body of the painter' and the 'feminine body'. Women want to make art, they want specifically to paint, a desire which is as much about wanting the right to enjoy being the body of the painter in the studio – the creative self in a private domain – as it is about wanting to express individualistically the none the less collective experiences of women. These are potently connected with and represented by aspects of our bodies, life-cycles and sexualities. There are different theories about how much and what of this 'body of woman' women can represent against the grain of the dominant culture's trope of the active male creative body and the supine female object body, narratively figured in Matisse's reflexive modernist painting. The field is thus triangulated – the painter's body, the feminine body and the contestation of both through feminist discourse and practice of 'the woman's body'.

But in that formulation some 'women's bodies' are effaced in a false universalism. If the white woman's body has been objectified and priced as the material of fantasy and art, the black woman's body, brutalized and violated under slavery and racism, has not been figured so extensively in this privileged exchange.[1] However negatively present, indeed over-present, the white body of woman has been part of the spectacle.[2] The politics of white feminist resistance may thus involve a set of strategies of calculated invisibility and its corollary insistence on *presence* signified 'an-iconically'. For black women, however, the outrage against their absence in hegemonic cultures, and the insistence upon other traditions in the representation of women, dictate the necessity for a creative production of *presence*. This involves strategies for insisting on visibility through figuration and the production of icons.[3]

> I am a Blackwoman and my work is concerned with making images of Blackwomen. Sounds simple enough – but I'm not interested in portraiture or its tradition. I'm interested in giving space to Blackwomen presence. A presence which has been distorted, hidden and denied. I'm interested in our humanity, our feelings and our politics; somethings which have been neglected ... I have a sense of urgency about our 'apparent' absence in a space we've inhabited for several centuries.[4]

There is no doubt that the body is a critical site of our oppressions and exploitations, the locus of social disciplines and violations, the field of pleasure and desire as all are traversed and differentially lived across the wounds of class, race, gender and sexuality. Diverse political campaigns and opposing theoretical programmes converge – in distinctively post-modernist fashion – upon this social, psychic, political, physical and metaphorical image of ourselves – the body, which is not inert matter or irreducible physicality, but figure, sign, space, name. The questions I want to pose are preliminary and strategic in character, mapping some of the contradictory pressures since the early 1970s which have shaped western feminist thought and cultural practice by reading a series of images of bodies in the studio.

THE ARTIST IN THE STUDIO

A photograph by Hans Namuth of Jackson Pollock (d. 1956), perhaps as a result of these very photographs the most famous 'body of the painter', frames the producing body and the arena of his activity, the canvas itself, supine on the floor receiving from his flurry of gestures the marks and traces of his presence and action. The sexual hierarchy pictured in Matisse is not visualized directly in Namuth's photographs of Pollock at work. But the legacy is there in the potency and activity of the masculine body now directly mastering the supine feminine space of the canvas, patterning that surface, that imaginary body, with his inscriptions.

Abstract Expressionism (the artistic movement epitomized by Pollock's manner of painting) reduced reference to a world, however stylized or oblique, and substituted these vivid, metonymic traces of the 'body of the painter', epitomized by 'the gesture'. Pollock's practice was critically valorized in different ways, all of which celebrate, however subtextually, a colonizing masculine mastery. Harold Rosenberg, who coined the phrase 'Action Painting', redefined this new art process as a kind of existential drama acted out in the theatre of the canvas's fictive space. Clement Greenberg defined Pollock in relation to his theory that the destiny of each modern art was its sacrifice of all ambitions for painting save those dictated by the material character of its medium. Painting, quintessentially defined by its flat, two-dimensional surface covered with coloured liquids which induce optical effects, achieves its modernist purity when it has banished literary subject matter, narrative and social content. Greenberg defined the law of modernism as the purification of each art: that 'the conventions not essential to the viability of a medium be discarded as soon as they are recognized.'[5] This process, however, did not in fact result in abstract art as such. The purity of the visual signifier, seemingly emptied of all reference to a social or natural world, is still loaded with significance through its function as affirmation of its artistic subject.[6] Abstract Expressionism is a celebration of the 'expressivity' of a self which is not to be constrained by expressing anything in particular except the engagement of that artistic self with the processes and procedures of painting. Thus 'painting' is privileged in modernist discourse as *the* most ambitious and significant art form because of its combination of gesture and trace, which secure by metonymy the presence of the artist. These inscribe a subjectivity whose value is, by visual inference and cultural naming, masculinity.[7]

**Plate 3**   Hans Namuth, *Jackson Pollock at Work*, 1950. Photograph New York, Studio © Hans Namuth 1990.

The subject encountered through traces of his action upon the canvas is a self, imagined to be capable of total self-expression, free from division and articulation, producing meaning directly without the mediation of symbol or sign.[8] At a psychic level this must be read as a regressive fantasy to a moment when the proto-subject first imagines itself unified. It invents an imagined memory of being able to communicate spontaneously and fully by means of the infant's primitive but psychically freighted tools, the look and the gesture. For this reason the fantasy exerts a powerful appeal to all artists irrespective of their sex, for it evokes the imaginary phase, a moment in the process of being made a human subject which is common to us all, despite the fact that the inflections of culturally ordained sexual difference are already shaping different trajectories which will match our forming subjectivities to the positions of masculinity and femininity. But for all that this ideology of art services bourgeois mythologies of the self-possessing and self-realizing individual in this imaginary form, we must recognize that its function is also decisively on the side of the Symbolic; that is, the cultural-social-political order. The imaginary individual, as all the images so starkly insist in their iconography, is a man, empowered by his privileged place on the symbolic side of the division theorized as 'sexual difference'.[9]

### 'WHERE ARE THE WOMEN?'

In our book *Old Mistresses* (1981),[10] Roszika Parker and I juxtaposed a photograph by Ernst Haas of Helen Frankenthaler, a second-generation abstract expressionist, to Namuth's Pollock. The pairing iconically suggested what we dared not write. Is there a visible difference between men and women artists? Do Pollock's slashing and throwing of paint, his gyrations around a supine canvas, enact a macho assault upon an imaginary, feminine body? Are the traces of paint on canvas the residues of a psychic performance? Is this *'écriture/peinture masculine'* at its most vivid? How could we then read Frankenthaler's pouring, pushing, smoothing gestures as she knelt on or near the canvas as a surface continuous with her space and movements? Is this a feminine modality inviting us to invent metaphors uniting femininity and fluidity for these luscious effects? Do these gestures of the labouring, painting bodies register some profoundly different way of being in the body and being in artistic space which the viewer might then read in terms of the signs of gender and sexuality? Are the procedural and hence the resulting formal differences within a modernist discipline symptoms of sexual difference? Are sexual politics there in the formal and technical processes of high modernist art?

At that moment we had no language in which to raise these questions, let alone answer them. The problem then, as now, is to find terms in which to analyse the *specificity* of women as subjects in a social and historical world without confirming that particularity as nothing more than difference; that is, that women are just women. It would be easy now to mobilize Irigaray and Kristeva to create a feminine poetics of

**Plate 4**   Ernst Haas, *Helen Frankenthaler at Work*, 1969. Photograph New York, Studio Ernst Haas.

painting through which to commend the specific qualities of Frankenthaler's practice of abstract painting. (See the section on 'Post-modernist Feminist Modernisms' below.) But affirmative action, however theoretically inspired, cannot spring us out of the still powerful model of modernism which is a historically specific enunciation of sexual difference.

Of course women share the fantasy of the creative self, desire that privileged space of imaginary freedom called the studio. Feminism and the discourses of art are, however, locked in a profound contradiction at the site of the expression of the creative self. Feminist theory problematizes notions of the self, of woman, of the subject, arguing that these are not essences, the pre-social sources of meaning, but intricate constructions in social and psychic space. Furthermore, feminist cultural theory refuted absolutely the idea that art was a kind of blank space upon which to deposit meanings through the singular look and self-affirming gesture. A historical and materialist thesis challenged affirmative and expressive theories of art by insisting that the materials for art are social, part of socially and historically determined signifying systems.[11] Art is not the privatized space of self-generated significance; it is a form of textual politics.

Textual practice is, furthermore, institutionally constituted. Modernist art theory, as the images discussed above suggest, privileges the studio as *the* discrete space where art is made, relegating gallery or exhibition, journal or art lecture to a subsidiary role of circulation and consumption, an act of interpretation or use coming after the singular creative event. Feminist materialist theory suggests that the studio, the gallery, the exhibition catalogue are not separate, but form interdependent moments in the cultural circuit of capitalist production and consumption. They are also overlapping sets within the signifying system which collectively constitutes the discourse of art. While the spaces of art have specific and local determinants and forms, they are, furthermore, part of a continuum with other economic, social, ideological practices which constitute the social formation as a whole. The interconnection between art as text and art as institution no longer permits the galleries alone to be blamed for sexism. It is necessary to interrogate the political effects of images of art as symbolic presence, as figuration of the artistic self, no longer present in person as 'he' was when, as 'master' of 'his' world, he made 'his' art-work. The sociality of art is 'the question of institutions, of the conditions which determine the reading of artistic texts and the strategies which would be appropriate for interventions (rather than "alternatives") in that context'.[12] Feminism, therefore, provides a theory of interventions within a field of signification, rather than an alibi for female expressivity; that is, for seeking to secure women's equal right to the 'body of the painter'. A critical debate hinges on this distinction and it is the purpose of this chapter to examine the politics of it.

SEXUALITY IN THE FIELD OF VISION

Feminism and politics have been common-sensically associated with the content of art, not with formal issues. But this is a misapprehension. Judy Chicago, for instance, wanted to create not merely a feminist iconography but a visual language, a semi-abstract imagery based on the metaphor of female sexuality. Refusing the repression of its physical form in the visual arts (all those nudes without pubic hair or any indication of genitals), she portrayed the history of women through ceramic evocations of female genitalia. 'The Dinner Party' (1978) opposed the silencing of women; women could speak through their labia, as it were. Powerful as a statement, the implications have troubled feminists, for the equation of woman with body, of sexuality with the genitals, seemed too limiting and indeed dangerous.

In contrast, feminist theory derived from psychoanalysis and film studies worked on what Jacqueline Rose defined as 'sexuality in the field of vision'.[13] Sexuality is understood not to be tied to genitals and gendered bodies. Sexuality is a representation. The 'sexual component of the image' goes beyond merely recognizing that figurative images play a part in the production of norms and stereotypes of gender. There is a cultural politics of sexuality in visual form and space itself, as well as in the practices of looking: 'the aesthetics of pure form are implicated in the less pure pleasures of looking.'[14] Psychoanalysis has provided an account of a politics of sexual difference secured in that relation between looking/seeing/form, especially in its analyses of fetishism, voyeurism, narcissism and exhibitionism. The 'body of woman' is perpetually figured in multifarious spaces of representation as both a threat of lack (bodily mutilation standing as metaphor for psychic disintegration) and an aesthetically super-perfect body whose beauty or harmony displaces the threat of lack. Matisse's painting narrates the threat, in the punishing dehumanization of the model, while it is disavowed and compensated for in the formal, almost abstract harmonies, the aesthetic beauties reworked by his artistry in the painting-within-the-painting of that model.

Rose states: 'We know that women are meant to *look* perfect, presenting a seamless image to the world so that man, in that confrontation with difference, can avoid any comprehension of lack. The position of woman in fantasy therefore depends upon a particular economy of vision.'[15] Much art can be seen to submit to that economy of vision – a fixed difference in which man is empowered with the look, rendering his fantasy of perfection, art formally beautifying the threatening otherness of woman. This is the sexual economy circulated through paintings and photographs of the man artist in his studio with his woman model. Indeed, part of the political force of critical, feminist art practices has been a purposeful strategy of fracture, of disruption of aesthetic perfection and the ease and fullness of familiar cultural pleasures. What has characterized a diversity of feminist modes is a refusal of an exclusive 'visuality', with its fantasies of looking, and a concurrent exploitation of a wider range of semiotic forms which call upon other drives, such as the invocatory, and other sign systems, including writing/inscription, incantation, rhythm, memory, echo.

Yet modernist painting at its height, Pollock's for instance, put that drive for aesthetic perfection at risk. The studio became the site of

a terrifying and heroic struggle in which the artist abandoned every
support, instrument, convention and tradition – even the body of the
woman.[16] Reducing his means to himself and the paint, he set out to see
if he could still make a picture work, conquer lack and recreate aesthetic
unity. This battle was represented publicly in the language of avant-
gardism – a great new endeavour, shedding the habits of the past,
adventuring to create a future, pushing culture onwards into uncharted
spaces: heroic, progressive, individualistic, it celebrated modernity's
promise of freedom, which, read from other perspectives, signalled
conquest, colonization and violence. Spurious and partial, freedom was
enjoyed in imaginary, aesthetic spaces figured by the western, avant-
garde, masculine artist; but that freedom was a powerful attraction, as
sometimes the only freedom on offer.


### MODERNISM'S APPEAL FOR WOMEN

The tradition of modernist painting is still significant and alive, and
there are plenty of important women practising there. But it is interesting that there has been little serious feminist work on it. Few feminists
have thought of putting on an exhibition of these modern 'mistresses',
while Victorian or baroque art by women has been fertile ground for
exhibitions and publications. But in 1988–9 The Arts Council of Great
Britain circulated an exhibition, 'The Experience of Painting: Eight
Modern Artists', of which, significantly, half the artists were women:
Gillian Ayres, Jennifer Durrant, Edwina Leapman and Bridget Riley.
  The very title already declares the liberal humanist character of its
project. 'Before we speak of the experience of painting let us consider
our experience of the world', writes Mel Gooding in the exhibition
catalogue. That 'our' is inclusive, suggesting a condition in which we all
share experience of the world: 'Memories, dreams, desires, our imagin-
ings of history, our projections of futurity, our sense of what is true and
what is false, all converge upon this moment, as we stand, say, upon a
beach, and looking seawards, smell the salt upon the air and feel the
wind cold upon our cheek.'[17] History and time evaporate before the
timeless moment of being in nature – a highly romantic concept which
typically enlivens the technical procedures of painting to give them
metaphysical resonance: 'Art may reflect something of this evanescence
but its purposes are deeper than a mirroring of the actual. It is an
imaginative and metaphorical interaction with the world and its objects,
answering to the deepest human impulse.'[18] This apologia is far from

Greenberg's rigorous, disciplined, modernist project for abstract paint-ing. Indeed it echoes the romanticism by which women's work is often 'feminized' and dehistoricized in one lyrical movement towards the monumental time of nature.[19]

The catalogue is prototypical in other ways, presenting each artist as an individual in his or her aesthetic cell, prefaced by a photograph of each person at work in her or his studio. The image is accompanied by the familiar artist's statement, couched in individualistic terms, project-ing this liberal humanist vision through the aesthetic vocabulary of pure formalism. The major presence is Gillian Ayres, featured on the cover – not active as is Pollock in Hans Namuth's evocation of the painting body in the studio – but seated like Matisse's model, compressed against the overwhelming colour and activity of paintings and paint-pots which seem not to be the product of this contemplative figure. She states her lifelong commitment to abstract painting:

> Abstract art has been the vital force in visual art in this century. This is nothing to do with myself, with my own commitment to abstraction. Modernism meant a lot of different things, and some of those things one may not like or agree with. But what it meant above all was hope in a brave new world. And what did go on under modernism was a *question-ing and thinking* . . . And under modernism that questioning was almost the condition of being creative.[20]

What I am trying to discern here is the contradictory formation in which a woman like Gillian Ayres has worked for thirty years, em-powered by the possibilities of modernism which allowed her to be an artist while not prescribing what she should paint as a woman. She is also sharing in the project of modernity, a belief in progress, a critical sense of how that progress is created by 'questioning and thinking'. Artistic practice is posited as a privileged site of such open experiment: 'You could simply say that imagination is *anti-cliché*, against known experience. You're always trying to find something you haven't seen before, an experience that is true to oneself.'[21]

What interests me is the way in which imagination and the critical faculty are captured within an exclusively aesthetic domain. Jürgen Habermas has characterized modernity precisely by such divisions of social life into specialist compartments – science, morality, aesthetics.[22] Mainstream twentieth-century modernism, the extreme bourgeois real-ization of the autonomy of art, offered to women a means, but a vicarious one, to experience freedom. That is why they embraced it and,

**Plate 5** Martin Charles, *Gillian Ayres in her Studio*, 1988. Photograph Isleworth, Studio Martin Charles.

despite all, dedicated their lives to 'painting'. In that studio, with the canvas on floor or wall, women imagined themselves free; if not from being women, free from being seen and defined exclusively in those terms. Once outside the door, they would once again have to be women, forgotten or ignored, condescendingly acknowledged until such time as the particular practice lost its place as culturally dominant. British abstract art in the 1990s is not where culture is at, and so the women who gave it vitality achieve belated recognition for their work in the house of culture, when everyone else has moved to another room.[23]

When Charles Harrison reviewed this show, he suggested that post-modernism might represent a shift as significant as that which ushered in modernism itself (which happened in the late nineteenth century for painting) and left many nineteenth-century academic painters desiring to continue to explore the still rich resources of their tradition, yet, as a result of the substantial reorientation signified by modernism, 'deprived of cultural and historical authenticity'.[24] Harrison's argument seems particularly pertinent to the feminist debate about painting. History, not feminism itself, has altered the terms and conditions of cultural practice. Yet feminist politics insists that within the community, we take seriously women's demands and do not judge their viability according to any given orthodoxy. Painting is not only very much on the agenda in art education, but it answers to many women's powerful desire for a way to represent women's experience as whole, human and thus equally important. Indeed that is what I think the call for feminist painting is about. It registers a demand for a permitted space in which the women who wish to be artists can experience, in the creative freedom of the studio and canvas, those expanding and personally challenging adventures symbolized through an encounter with the blank canvas, aided only by one's brushes and paints and fired by ambition and a sense of limitless possibility. In the name of what can feminists argue against such claims for women's right to participate in the modernist project, especially now that the formalism of Greenberg's modernism has been suspended and post-modernist painting allows the painter to enjoy the grand gesture, expressive figuration and, most importantly, historical and personal reference?

The answer is whatever we mean by post-modernity. But that is too trite, for we have only just begun to analyse post-modernity from a feminist perspective.[25] Modernism offered to women a delusive freedom from being defined as 'the sex', as woman. Yet in its institutions and critical discourses modernism patrolled the boundaries of masculine hegemony not so much by an overtly gendered discourse, but obliquely.

In an article entitled 'Mass Culture as Woman: Modernism's Other', Andreas Huyssen identifies the force of gender politics in the rigidly policed divide between mass culture – defined as engulfing, dangerous, trivial, easy, feminine – and authentic, high culture, which is represented in masculine terms as a project requiring steely determination and single-minded dedication to preserve true art against the diluting threat posed by popular art.[26] The gendering of mass culture bespeaks a sexual politics, but it is also the form of a division created by capitalism of which both high modernism and popular culture are fragmented pieces. Huyssen writes: 'I know of no better aphorism about the imaginary adversaries, modernism and mass culture, than that which Adorno articulated in a letter to Walter Benjamin: "Both [modernist and mass culture] bear the scars of capitalism, both contain elements of change. Both are torn halves of freedom to which, however, they do not add up".'[27]

Huyssen's suggestion of a 'masculine mystique', secured across the division of high and popular culture, has direct repercussions for feminist theory and practice in the post-modern moment. Huyssen, for instance, questions the fashionable idea of the 'femininity' of avant-garde writing proposed by Kristeva, who argues that femininity signifies the repressed and the transgressive (a point taken up later as a possible route to a feminist theory of abstract painting). Huyssen reminds us of the pervasive fantasy of a 'male femininity', in the work of Flaubert for example, a fantasy induced perhaps as a necessary reaction against the excessive masculinity demanded by the discipline of high art with its relentless abstention from pleasure – 'the suppression of everything that might be threatening to the rigorous demands of being modern and at the edge of time'.[28] Kristeva, celebrating the femininity of Mallarmé's and Joyce's negative aesthetics, was dealing in imaginary sexualities and disregarded a tradition of writing by women and their complex social, ideological and semiotic inscriptions within modernism, produced under the sign of woman. Huyssen points out that 'the universalising ascription of femininity to mass culture always depended on the real exclusion of women from high culture and its institutions.'[29] Now that women are visible as practitioners in high art, the gendering device becomes obsolete but only because 'both mass culture and women's (feminist) art are emphatically implicated in any attempt to map the specificity of contemporary culture and thus to gauge this culture's distance from high modernism.'[30]

Huyssen falters just where we must not – is there not some significant distinction between 'women's art' and 'art' qualified by feminism? The practices which constitute the most visible *feminist* interventions in culture are not to be defined according to the gender of their expressive subject, and not through residual modernist terminology as scripto-visual, photographic, video, or whatever other medium. By the same token we cannot be debating women's right to use oil or acrylic paint on canvas. To do so would be to renege on such political distance as we have achieved through the last two decades of feminist theory and practice in the cultural sphere.

In mass culture the manifest body, however, is the body of the woman, which becomes the very antithesis of individuality celebrated in high culture's body of the artist. The feminine body in mass culture is the symbol of saturation by the commodity, the field of play for money, power, capital and sexuality. As the body of woman lost its necessity and supremacy within modernist formalism, it continued to be cease-lessly circulated by its corollary, mass culture, which further devalued this body because it was produced without the authorizing signature of the artist.[31] Thus two bodies – the body of the painter and the body of woman – the signs of difference – stand opposed in modernist culture, caught up in the series of binary oppositions which figure sexual differ-ence to us across these inter-related domains.

Feminist practices cannot simply abandon either of these bodies, but whatever constitutes the feminism of the practice results from the necessity to *signify* a relation to this complex.[32] That is not the same as desiring somehow to have a share in the painter's body while producing new meanings for the feminine body. They exist as a relation, fabricated interdependently across the disparate spaces which make up culture. Thus feminist interventions in the spaces of representation have begun to qualify and differentiate the feminine bodies fabricated in culture's inter-facing hierarchies of race, class, gender, sexuality and age. But such practices are rarely single works, or merely series. They form complex installations, documentations and events, which aim to create a signify-ing space in which the historical changes wrought by feminism can be perceived and represented while others still more radical can be im-agined. The freedom here is not imaginary self-realization within the confines of the canvas, but the register of concrete struggles on and beyond the battlefield of representation.

## AFTER MODERNISM, FEMINISM?

Political feminist culture of the sixties and seventies was a part of a critique of modernism which in turn was symptomatic of a scepticism

about *modernity*. Its legacy of belief in human progress and the humanist, rationalist ideals of freedom have been savaged by the revolt of those
it had enslaved, violated, and repressed. But feminism itself, taken in
a long historical perspective, is also a product of the Enlightenment
project and of modernity.[33] Originally named the Women's *Liberation*
Movement, its project was conceived of by the second wave in terms of
emancipation from social structures of inequality. What the narratives
of modern art paradigmatically represent finds echoes in the project of
feminism – the self-realization of women/subjects/selves liberated from
the constraints of external pressures and socially induced limits. Just as
the materialist thesis on culture suggests an interdependence of text,
institution and the production of sexual difference, materialist feminist
theory has moved from this inside/outside dichotomy of individual
caught in a web of social oppression to a structural mode of analysis of
our condition as systematically social, political, linguistic, cultural and
psychic. In place of utopian dreams of the new society of post-liberation
times, there is a stress on enacted resistances, oppositions, negotiations
and the accumulation of local and particular strategies of intervention
and redefinition.

I do not, however, think it is sufficient to suggest that we have
witnessed a shift in feminist theory over two decades which has, as it
were, propelled feminism across a frontier, from its modernist liberation
theology into some post-modernist relativism. Indeed, it is the predica-
ment and paradox of women's struggles which constantly disrupts both
neat historical narratives and theoretical constructs.

Since they seem to have much in common, feminism has been cited
as a prototypical form of post-modernism. Indeed, much recent feminist art has been assimilated to post-modernism, especially those self-
consciously 'strategic practices' conceived by Barbara Kruger, Mary
Kelly, Cindy Sherman, Lubaina Himid, Susan Hiller, Jenny Holzer,
Marie Yates, Yve Lomax, Martha Rosler, Sutapa Biswas, Mitra Tabri-
zian, Jo Spence, Zarina Bhimji, Mona Hatoum and so forth.[34] Their
work is a site for a sustained analysis of the meanings of sexual difference authored by culture, across which 'cultural body' they inscribe
feminist readings.[35] Each artist has a 'project', a defined set of concerns
and resources, but they cannot be assimilated to the paradigm of the
expressive, self-affirming artist signified by 'the painter'. Wherever their
work is made, the point at which its meanings are produced is a public
space where viewers read its signs in relation to a wider field of representations and histories, collective as much as individual. While being
exhibited, even in an art gallery, such work implies the social spaces and

semiotic systems of both culture as a whole, and specific, often repressed or silenced constituencies to which the work so calculatedly
refers, and which it reworks to produce as critical *presence* in culture as
a whole. It is this radical reconceptualization of the function of artistic
activity – its procedures, personnel and institutional sites – which is the
major legacy of feminist interventions in culture since the late sixties.
What distinguishes such practices from the generality of post-
modernism is the refusal to abandon a sense of history and political
effect.

### POST-MODERNIST FEMINIST MODERNISMS

Nothing reveals more clearly the perverse trajectory of the last two
decades than the fact that this legacy is now seriously contested within
some sections of the feminist art community. What was but a decade
ago hailed as the feminist gesture of liberation in art is now felt to be
oppressive, elitist and avant-gardist. There is an explicit call to reunite
feminism and painting. Such debate between feminist definitions of
appropriate cultural forms and practices takes place, however, against a
shifting cultural landscape which includes a major *post*-modern reinvest-
ment (economically as much as curatorially and critically) in painting
and the privileged identities the term *embodies*. Neo-expressionism, new
figuration, gesture painting: a diverse array of practices restored to the
markets and the galleries their prize commodity – the body of the artist
through look and gesture now marketed as style.[36]

The new appraisals of women's painting represent it as radically
'different' from post-modern painting by men. Gender is thus positioned as outside the process of representation but expressed through its
evocation of the gendered author. Sarah Kent writes:

> Postmodern painting is often referred to as post-political. One might
> equally name it post-moral, post-idealist or retro-visionary. It is a form of
> mourning for lost power, lost belief and lost confidence, in which actual
> significance is replaced by overblown self-importance, inflated scale and
> hysterical bombast. It is a masculine art form, a witness to the crumbling
> of certainty and centrality.
> Women do not share this sense of dislocation and despair.[37]

On the contrary, Sarah Kent writes that women painters feel strong,
optimistic and rooted, and quotes Alexis Hunter, who claims that
women are working from a 'position of integrity'. While gender is the

basis for a 'difference' within post-modernist culture, it is so through a modernist conception of the wholeness of the artistic subject, which is now only possible for a woman artist. The power comes from the celebratory revelation of the feminine, usually negatively connoted and othered.

Sarah Kent's introduction to a recent exhibition of the work of the painter Rosa Lee opens with a reference to Luce Irigaray's critique of western rationalism as founded on identity, stability and binary opposition. Femaleness is typically placed on the side of the unbounded, irregular, disorderly. Painting becomes a means to express this other, feminine imaginary: Rosa Lee's paintings can be seen as an attempt to give form to those areas of experience and knowledge suppressed by the constraints of rationalism . . . Cradled within the geometry of Lee's paintings are flashes of the unruly, dark, wanton or barbarous aspects or the irrational that are associated with the feminine.'[38] In 1987 *Feminist Review* published a paper by Rosa Lee which conjoined feminism, painting and post-modernism in its title. Her question was this: 'Is it possible to produce a radical art form without recourse to the strategies of deconstruction adopted by feminists such as, for example, Mary Kelly, Rose Garrard, Susan Hiller or Nancy Spero?[39] Rosa Lee devoted much of her article to the work of Therese Oulton, a celebrated British painter who is not so much abstract as non-figurative. Her vast canvases are represented as critical attempts to renew artistic language by a subversion of the grand tradition of painting from Titian to Pollock. These claims are based upon structuralist theory about the radicalness of insisting that art is nothing but its means; structuralism is often a merely theoretical formulation of what we know as modernism. Oulton's work is also appraised via French feminist theory, which associates femininity with negativity and transgression of patriarchal languages. 'In these paintings the quest for renewal rests upon a series of "refusals" which result from a critique of painting's traditions . . . the paintings refuse any one fixed interpretation . . . It is through the subversive juxtaposition of paradoxes that the possibility of creating a new, non-representational artistic language emerges.'[40]

Painting by such women is characterized as feminine precisely because it resists representation, a claim that draws upon Kristeva's thesis that femininity is unrepresentable within a phallocentric symbolic. But for Kristeva, femininity is not synonymous with women or their bodies. It is a specificity complexly produced in the psychic and social semiotics of culture, lived out, experienced by those designated thereby as women. This is a profound distinction between notions of gender as rooted in essential properties named being a man or being a woman (which can be defined biologically, psychically or sociologically) and notions of sexual difference as an effect of a process always already written upon us, but which can be theoretically grasped as a projection only fixed at a relatively late stage of our formation as human subjects. It is the gap between the making of sexual difference, the signifying of sexual difference and identities construed across the process and the naming that gives us hope – for there it is that transformation and revolution are possible.

Indexed only to art, annexed to a still modernist art theory, the subtle misreadings of French feminism provide an updated alibi for the model of the artist in the studio producing a singular, individual practice, whose traces define the painting, and give spectators access back to the artistic subject. Lee, Oulton or Newman: these names, like those of Matisse and Pollock, are moments of a gender category, in the former case, women. The fact of the gender of the artist invites a reading of the work as an expression of femininity. Negatively positioned in patriarchal culture, it is celebrated for its negativity in this critical discourse. At the level of experiential and aesthetic effect these readings are seductive and enriching. But the use of French feminism's reworking of the term 'feminine' within the paradigm of 'the artist in the studio' tends to confirm, because it so confidently affirms, a fundamental difference of the feminine, or femininity only as fundamental difference. The binary opposition remains in place and the feminine, however much it is locally valorized by women painters and viewers, continues its prescribed role as cipher against which masculinity erects its domination. While we may try to insert the woman's body into the space of the studio – both practically and symbolically in discourse – the project easily succumbs to merely replaying the deep structures of that system: woman as difference, inchoate, unspeakable, enigmatic, metaphor for all that is outside representation and meaning except as lack. The formal achievements of these undoubtedly marvellous painters paradoxically confirm it. Now it is women's painting, not their body alone, that must be beautiful, formally satisfying, managing the risk of chaos to secure pictorial unity.

The implicit binarism also has effects in relations to other distinctions, differences between women with regard to race, class, sexuality, age, disability. Black women artists assert the need for definition as a priority. The difference their bodies have been forced to signify allows little of the pleasures of inchoateness and abandon. Oversensualized and underdefined in relation to the term woman – both sexually brutalized and enslaved as the anonymous labouring body – other representational strategies are demanded to negotiate spaces for their occupation and redefinition of the term femininity to accommodate their history and desire.[41] Each community inscribes its values and meanings upon the terms woman and femininity, which circulate promiscuously, seeming to refer to shared meanings when, in fact, as signifiers, they are often indeterminate, chronically historical and variable. Yet Denise Riley cogently argues: 'These difficulties can't be assuaged by appeals to the myriad types and conditions of women on this earth. They are not a matter of there being different *sorts of* women, but the effects of the designation, "women".'[42] Any strategy that relies on the givenness of meaning, woman, women, femininity, must find itself potentially confirming the dominant, preferred meanings, once more conjuring up a false universality, itself a touchstone of modernism's liberal lie.

Of Lubaina Himid's *Freedom and Change* (1984), Gilane Tawadros writes:

> Himid's women displace what Stuart Hall has called the 'centred discourses of the West', but this does not simply imply that the grand narratives of the West are simply to be replaced by an alternative, totalising narrative. Rather this process of displacement 'entails putting in question (Western culture's) universalist character and its transcendental claims to speak for everyone, while being everywhere and nowhere' ... In opposition to the universalising tendencies of modernism, *Freedom and Change* assigns central importance to the position of difference.[43]

To make a difference is to work to create the means to signify difference, and that cannot mean merely changing sides or perspectives. It means taking on the systems which themselves make sexual difference and hinge that formation to so many other social differentiations. This involves recognizing the specificity of the level and effect of sexual difference, however differently various social communities live it. There are neither hierarchies of oppression nor synchronous listings – race, gender, class and so forth. There are specific configurations, each of which formations – gender, class, race – occurs through particular processes requiring appropriately forged methods of analysis and strategies of opposition.

Gilane Tawadros argues that Lubaina Himid articulates 'a positive conception of the ethnicity of the margins, or the periphery ... a recognition that we all speak from a particular place, out of particular history, out of a particular experience, a particular culture, *without being contained by that position*'.[44] Particularity is a strategy of resistance to modernism, which, with western feminism, shares the western discourse of centrality. Yet western feminism, in pursuit of the means to analyse the particularity of some women (which it oft-times imagined were all women, admittedly), has identified a formation – sexual difference – which, however configured through the prism of many particularities, is a determinant on all of us. Denise Riley writes:

> The now familiar device for challenging essentialism from a feminist perspective attacks its false universalism in representing the experiences of, usually, middle-class, white western women as if they embraced all womankind. But this move to replace the tacit universal with the qualified 'some women's experience' is both necessary and yet in the end inadequate. Below the newly pluralized surfaces, the old problems still linger.[45]

### POST-MODERNIST FEMINIST POST-MODERNISMS

In 1987 Katy Deepwell also wrote an article 'In Defence of the Indefensible: Feminism, Painting and Post-Modernism'. She polemically intervened against what she took to be a theoretically inspired prescription of feminist art practice – an orthodoxy of scripto-visual work – and she initiated a reconsideration of the admittedly problematic relation between feminism and figurative painting. 'What is at issue here is the potential of painting as a medium through which feminists can mount a challenge to notions of art prevalent today: a challenge in images, methods, and readings, different to the existing order.'[46] 'Painting as a medium' evokes shades of Greenberg's modernist definition of art by its materials. But 'painting' is much more than an artistic technique, a medium. Since the late eighteenth century, and certainly since the beginning of this, the term has referred to the hegemonic cultural form which is constituted by the combination of a subject (the artist), an activity (the practice in the studio) and a web of symbolic meaning woven through that figure in that space by means of the economic investment in the commodity it produced.[47] It is a historical naivety to imagine that the debate about feminism and cultural practice is reducible to whether it is OK to use acrylic on canvas as well as video or photographic montage.

But Katy Deepwell focuses on questions of the means of signifying women's particularity – not theorized as negativity, but as materials of lived experience and specific interests. The space of art is one which narrates and in doing so legitimizes that which is made visible in its recurring stories. The script of figurative painting in the west has been massively masculine, servicing its fantasies and representing its white dominance. Women desire to write new stories, their stories, into this narrative. In the Victorian period, as in the moment of surrealism with its echoes of that earlier bourgeois age, narrative, figurative painting offered space for women's inscriptions, as often supportive of dominant ideological formations as against the grain.[48] Under a post-modernist cultural dispensation, strict Greenbergian formalism has been displaced. Reference and figuration are permitted. As Sarah Kent suggests, women are placed differently from men in this moment. Feminist liberation politics, affirmative, experiential and revelatory, comfortably cohabits with a positive adoption of the new possibilities of figurative painting. But again, it seems that while recolonizing painting with specific meanings for and of women, both the notion of woman and the notion of art as self-expression – however collective a self; that is, women – are unexamined. As a result the positivity of what is expressed (women's experience and viewpoint) will continue to be determined negatively as a subcultural expression (only women's, only black women's, only lesbians, only mothers' experience and viewpoint) by the structural sexism of the institution within which the work, like all art as text, will signify.

WHERE HISTORIES CONVERGE

To take the issue beyond the troubling and impossible relation between 'feminism' and 'painting' we need a third term, 'history'.[49] The women's movement is predicated upon a seemingly self-evident collectivity, women. We have not, however, always been and are never only 'women'. Indeed feminism in the western form is a historical product of the fact that sex has a history.[50] The historian Denise Riley has argued for the necessity of a historical understanding of the formations and alterations of the collectivity 'women' in European history. From the seventeenth century and reaching a culmination in the nineteenth century, female people in the west undergo a historical process of increasing sexualization, whose effects are uneven according to hierarchies of power called class, race and gender. Riley's phrase 'the long march of the empires of gender over the entirety of the person' points to the redefinition of women as 'the sex', as only their sex – or rather 'the sex he uses'. Ruled by reproductive biology, white bourgeois women were subjected through a range of new disciplines and social practices which resulted in what we could name 'overfeminization'. Women – the name already encoding class- and race-specific references – became extensions of Woman, weighted with a sexuality that excluded from the definition of 'woman' most forms of political or economic power. In the formation of this highly sexualized division in western bourgeois society between masculine and feminine spheres, cultural forms, institutions and practices played a significant part at the level of representation. The femininity of 'women' was negotiated both by their inclusion in cultural narratives and imageries, though in a restricted range of types and settings, and by their exclusion from culture's most prestigious practices and institutions, such as the Royal Academy or History painting. None the less, women did practise professionally as artists, but in ways which as often reinforced as much as they criticized the sexualized, gendered vocabulary of bourgeois society. But, paradoxically, if femininity was on the cultural agenda, it meant there were cultural opportunities in which to examine the question of sexual difference and to speak out both from, and of, the specific psychic spaces and social bodies bourgeois culture *engendered*.[51]

Feminism emerged as a protest from within this overfeminization of bourgeois sexual order. An immediate if not simultaneous historical effect, it disputed the enunciations of femininity, but from within the boundaries of this sexually divided universe. But by the beginning of this century, to claim space in modernity, it became necessary for women to distance and denounce both bourgeois and nineteenth-century feminist enunciations of femininity. For women artists, for example, wishing to escape the possible but always limiting sphere of feminine art, the spaces and practices of cultural modernism permitted an apparent liberation from the culture's traditional overfeminization of women.[52] Women artists aligned themselves with the modernist project, which seemed to offer them access to freedom, equality, the chance to be just an artist – to be the body in the studio, free like Matisse's from time, place and, however momentarily, gender. In contrast to the highly gendered modes of the nineteenth-century bourgeois culture, the emergent modernist community appeared to embody the liberal ideal of humanity blissfully indifferent to gender.

Indifferent it was – to women, and any other community. Without any serious deconstruction of the masculine power it had sustained, this liberal ideal reinscribed that gender's privilege. What it offered women and the white bourgeoisie's colonial others was participation in modernism, on condition that they effaced their gender/cultural particularity. Well known in the study of racism, the discourse of tolerance has also functioned within the modern politics of gender.[53] Women had to

choose between being human and being a woman.[54] As artists this was a
paradoxical experience. In her probing interviews with women artists
of the modernist generations, Cindy Nemser repeatedly recorded the
pressures these women experienced to 'become one of the boys' in order
to have access to the profession they desired.[55] Throughout the twentieth century, with honourable exceptions, women artists forged artistic
identities under this modernist arrangement, signing their initials or
defeminizing their names, like Lee Krasner, the painter who was
married to Jackson Pollock.[56] The process of becoming an artist did not
tolerate public avowal that being a woman made any difference. But
being a woman made all the difference to the size of the studio you got
to work in, to whether you got exhibitions, or to the terms in which
your work was written about.

Helen Frankenthaler, for instance, was an up and coming post-
graduate painter when she attracted the attention of leading modern art
critic Clement Greenberg. He sent her to visit Jackson Pollock in his
studio at East Hampton and she was duly astounded by his novel
painting methods and the solutions his work was suggesting to the
impasse of post-cubist art. It is generally agreed that Frankenthaler
learnt that lesson well and in her immediate exploitation of techniques
of staining and soaking unprimed canvas, in paintings such as *Mountains and Sea* (1952, Washington National Gallery), effectively created
the next move in the game of avant-garde painting, a move which was
taken up in the later 1950s by Kenneth Nolan and Morris Louis. In 1960
Clement Greenberg hailed Louis and Nolan as the leading American
painters, the only ones who moved the art game on. His article is
shadowed by a presence – Frankenthaler's. She is not acknowledged
in his history of modernism, except obliquely in this passage securing
Louis's pedigree: 'His first sight of middle period Pollocks, and of a
large, extraordinary painting done in 1952 by Helen Frankenthaler
called *Mountains and Sea*, led Louis to change his direction abruptly.'[57]
That is the sum of her historical presence in a kind of art writing that is
all about a league table of goals and innovations. In other books which
have discussed her work, she is removed from the linear, historical time
of Greenberg's modernism. Her work is lyrically associated with landscape and nature – projecting Frankenthaler out of art historical time
into a monumental temporality of eternal femininity.[58] Greenberg at
least did not subject Frankenthaler to that fate, but his virtual silence
eradicated her as effectively from history. While this may well be a
product of his sexism, it is also an effect of modernism itself – how can
gender be said to inflect facture, strategic painterly moves on late cubist

space, relations between geometry and colour on a flat surface? It obviously can, as I have argued above, but it has required the perspective of feminist critique to found a vocabulary with which to deconstruct the in*difference* of modernist discourse.[59]

Late twentieth-century western feminism can be named a reaction against modernist liberalism's 'underfeminization'. Bourgeois society made sex a central categorization, an extremity which framed the resistance – a desire to escape being a woman. Art, like money and power, offered a respite for the lucky few. But the categorization remained, if not at the political level then economically, legally, in employment and social welfare, etc. Being a woman made a difference, and feminism has, since the late sixties, worked to repoliticize femininity.[60] The problem is how to develop enunciations of femininity that can cut across the twin poles of femininity as absolute difference (the nineteenth-century model) and femininity as a social disadvantage to be overcome in the ambition for equality with men (the twentieth-century liberal position). As Toril Moi has argued, western feminism is an impossible undertaking, a political struggle in the name of women, aiming either to render such a nomination a matter of indifference or to valorize difference with a system of binary oppositions which systematically values one term, man, over its negative other, woman.

> Given this logic, a feminist cannot settle for either equality or difference. Both struggles must be *aporetically* fought out. But we also know that both approaches are caught in the end in a constraining logic of *sameness* and *difference*. Julia Kristeva therefore suggests that feminism must operate in a third space: that which deconstructs all identity, all binary oppositions, all phallologocentric positions.[61]

This third space, projected in Julia Kristeva's essay 'Women's Time' (1979), is the theoretical space associated with the feminist analysis of sexual difference – that is, of a system by which human subjectivity is constituted and which no one can escape. This is perhaps also the space in which to think the issues of difference which feminism in its late twentieth-century form has not.

Femininity has also to be thought beyond its imperial bourgeois origins.[62] If women are not a stable or given unity but a historical category, a designation, we must think that for each aspect of social existence the same applies: class, race, sexuality. Each one person is captured by a plurality of categorizations, each of which works over, to reconfigure, the other categorizations. At the same time the dominant categorizations encounter and negotiate with historical residues, as well as emergent formations, which may be simply alternative or actively oppositional. Thus identities are not just plural (an idea typical of post-modern indifference). They are historical complexes of textured difference. The confrontations between imperial feminism and black feminists hinge on the misrecognition of the historical conditions of both attitudes. Feminism, a politics privileging gender, is the troubled effect of western bourgeois sexualization with its phony universals. The phrase 'black women' can be read to emphasize women as the category and black as the qualifier, as a composite noun; or to put the stress on black as the category and woman as the minor term, qualified by belonging to a larger community of the diaspora. These are the registers of historical and political affiliations and experiences which speak of the necessity to grasp persons as living, specific configurations of historical placement around deeply and mutually interactive categorizations – race, class, gender – which are never discrete totalities, but complex formations operative as much at the level of psychic as of socio-economic construction.

BODY, SIGNS AND HISTORY

In 1986 Lubaina Himid produced a major installation work, 'A Fashionable Marriage'. Her strategy for signifying her presence as an artist, and that of the political community she represents, is based not on essentialist notions of expression, but on historically and semiotically strategic plays with signs. She names this 'gathering and re-using': 'Gathering and re-using is an essential part of Black creativity, it does not mimic and it is inextricably linked to economic circumstance. Each piece within the piece has its own history, its own past and its own contribution to the new whole, the new function.'[63] In the installation Himid uses large cut-outs, objects and paintings to rewrite creatively the scene of the Countess's Levée from the British eighteenth-century artist William Hogarth's series 'Marriage à la Mode' (1745). That painting included an African man serving hot chocolate and a small African child unpacking various trophies of colonial theft. Recostuming each figure in contemporary identities, Himid's complex piece produced a discourse on history, politics and art, shifting these black presences from being traces of colonial violation to being the protagonists of contemporary historical consciousness. On the left side is the white British art establishment of critics, journalists and funding bodies, and attentively listening to them a white feminist artist – a body compositely constructed through references to the work of Helen Chadwick, Susan Hiller and Mary Kelly. On the right side, Mrs Thatcher entertains her lover, Ronald Reagan, who offers an invitation to the Third World War as they recline beneath Picassoid replicas – themselves evidence of cultural appropriations definitive of modernism. The two key figures who stand as commentators and points of identification are the small child, unpacking now nuclear weapons, who represents a black consciousness of what is really going on, and the black feminist artist, positioned where the man serving chocolate had been; but now, instead of servicing the white feminist, the black feminist artist is standing resolutely apart, refusing to lend her energies to the careers of white art, because of the pressures of a real history.

This is a history piece, a work about and generically of that ambition the term 'history painting' in the west signified. But it also has a connection with orature, an African discourse on history as a community's necessary and collective memory in the present. It speaks the urgency of the historical, at a moment when post-modernism is characterized as a loss of historicity, and of difficulty in mapping ourselves within a global capitalist order.[64] Indeed this insistence on the historical is claimed as a defining characteristic of contemporary black art practices by Gilane Tawadros. She puts post-modernism at a distance from black artists, following Habermas, who sees post-modernism's break with modernism as a mere feint, which leaves a continuity in western thought and power systems in place. Tawadros also argues that modernism banished history for a sense of timeless novelty and of modernity as the achievement and end of history. Importantly she sees the strategies of the artists she analyses as creating what she calls the '"populist modernism" of black cultural practice, which signals a critical appropriation of modernity which stems from the assertion of history and historical process'.[65] Insisting on the ambivalence of identities and the impossibility of fixed boundaries, the artists she discusses – Lubaina Himid, Sutapa Biswas and Sonia Boyce – operate in a 'zone of indiscernibility', 'which does not attest to the primacy of difference and dispersion over and above historical and political exigencies'.[66]

Himid's 'Fashionable Marriage' makes the installation itself the site of work. It is an event in history as well as a critical representation of it. It is a multi-layered text there to be deciphered and read by the spectator, who must recognize and rework her identifications in the encounter with these large-scale figures. There is no sense of the privatized studio where meaning is traced on to inert matter by the creative subject. But there are representations of artists in this public space, embodiments of conflicted and antagonistic positions, placed in social, cultural and historical relations, not separated into discrete apartments of identity and expressivity.

The composite white feminist artist, located by this text inside the world of art, looking only to it and not to the wider historical emergency, is defined by traces of work by white feminist artists which deal above all with femininity and the configurations of the feminine body. This implies that strategic practices on signifying systems are somehow less historical and removed from political effect, are ultimately only modernist in their concern with intervening in a specific domain. But it has been one of the major effects of feminist theory and practice both to expand what is understood as political, and to grasp the realm and institutions of representation as decisive in social and historical formations of all constructions of difference.

One of the feminist practices critiqued in Lubaina Himid's 'body of the feminist artist' is Mary Kelly's installation on the temporality of femininity, 'Interim', a work which examines the question of ageing. Including both these pieces here is not a move to create false continuities by finding common artistic tendencies. Both Himid and Kelly are obliged to generate signifying systems and signifying spaces by strategic intervention in the field of modernism, post-modernism and popular cultural forms. Lubaina Himid's popular is of course more extensive than western mass media, though African culture has been part of western modernism, and western mass media have colonized African culture. What the distinct practices of Mary Kelly and Lubaina Himid share is the necessity to locate their practice as an intervention on this historically constituted semiotic territory and its institutional sites.

'Interim' is a historical project which continues Mary Kelly's investigations of culture's *figurations* of femininity. In this piece she asks if being a woman is only one moment in our lives. She is examining 'women's' relation to the ageing body, women entering a stage in their lives marked negatively by the culture's alignment of femininity with an image of either nubile sexuality or maternal bliss. What is our identity when our relation to the enunciations of femininity falter, and how has this been transformed by the lived histories of women since 1968? That is, what difference has feminism made?

'Interim' identifies four key themes which constitute enunciations of femininity: the body, money, power and history itself. The multi-part installation comprises perspex panels with silk-screened photographs of women's clothing arranged in styles which evoke the dominant dis-

courses on the feminine body, fashion, medicine, romance; with gal-
vanized steel greeting cards ironically and humorously reworking the
sentimentality which mystifies women's life-cycles in their positions
as mother, wife, daughter and sister; with steel books opened as in a
newspaper library telling the stories of women who were aged 30, 20, 10
and 3 respectively in 1968; with monumental forms which schematically
present UN statistics on gender and wealth, labour and population. At
once spectacle and presence, the signifying space it generates refutes the
pure visuality of modernist art. Like painting it provides striking and
emblematic imageries. Like classic cinema its meanings build up by
repetition and stylistic rhyme, plot and sub-plot, character and narrative, expressive *mise-en-scène* and dramatic moment. Like sculpture with
glinting surfaces and tactile forms, it plays with minimalist formalities
and rebus-like assymetries. Like Godard's social cinema it gives us
snatches of lives and fragments of fantasies generated across familiar
social spaces.

'Interim' provides no icons but many images, no single text but many
textualities. In its totality, the project politically reconceptualizes the
rhetorics of the highest of high modernisms as well as the spectacles
of post-modern sign systems, and it is here that the decisively feminist intervention is made. Extruded from modernism, femininity was
allied with popular culture, sharing its triviality, decorativeness and easy
pleasure. Post-modernism has challenged the negative evaluation of
popular culture by appropriating its forms as the signifying materials of
a high art practice. Mary Kelly does not merely quote or recycle. She
originates new forms, which defy the great divide and force both sides
into politically explicit confrontation on the territory defined by feminism's insistent but critical enunciation of femininity. The work speaks of
repressed femininities by evoking in the art gallery the reviled cultural
forms of the woman's magazine or the supermarket, the doctor's waiting room or the pages of romantic fiction. The point is neither to
celebrate nor to validate, a reversal of negative evaluations. The effect
is to question both the anxieties and the pleasures of femininity as
it is lived and as it has been politically reconstrued through political
transformation of the category of 'women' since 1968. Suspending the
dichotomy between the masculine mystique of high culture and the
pejoratively effeminate lures of popular culture, Mary Kelly maps the
specific points at which the regime of sexual difference shapes both
modernism and its post-modern offspring alike. This involves a specific
theoretical input, linked, in the 'History' section, to the growing interest
in psychoanalysis within sections of the feminist community. 'Sexual

difference' is not a synonym for gender; it signals a conceptualization of human subjectivity which (1) helps understand the sexing of the subject – that is, that masculinity and femininity are psychic constructions – and (2) defines the human subject as split between conscious and unconscious. The latter makes it clear that the former, sexing, is incomplete and that all subjectivity is a construction fissured and unstable, shaped by the unconscious and desire. Feminist interest in psychoanalysis does not privilege sex over other forms of social oppression, but insists that we consider the level at which subjectivity is formed, and therefore the level and the mechanisms of identity which social formations operate across.[67]

The events staged by 'Interim' and 'A Fashionable Marriage' create 'signifying spaces' for specific and distinct enunciations of both the political and the aesthetic. The phrase is Julia Kristeva's. In her essay 'Woman's Time',[68] she defines western feminism as being made up of three generations, two historically current, a third in the process of being imagined. The first generation campaigns for equal rights and legislative redress against discrimination in the name of women's human rights. A second, concurrent generation rejects political solutions and insists on the radical specificity of woman's difference, using art and literature to found a language for the 'intrasubjective and corporeal experiences left mute in culture in the past.' Either effacing the issue of difference or extravagantly insisting upon it in a kind of reverse sexism, this paradox can also be seen to shape debates on race and ethnicity. Kristeva wanted then to imagine a moment of feminism which will effect a radical questioning of the system by which all subjectivity, all identity, every sex is necessarily formed. That is to say that the division (the saga of separation and loss which produces the split unconscious/ conscious condition we call subjectivity) is to be prised away from its self-presentation as a product of given sexual division, so that we can articulate the inevitable fact of difference not as binary opposition but as specificity and heterogeneity.

What this means is that such new significations will not emerge either from a repressed culture of those always-already women, nor from a position of radical alterity, outside the system. They can only be the effect of a calculated strategy of transgression of the system's own divisions and orders. For Kristeva, meaning is the product of a perpetual play between unity (those forces like the state, family, religion, which try to fix meanings to a particular arrangement of power) and process (the drives and semiotic potential of sound and form, which unity tries to harness to its systematization). Thus in any system there is both order and the possibility of disruption and transformation. Signifying practices such as a new kind of text or art-work mean 'the acceptance of the symbolic law together with the transgression of that law for the purpose of renovating it'.[69] This theory of meaning and change allows for little of either the affirmative or expressive theses of various feminist cultural practices.

Kristeva hailed certain avant-garde writing strategies as transgressive and made them synonymous with femininity as a patriarchal order's obvious negative. She failed to acknowledge that the heroic revolutions of modernism against the state, family and religion were executed in a concretely powerful system of sexual and racial power, so that the revolutions were effected only in the name of men, unable and unwilling seriously to dispute the basis of their own privilege. As neither modernism nor post-modernism, the women's movement, with its complex relations to both moments and cultures, intervenes in signifying practice as the historically necessary realization of Kristeva's reconceptualization of modernism. This is a possibility only now being generated or recognized in the practices of those women who mount a feminist intervention at the level of the textual, the subjective and the historical.

Kristeva attributes a particular significance to aesthetic practices – and not as a minor field colonized by feminism for women's edification. In the historical project of the resistance movements, we can counter the scars of imperial capitalism in culture, where modernism's utopian ambitions for renewal, change, unforeseen possibilities were stunted by their confinement to an imaginary realm of subjective freedom (the studio). Semiotic understanding of the place of signification in the process of power attributes a strategic function to aesthetic practices, which remain a necessary realm for individual enunciation and creation.

> It seems to me that the role of what is usually called 'aesthetic practices' must increase not only to counterbalance the storage and uniformity of information by present day mass media, data-bank systems, and, in particular, modern communications technology, but also to demystify the identity of the symbolic bond itself, to demystify, therefore, the *community* of language as a universal and unifying tool, one which totalizes and equalizes. In order to bring out – along with the singularity of each person, and, even more, along with the multiplicity of every person's possible identifications . . . – the *relativity of his/her symbolic as well as biological existence*, according to the variation in her/his specific symbolic capacities.[70]

The ideological individualism of modernist culture gives way to an acknowledgement of a concrete historical singularity, itself both social and psychic, both symbolic and particular to a kind of existence of and in the body. Thus we achieve a sense of sexual particularity in lieu of being tied to bodies that are only allowed to speak of a monolithic difference. For Kristeva the socially produced and semiotically signified singularity of the subject is set up as an active agent against the galloping forces of modernization, the information society in which individuation is a means of administration of power. Overcoming the specializations through which modern society has oppressed its populations, aesthetic practices are necessarily allied to politics, not secreted in the studio escaping from contamination as the condition of defending the purity and purpose of art.[71]

The burden of Kristeva's piece, like the complex forms of feminist art practices, is to represent the stakes for feminism in terms of ambition clearly indebted to the project of modernity.[72] We cannot fail to sense the gravity of the undertaking nor the pleasures it promises. The debate for feminists involved in 'aesthetic practices' cannot be reduced to a question of 'painting' or scripto-visual forms. It is a historical project, an intervention in history, informed by historical knowledges, which means not forgetting, in the act of necessary critique, the history of western feminism.

### NOTES

1 There is of course some representation of black women in western art, and a substantial iconography associated with sexual services and fantasized erotic scenarios. But it is indicative that in orientalist painting, for instance, where a European and an African woman are represented in a harem or bath-house, the two bodies are very differently treated to locate the white body as the object of desire. This point needs much more careful analysis and documentation than is possible here.

2 See R. Dyer, 'White', *Screen*, 29 (1988), pp. 44–65, and *Heavenly Bodies* (Macmillan, London, 1986) for further analysis of the relations between femininity, whiteness and representation.

3 In the work of Sutapa Biswas for instance, 'Housewives with Steakknives', the Hindu goddess Kali is represented to oppose western definitions of femininity as passive and powerless. On the notion of icons see Frederica Brooks, 'Ancestral Links: The Art of Claudette Johnson', in Maud Sulter (ed.), *Passion: Discourse on Blackwomen's Creativity* (Urban Fox Press, Hebden Bridge, 1990), pp. 183–90; also quoted in Lubaina Himid (ed.),

*Claudette Johnson: Pushing Back the Boundaries* (Rochdale Art Gallery, Rochdale, 1990), p. 5. See also Maud Sulter, 'Zabat: Poetics of a Family Tree', in Sulter, *Passion*, pp. 91–105.

4  Claudette Johnson, quoted in Himid, *Claudette Johnson*, p. 2.

5  Clement Greenberg, 'American-type Painting', *Art and Culture* (Beacon Press, Boston, Mass., 1961), p. 208.

6  On the notion of the artistic subject as the subject of art see Griselda Pollock, 'Artists, Mythologies and Media', *Screen*, 21 (1980), pp. 57–96, reprinted in Philip Hayward (ed.), *Picture This: Media Representations of Visual Art and Artists* (John Libbey, London, 1988), pp. 75–114.

7  That this operation was Eurocentric is specified by Rasheed Areen in *The Other Story* (Hayward Gallery, London, 1989); that his challenge to a white hegemony in modernism remains masculinist underscores the sexual politics of this formation. See Rita Keegan, 'The Story So Far', *Spare Rib*, February 1990; Sutapa Biswas, 'The Wrong Story', *New Statesman*, 15 December 1990, pp. 41–2.

8  For an extensive analysis of this typical art school ideology, see Terry Atkinson, 'Phantoms of the Studio', *Oxford Art Journal*, 13 (1990), pp. 49–62.

9  Michèle Barrett, 'The Concept of Difference', *Feminist Review*, 26 (1987), pp. 29–42.

10  R. Parker and G. Pollock, *Old Mistresses: Women, Art and Ideology* (Pandora, London, 1981), p. 147.

11  This can be understood in one of two ways. Taken in terms of communication, it suggests that social practice and use invest things or sounds or images with the capacity to function as tokens of exchange between members of a group or system. These tokens are bearers of value and significance; meaning is produced by them in a transaction that involves the receiver as much as the sender. Taken in stricter semiotic terms, the idea of signification excludes the sender and receiver as agents of making meaning and throws meaning on to the effect of the chains of signifiers, which produce positions for us to occupy as speakers (I, you, he, she, it). Thus man, woman, artist, are not meaningful because of a relation to, a reference from sound or word to, something already there, with its innate meaning, but only in their relations as signifiers within a system. That system then defines us as we occupy the places, the terms, that it sets. The signifying systems are not abstract or ahistorical, but the place where the culture, the social system is, as it were, written and thus writes itself upon us as both its users and its effects. See Christine Weedon, *Feminist Practice and Post-structuralist Theory* (Basil Blackwell, Oxford, 1987).

12  Mary Kelly, 'Reviewing Modernist Criticism', *Screen*, 22:3 (1981), pp. 41–62; p. 57.

13  Jacqueline Rose, 'Sexuality in the Field of Vision', in Rose, *Sexuality in the Field of Vision* (Verso Books, London, 1986), pp. 225–34.

14  Ibid., p. 231.

15 Ibid., p. 232.

16 The female nude had become in early modernist art the image for the ambitious artist to dominate and excel with. Modernists continue to perform this initiation ritual: Manet's *Olympia*, Picasso's *Demoiselles d'Avignon*, Matisse's *The Blue Nude*, De Konning's *Woman* series, F.N. Souza's *Black Nude* and so forth.

17 Mel Gooding, *The Experience of Painting* (Arts Council, London, 1988), p. 2.

18 Ibid.

19 See J. Kristeva, 'Women's Time' (1979), in T. Moi (ed.), *The Kristeva Reader* (Basil Blackwell, Oxford, 1986), pp. 186–213.

20 Gillian Ayres, statement, in Gooding, *The Experience of Painting*, p. 13.

21 Ibid.

22 Jürgen Habermas, 'Modernity – An Incomplete Project', in Hal Foster (ed.), *The Anti-Aesthetic: Essays in Postmodern Culture* (Bay Press, Townsend, Wash., 1983), pp. 3–15; p. 9.

23 This brilliant insight into women's perpetual fate in art was first developed by the late Buzz Goodbody in a lecture at Bedford College, London, in 1973.

24 Charles Harrison, 'The Experience of Painting', *Artscribe International*, 75 (1989), pp. 75–7; p. 76.

25 I define post-modernity as the socio-economic and ideological processes which currently define our horizons. Post-modernity refers to an epochal shift, whereas post-modernism refers to the cultural forms generated in this larger social transformation, which are the site for both affirmative and critical cultural responses to post-modernity. The distinctions are drawn from Clive Dilnot, 'What is the Post-modern?', *Art History*, 9: 2 (1986), pp. 245–63, and Hal Foster, 'Postmodernism: A Preface', in Foster, *The Anti-Aesthetic*, pp. ix–xvi.

26 In 1939 Clement Greenberg wrote a mighty defence of the avant-garde culture threatened by fascism, in terms which implicitly feminize the masses and the ersatz culture, kitsch, which capitalism served up to them: 'Avant-garde and Kitsch', in Greenberg, *Art and Culture*, pp. 3–21.

27 Andreas Huyssen, 'Mass Culture as Woman: Modernism's Other', in Huyssen, *After the Great Divide: Modernism, Mass Culture and Postmodernism* (Macmillan, London, 1986), pp. 44–64; p. 58.

28 Ibid., p. 55.

29 Ibid., p. 62.

30 Ibid., p. 59.

31 Of course it was never really lost to high culture and makes a major reappearance in surrealist discourse, and again after Greenbergian modernism by means of pop art's deceitful appropriations of comics and movie stars. Post-modernism represents yet another way high art has tried to get back to the feminine body – but only by confirming that mass culture is now almost synonymous with it.

32 I use the term here to mean the production of meaning by the production

of new means to produce meaning. Most theories of art are referential, using terms like reflect or express, or even represent. These imply that there is something, a person, a thing, a world, with its already formed meaning, which art, as a secondary system, reflects, expresses or re-presents. Signification is a theory that argues that meanings are produced by the relation of signifiers, sounds or letters, in systems. Meaning is produced for the world, not derived from it. Feminism does not merely express already known meanings that real women know. As a movement we are making new meanings, enunciating, from a specific place and historical condition in the world, a femininity that has to be signified.

33  Alice Jardine, 'At the Threshold: Feminists and Modernity', *Wedge*, 6 (1984), pp. 10–17; Gayatri Chakravorty Spivak, 'Imperialism and Sexual Difference', *Oxford Literary Review*, 8 (1986), pp. 225–39.

34  Craig Owens, 'The Discourse of Others: Feminists and Postmodernism', in Foster, *The Anti-Aesthetic*, pp. 57–82.

35  Many of these artists are specifically concerned with issues of identity, race, class, imperialism. I do not mean to subsume these within feminism, but hopefully to suggest that feminism is a variable term, not the property of those who privilege gender over everything. The meanings of feminism are constantly being expanded by women as they politically reconceive that identity in relation to other formations of power and consciousness.

36  See Kelly, 'Reviewing Modernist Criticism', p. 45.

37  Sarah Kent, 'Feminism and Decadence', *Artscribe*, 47 (1984), pp. 54–61; p. 61.

38  Sarah Kent, 'An Introduction', *Rosa Lee* (Todd Gallery, London, 1990), n. p.

39  Rosa Lee, 'Resisting Amnesia: Feminism, Painting and Postmodernism', *Feminist Review*, 26 (1987), pp. 5–27; p. 25.

40  Ibid., p. 24.

41  The issue of black women and visibility in relation to modernist and oppositional cultures was proposed by Michelle Wallis in her response at the panel 'Firing the Canon', College Art Association, New York, 18 February, 1990.

42  Denise Riley, *Am I that Name? Feminism and the Category of 'Women' in History* (Macmillan, London, 1988), p. 111.

43  Gilane Tawadros, 'Beyond the Boundary: The Work of Three Black Women Artists in Britain', *Third Text*, 8/9 (1989), pp. 121–50; pp. 122–3.

44  Stuart Hall, 'New Ethnicities', in *ICA Documents 7: Black Film/British Cinema* (Institute of Contemporary Arts, London, 1988), p. 29, cited Tawadros, 'Beyond the Boundary', p. 123.

45  Denise Riley, *Am I that Name?*, p. 99.

46  Katy Deepwell, 'In Defence of the Indefensible: Feminism, Painting and Post-Modernism', *Feminist Art News*, 2 (1987), pp. 9–12; p. 9.

47  Painting is thus simultaneously a medium, an expressive resource, an institutional practice, a critical category, a form of economic investment, a

curatorial term and a symbolic system. Any analysis which selects only one of the inter-related facets, such as medium or resource of expression, is smuggling back a covert form of modernism.

48  Deborah Cherry, *Painting Women: Victorian Women Artists* (Rochdale Art Gallery, Rochdale, 1987); soon to be published in an expanded, book-length study.

49  History means more than an authoritative narrative of events. History stands for three things: first, an archive, what a culture remembers. It matters what is in the archive and how it is recorded. History refers to remembering what has been happening. History refers to a context, a way of understanding where we are, because there has been a process creating the present conditions, forces and problems. This makes for historical consciousness. But this is not a consciousness of change as progress and development, some alibi for the present. History also means understanding discontinuity and fracture; it also implies recognizing continuities where we seem to see change. Post-modernism itself may be one such delusion. Feminism is a historical event, but it has historical conditions, knowledge of which we need to inform current practices and decisions. History then is strategic understanding of location and the stakes.

50  The statement is taken from Denise Riley's paper, 'Does Sex have a History?', reprinted in her *Am I that Name?*, pp. 1–17.

51  See Tamar Garb, 'L'Art Féminin: The Creation of a Cultural Category in Late Nineteenth Century France', *Art History*, 12 (1989), pp. 39–65.

52  It is significant that so many women of the early twentieth century emigrated to Paris, the city of modernism, where through some aspects of its precocious metropolitanism they could have access to a serious art education, exhibition and a literary culture. Gwen John is only one of the better-known artists who joined the phenomenon Sheri Benstock called *The Women of the Left Bank* (Virago Press, London, 1987). Modern Paris also hosted a protest against the heterosexuality of the overfeminized bourgeois societies that women artists and writers fled. There were many Afro-American women who were drawn to its modernist spaces.

53  Bill Williams, 'The Anti-semitism of Tolerance: Middle Class Manchester and the Jews 1870–1900', in A.J. Kidd and K.W. Roberts (eds), *City, Class and Culture* (Manchester University Press, Manchester, 1985), pp. 74–102.

54  This argument has resurfaced in the challenge recently made by the exhibition *The Other Story*, curated and introduced by Rasheed Areen, Hayward Gallery, London, 1989. Critics found themselves unable to negotiate the worlds of art and the worlds fissured by racism: to be taken seriously as artists, critics advised artists to forget their skin colour – the key term. No idea of the arguments about hegemonies, ethnicities, cultural imperialism, 'coloured' (a term advisedly used) the mainstream critics' discourse. There was art without colour, there was colour without art. The point Rasheed Areen intended to make was that they interfaced historically in the produc-

tion of art by Asian and Afro-Caribbean artists and politically in negative appraisal by white critics.

55  Cindy Nemser, *Art Talk: Conversations with Twelve Women Artists* (Charles Scribner, New York, 1975).

56  Anne Wagner, 'Lee Krasner as L.K.', *Respresentations*, 25 (1989), pp. 42–57, is an excellent study of the contradictions of women and modernism through the case of Leonore Krasner, alias Mrs Jackson Pollock and latterly a celebrated figure in the feminist canon.

57  Clement Greenberg, 'Louis and Nolan', *Art International*, IV (1960), pp. 27–30; p. 28.

58  See Parker and Pollock, *Old Mistresses: Women, Art and Ideology*, pp. 145–51.

59  I have elsewhere argued precisely that modernism is to be read as a sexual politics at all levels including the technical and aesthetic devices and use of space and facture. But the increasing pre-eminence given to such apparently neutral facets of an artistic process serve to efface the sexual order they represent, and the only visible evidence is the persistent celebration of artistic 'mastery'. See my 'Modernity and the Spaces of Femininity' in Griselda Pollock, *Vision and Difference* (Routledge, London, 1988), pp. 50–90. This problem is reflected in the unevenness of feminist art history as a whole. Certain periods have solicited thorough-going analyses of women's practice in art and their relation to institutions as much as their use of imagery, composition and relation therefore to ideology and meaning. Sexuality and gender can be complexly discussed for the art of the Victorian period, but what does a feminist say when confronted with a woman's practice in mainstream modernist abstract painting, such as that of Gillian Ayres, Britain's leading exponent?

60  In 1963 Betty Friedan wrote of 'the problem that has no name' in her famous, silence-breaking book, *The Feminine Mystique* (Bantam Books, New York, 1963).

61  Toril Moi, 'Feminism, Postmodernism and Style: Recent Feminist Criticism in the United States', *Cultural Critique*, 9 (1988), pp. 3–22; p. 6.

62  Valerie Amos and Pratibha Parmar, 'Challenging Imperial Feminism', *Feminist Review*, 17 (1984), pp. 3–20; pp. 9–12.

63  Lubaina Himid, 'Fragments', *Feminist Art News*, 2 (1988), pp. 8–9; p. 8.

64  F. Jameson, 'Postmodernism, or the Cultural Logic of Late Capitalism', *New Left Review*, 146 (1984), pp. 53–93.

65  Tawadros, *Beyond the Boundary*, p. 150.

66  Ibid.

67  For instance, see Homi K. Bhabha's use of the psychoanalytical category of fetishism in relation to the power and effects of the colonial stereotype, 'The Other Question – the Stereotype and Colonial Discourse', *Screen*, 24: 6 (1983), pp. 18–36.

68  Kristeva, 'Women's Time', pp. 186–213.

69  Julia Kristeva, 'The System and the Speaking Subject' (1973), in Moi, *The Kristeva Reader*, pp. 24–33; p. 29.
70  Kristeva, 'Women's Time', p. 210.
71  'At this level of interiorization with its social as well as individual stakes, what I have called "aesthetic practices" are undoubtedly nothing other than the modern reply to the eternal question of morality' (ibid.).
72  The phrase indicates the thesis of Jürgen Habermas, 'Modernity – An Incomplete Project' in H. Foster (1987), pp. 3–15.

# 9

# The Politics of Translation

## Gayatri Chakravorty Spivak

The idea for this title comes from Michèle Barrett's feeling that the politics of translation takes on a massive life of its own if you see language as the process of meaning construction.[1]

In my view, language may be one of many elements that allow us to make sense of things, of ourselves. I am thinking, of course, of gestures, pauses, but also of chance, of the sub-individual force-fields of being which click into place in different situations, swerve from the straight or true line of language-in-thought. Making sense of ourselves is what produces identity. If one feels that the production of identity as self-meaning, not just meaning, is as pluralized as a drop of water under a microscope, one is not always satisfied, outside of the ethico-political arena as such, with 'generating' thoughts on one's own. (Assuming identity as origin may be unsatisfactory in the ethico-political arena as well, but consideration of that now would take us too far afield.) One of the ways to get around the confines of one's 'identity' as one produces expository prose is to work at someone else's title, as one works with a language that belongs to many others. This, after all, is one of the seductions of translating. It is a simple miming of the responsibility to the trace of the other in the self.

Responding, therefore, to Michèle with that freeing sense of responsibility, I can agree that it is not bodies of meaning that are transferred in translation. And from the ground of that agreement I want to consider the role played by language for the *agent*, the person who acts, even though intention is not fully present to itself. The task of the feminist translator is to consider language as a clue to the workings of gendered agency. The writer is written by her language, of course. But the writing of the writer writes agency in a way that might be different from that of the British woman/citizen with the history of British feminism, focused on the task of freeing herself from Britain's imperial past, its often racist present, as well as its 'made in Britain' history of male domination.

### TRANSLATION AS READING

How does the translator attend to the specificity of the language she translates? There is a way in which the rhetorical nature of every language disrupts its logical systematicity. If we emphasize the logical at the expense of these rhetorical interferences, we remain safe. 'Safety' *is* the appropriate term here, because we are talking of risks, of violence to the translating medium.

I felt that I was taking those risks when I recently translated some late eighteenth-century Bengali poetry. I quote a bit from my 'Translator's Preface':

> I must overcome what I was taught in school: the highest mark for the most accurate collection of synonyms, strung together in the most proxi-mate syntax. I must resist both the solemnity of chaste Victorian poetic prose and the forced simplicity of 'plain English,' that have imposed themselves as the norm . . . Translation is the most intimate act of reading. I surrender to the text when I translate. These songs, sung day after day in family chorus before clear memory began, have a peculiar intimacy for me. Reading and surrendering take on new meanings in such a case. The translator earns permission to transgress from the trace of the other – before memory – in the closest places of the self.[2]

Language is not everything. It is only a vital clue to where the self loses its boundaries. The ways in which rhetoric or figuration disrupt logic themselves point at the possibility of random contingency, beside language, around language. Such a *dis*semination cannot be under our control. Yet in translation, where meaning hops into the spacy empti-ness between two named historical languages, we get perilously close to it. By juggling the disruptive rhetoricity that breaks the surface in not necessarily connected ways, we feel the selvedges of the language-textile give way, fray into *frayages* or facilitations.[3] Although every act of reading or communication is a bit of this risky fraying which scrambles together somehow, our stake in agency keeps the fraying down to a minimum except in the communication and reading of and in love. (What is the place of 'love' in the ethical?) The task of the translator is to facilitate this love between the original and its shadow, a love that permits fraying, holds the agency of the translator and the demands of her imagined or actual audience at bay. The politics of translation from a non-European woman's text too often suppresses this possibility because the translator cannot engage with, or cares insufficiently for, the rhetoricity of the original.

The simple possibility that something might not be meaningful is contained by the rhetorical system as the always possible menace of a space outside language. This is most eerily staged (and challenged) in the effort to communicate with other possible intelligent beings in space. (Absolute alterity or otherness is thus differed-deferred into an other self who resembles us, however minimally, and with whom we can communicate.) But a more homely staging of it occurs across two earthly languages. The experience of contained alterity in an unknown language spoken in a different cultural milieu is uncanny.

Let us now think that, in that other language, rhetoric may be disrupting logic in the matter of the production of an agent, and indicating the founding violence of the silence at work within rhetoric. Logic allows us to jump from word to word by means of clearly indicated connections. Rhetoric must work in the silence between and around words in order to see what works and how much. The jagged relationship between rhetoric and logic, condition and effect of knowing, is a relationship by which a world is made for the agent, so that the agent can act in an ethical way, a political way, a day-to-day way; so that the agent can be alive, in a human way, in the world. Unless one can at least construct a model of this for the other language, there is no real translation.

Unfortunately it is only too easy to produce translations if this task is completely ignored. I myself see no choice between the quick and easy and slapdash way, and translating well and with difficulty. There is no reason why a responsible translation should take more time in the doing. The translator's preparation might take more time, and her love for the text might be a matter of a reading skill that takes patience. But the sheer material production of the text need not be slow.

Without a sense of the rhetoricity of language, a species of neo-colonialist construction of the non-western scene is afoot. No argument for convenience can be persuasive here. That is always the argument, it seems. This is where I travel from Michèle Barrett's enabling notion of the question of language in post-structuralism. Post-structuralism has shown some of us a staging of the agent within a three-tiered notion of language (as rhetoric, logic, silence). We must attempt to enter or direct that staging, as one directs a play, as an actor interprets a script. That takes a different kind of effort from taking translation to be a matter of synonym, syntax and local colour.

To be only critical, to defer action until the production of the utopian translator, is impractical. Yet, when I hear Derrida, quite justifiably, point out the difficulties between French and English, even when he agrees to speak in English – 'I must speak in a language that is not my own because that will be more just' – I want to claim the right to the same dignified complaint for a woman's text in Arabic or Vietnamese.[4]

It is more just to give access to the largest number of feminists. Therefore these texts must be made to speak English. It is more just to speak the language of the majority when through hospitality a large number of feminists give the foreign feminist the right to speak, in English. In the case of the Third World foreigner, is the law of the majority that of decorum, the equitable law of democracy, or the 'law' of the strongest? We might focus on this confusion. There is nothing necessarily meretricious about the western feminist gaze. (The 'naturalizing' of Jacques Lacan's sketching out of the psychic structure of the gaze in terms of group political behaviour has always seemed to me a bit shaky.) On the other hand, there is nothing essentially noble about the law of the majority either. It is merely the easiest way of being 'democratic' with minorities. In the act of wholesale translation into English there can be a betrayal of the democratic ideal into the law of the strongest. This happens when all the literature of the Third World gets translated into a sort of with-it translatese, so that the literature by a woman in Palestine begins to resemble, in the feel of its prose, something by a man in Taiwan. The rhetoricity of Chinese and Arabic! The cultural politics of high-growth, capitalist Asia-Pacific, and devastated West Asia! Gender difference inscribed and inscribing in these differences!

For the student, this tedious translatese cannot compete with the spectacular stylistic experiments of a Monique Wittig or an Alice Walker.

Let us consider an example where attending to the author's stylistic experiments can produce a different text. Mahasweta Devi's 'Stanadāyini' is available in two versions.[5] Devi has expressed approval for the attention to her signature style in the version entitled 'Breast-giver'. The alternative translation gives the title as 'The Wet-nurse', and thus neutralizes the author's irony in constructing an uncanny word; enough like 'wet-nurse' to make that sense, and enough unlike to shock. It is as if the translator should decide to translate Dylan Thomas's famous title and opening line as 'Do not go gently into that good night'. The theme of treating the breast as organ of labour-power-as-commodity and the breast as metonymic part-object standing in for other-as-object – the way in which the story plays with Marx and Freud on the occasion of the woman's body – is lost even before you enter the story. In the text Mahasweta uses proverbs that are startling even in the Bengali. The translator of 'The Wet-nurse' leaves them out. She decides not to try to translate these hard bits of earthy wisdom, contrasting with class-specific access to modernity, also represented in the story. In fact, if the two translations are read side by side, the loss of the rhetorical silences of the original can be felt from one to the other.

First, then, the translator must surrender to the text. She must solicit the text to show the limits of its language, because that rhetorical aspect will point at the silence of the absolute fraying of language that the text wards off, in its special manner. Some think this is just an ethereal way of talking about literature or philosophy. But no amount of tough talk can get around the fact that translation is the most intimate act of reading. Unless the translator has earned the right to become the intimate reader, she cannot surrender to the text, cannot respond to the special call of the text.

The presupposition that women have a natural or narrative-historical solidarity, that there is something in a woman or an undifferentiated women's story that speaks to another woman without benefit of language-learning, might stand against the translator's task of surrender. Paradoxically, it is not possible for us as ethical agents to imagine otherness or alterity maximally. We have to turn the other into something like the self in order to be ethical. To surrender in translation is more erotic than ethical.[6] In that situation the good-willing attitude 'she is just like me' is not very helpful. In so far as Michèle Barrett is not like Gayatri Spivak, their friendship is more effective as a translation. In order to earn that right of friendship or surrender of identity, of knowing that the rhetoric of the text indicates the limits of language for you as long as you are with the text, you have to be in a different relationship with the language, not even only with the specific text.

Learning about translation on the job, I came to think that it would be a practical help if one's relationship with the language being translated was such that sometimes one preferred to speak in it about intimate things. This is no more than a practical suggestion, not a theoretical requirement, useful especially because a woman writer who is wittingly or unwittingly a 'feminist' – and of course all woman writers are not 'feminist' even in this broad sense – will relate to the three-part staging of (agency in) language in ways defined out as 'private', since they might question the more public linguistic manoeuvres.

Let us consider an example of lack of intimacy with the medium. In Sudhir Kakar's *The Inner World*, a song about Kālī written by the late nineteenth-century monk Vivekananda is cited as part of the proof of the 'archaic narcissism' of the Indian [sic] male.[7] (Devi makes the same point with a light touch, with reference to Krsna and Siva, tying it to sexism rather than narcissism and without psychoanalytic patter.)

From Kakar's description, it would not be possible to glimpse that 'the disciple' who gives the account of the singular circumstances of Vivekananda's composition of the song was an Irishwoman who became a Ramakrishna nun, a white woman among male Indian monks and devotees. In the account Kakar reads, the song is translated by this woman, whose training in intimacy with the original language is as painstaking as one can hope for. There is a strong identification between Indian and Irish nationalists at this period; and Nivedita, as she was called, also embraced what she understood to be the Indian philosophical way of life as explained by Vivekananda, itself a peculiar, resistant consequence of the culture of imperialism, as has been pointed out by many. For a psychoanalyst like Kakar, this historical, philosophical and indeed sexual text of translation should be the textile to weave with. Instead, the English version, 'given' by the anonymous 'disciple', serves as no more than the opaque exhibit providing evidence of the alien fact of narcissism. It is not the site of the exchange of language.

At the beginning of the passage quoted by Kakar, there is a reference to Ram Prasad (or Ram Proshad). Kakar provides a footnote: 'Eighteenth century singer and poet whose songs of longing for the Mother are very popular in Bengal'. I believe this footnote is also an indication of what I am calling the absence of intimacy.

Vivekananda is, among other things, an example of the peculiar reactive construction of a glorious 'India' under the provocation of imperialism. The rejection of 'patriotism' in favour of 'Kali' reported in Kakar's passage is played out in this historical theatre, as a choice of the cultural female sphere rather than the colonial male sphere.[8] It is undoubtedly 'true' that for such a figure, Ram Proshad Sen provides a kind of ideal self. Sen had travelled back from a clerk's job in colonial Calcutta before the Permanent Settlement of land in 1793 to be the court poet of one of the great rural landowners whose social type, and whose connection to native culture, would be transformed by the Settlement. In other words, Vivekananda and Ram Proshad are two moments of colonial discursivity translating the figure of Kali. The dynamic intricacy of that discursive textile is mocked by the useless footnote.

It would be idle here to enter the debate about the 'identity' of Kali or indeed other goddesses in Hindu 'polytheism'. But simply to contextualize, let me add that it is Ram Proshad about whose poetry I wrote the 'Translator's Preface' quoted earlier. He is by no means simply an archaic stage-prop in the disciple's account of Vivekananda's 'crisis'. Some more lines from my 'Preface': 'Ram Proshad played with his mother tongue, transvaluing the words that are heaviest with Sanskrit meaning. I have been unable to catch the utterly new but utterly gendered tone of affectionate banter' – not only, not even largely, 'longing' – 'between the poet and Kāli.' Unless Nivedita mistranslated, it is the difference in tone between Ram Proshad's innovating playfulness and Vivekananda's high nationalist solemnity that, in spite of the turn from nationalism to the Mother, is historically significant. The politics of the translation of the culture of imperialism by the colonial subject has changed noticeably. And that change is expressed in the gendering of the poet's voice.

How do women in contemporary polytheism relate to this peculiar mother, certainly not the psychoanalytic bad mother whom Kakar derives from Max Weber's misreading, not even an organized punishing mother, but a child-mother who punishes with astringent violence and is also a moral and affective monitor?[9] Ordinary women, not saintly women. Why take it for granted that the invocation of goddesses in a historically masculist polytheist sphere is necessarily feminist? I think it is a western and male-gendered suggestion that powerful women in the Sākta (Sakti or Kāli-worshipping) tradition take Kāli as a role model.[10]

Mahasweta's Jashoda tells me more about the relationship between goddesses and strong ordinary women than the psychoanalyst. And here too the example of an intimate translation that goes respectfully 'wrong' can be offered. The French wife of a Bengali artist translated some of Ram Proshad Sen's songs in the twenties to accompany her husband's paintings based on the songs. Her translations are marred by the pervasive orientalism ready at hand as a discursive system. Compare two passages, both translating the 'same' Bengali. I have at least tried, if failed, to catch the unrelenting mockery of self and Kāli in the original:

Mind, why footloose from Mother?
Mind mine, think power, for freedom's dower, bind bower with love-rope
In time, mind, you minded not your blasted lot.
And Mother, daughter-like, bound up house-fence to dupe her dense and
    devoted fellow.
Oh you'll see at death how much Mum loves you
A couple minutes' tears, and lashings of water, cowdung-pure.

Here is the French, translated by me into an English comparable in tone
and vocabulary:

> Pourquoi as-tu, mon âme, délaissé les pieds de Mâ?
> O esprit, médite Shokti, tu obtiendras la délivrance.
> Attache-les ces pieds saints avec la corde de la dévotion.
> Au bon moment tu n'as rien vu, c'est bien là ton malheur.
> Pour se jouer de son fidèle, Elle m'est apparue
> Sous la forme de ma fille et m'a aidé à réparer ma clôture.
> C'est à la mort que tu comprendras l'amour de Mâ.
> Ici, on versera quelques larmes, puis on purifiera le lieu.

Why have you, my soul [*mon âme* is, admittedly, less heavy in
   French], left Ma's feet?
O mind, meditate upon Shokti, you will obtain deliverance.
Bind those holy feet with the rope of devotion.
In good time you saw nothing, that is indeed your sorrow.
To play with her faithful one, She appeared to me
In the form of my daughter and helped me to repair my enclosure.
It is at death that you will understand Ma's love.
Here, they will shed a few tears, then purify the place.

And here the Bengali:

মন কেন জার চরণ-ছাড়া ।
ও মন, তার শক্তি, পায়ে স্মৃতি, বাঁধ দিয়ে ভক্তি-দড়া ॥
সময় থাকিতে, না দেখলে মন, কেমন তোমার কপালপোড়া ।
ছল ভক্তে ছলিতে, তনয়া রূপেতে বাঁচিন আমি ধারের বেড়া ॥
মায়ে যত ভালবাসে, বুঝা যাবে শেষ্যশেষে,
জোদের দুগ-দুচার কান্নাকাটি, শেষে দিবে গোবরছড়া ।

I hope these examples demonstrate that depth of commitment to
correct cultural politics, felt in the details of personal life, is sometimes
not enough. The history of the language, the history of the author's
moment, the history of the language-in-and-as-translation, must figure
in the weaving as well.

By logical analysis, we don't just mean what the philosopher does,
but also reasonableness – that which will allow rhetoricity to be
appropriated, put in its place, situated, seen as only nice. Rhetoricity
is put in its place that way because it disrupts. Women within male-
dominated society, when they internalize sexism as normality, act out a
scenario against feminism that is formally analogical to this. The rela-

tionship between logic and rhetoric, between grammar and rhetoric, is also a relationship between social logic, social reasonableness and the disruptiveness of figuration in social practice. These are the first two parts of our three-part model. But then, rhetoric points at the possibility of randomness, of contingency as such, dissemination, the falling apart of language, the possibility that things might not always be semiotically organized. (My problem with Kristeva and the 'pre-semiotic' is that she seems to want to expand the empire of the meaning-ful by grasping at what language can only point at.) Cultures that might not have this specific three-part model will still have a dominant sphere in its traffic with language and contingency. Writers like Ifi Amadiume show us that, without thinking of this sphere as biologically determined, one still has to think in terms of spheres determined by definitions of secondary and primary sexual characteristics in such a way that the inhabitants of the other sphere are para-subjective, not fully subject.[11] The dominant groups' way of handling the three-part ontology of language has to be learnt as well – if the subordinate ways of rusing with rhetoric are to be disclosed.

To decide whether you are prepared enough to start translating, then, it might help if you have graduated into speaking, by choice or preference, of intimate matters in the language of the original. I have worked my way back to my earlier point: I cannot see why the publishers' convenience or classroom convenience or time convenience for people who do not have the time to learn should organize the construction of the rest of the world for western feminism. Five years ago, berated as unsisterly, I would think, 'Well, you know one ought to be a bit more giving etc.', but then I asked myself again, 'What am I giving, or giving up? To whom am I giving by assuring that you don't have to work that hard, just come and get it? What am I trying to promote?' People would say, you who have succeeded should not pretend to be a marginal. But surely by demanding higher standards of translation, I am not marginalizing myself or the language of the original?

I have learnt through translating Devi how this three-part structure works differently from English in my native language. And here another historical irony has become personally apparent to me. In the old days, it was most important for a colonial or post-colonial student of English to be as 'indistinguishable' as possible from the native speaker of English. I think it is necessary for people in the Third World translation trade now to accept that the wheel has come around, that the genuinely bilingual post-colonial now has a bit of an advantage. But she does not have a real advantage as a translator if she is not strictly bilingual, if she merely speaks her native language. Her own native space is, after all, also class organized. And that organization still often carries the traces of access to imperialism, often relates inversely to access to the vernacular as a public language. So here the requirement for intimacy brings a recognition of the public sphere as well. If we were thinking of translating Marianne Moore or Emily Dickinson, the standard for the translator could not be 'anyone who can conduct a conversation in the language of the original (in this case English)'. When applied to a Third World language, the position is inherently ethnocentric. And then to present these translations to our unprepared students so that they can learn about women writing!

In my view, the translator from a Third World language should be sufficiently in touch with what is going on in literary production in that language to be capable of distinguishing between good and bad writing by women, resistant and conformist writing by women.

She must be able to confront the idea that what seems resistant in the space of English may be reactionary in the space of the original language. Farida Akhter has argued that, in Bangladesh, the real work of the women's movement and of feminism is being undermined by talk of 'gendering', mostly deployed by the women's development wings of transnational non-government organizations, in conjunction with some local academic feminist theorists.[12] One of her intuitions was that 'gendering' could not be translated into Bengali. 'Gendering' is an awkward new word in English as well. Akhter is profoundly involved in international feminism. And her base is Third World. I could not translate 'gender' into the US feminist context for her. This misfiring of translation, between a superlative reader of the social text such as Akhter, and a careful translator like myself, speaking as friends, has added to my sense of the task of the translator.

Good and bad is a flexible standard, like all standards. Here another lesson of post-structuralism helps: these decisions of standards are made anyway. It is the attempt to justify them adequately that polices. That is why disciplinary preparation in school requires that you write examinations to prove these standards. Publishing houses routinely engage in materialist confusion of those standards. The translator must be able to fight that metropolitan materialism with a special kind of specialist's knowledge, not mere philosophical convictions.

In other words, the person who is translating must have a tough sense of the specific terrain of the original, so that she can fight the racist assumption that all Third World women's writing is good. I am often approached by women who would like to put Devi in with just Indian women writers. I am troubled by this, because 'Indian women' is not a feminist category. (Elsewhere I have argued that 'epistemes' – ways of constructing objects of knowledge – should not have national names either.)[13] Sometimes Indian women writing means American women writing or British women writing, except for national *origin*. There is an ethno-cultural agenda, an obliteration of Third World specificity as well as a denial of cultural citizenship, in calling them merely 'Indian'.

My initial point was that the task of the translator is to surrender herself to the linguistic rhetoricity of the original text. Although this point has larger political implications, we can say that the not unimportant minimal consequence of ignoring this task is the loss of 'the literarity and textuality and sensuality of the writing' (Michèle's words). I have worked my way to a second point, that the translator must be able to discriminate on the terrain of the original. Let us dwell on it a bit longer.

I choose Devi because she is unlike her scene. I have heard an English Shakespearean suggest that every bit of Shakespeare criticism coming from the subcontinent was by that virtue resistant. By such a judgement, we are also denied the right to be critical. It was of course bad to have put the place under subjugation, to have tried to make the place over with calculated restrictions. But that does not mean that everything that is coming out of that place after a negotiated independence nearly fifty years ago is necessarily right. The old anthropological supposition (and that is bad anthropology) that every person from a culture is nothing but a whole example of that culture is acted out in my colleague's suggestion. I remain interested in writers who are against the current, against the mainstream. I remain convinced that the interesting literary text might be precisely the text where you do not learn what the majority view of majority cultural representation or self-representation of a nation state might be. The translator has to make herself, in the case of Third World women writing, almost better equipped than the translator who is dealing with the western European languages, because of the fact that there is so much of the old colonial attitude, slightly displaced, at work in the translation racket. Post-structuralism *can* radicalize the field of preparation so that simply boning up on the language is not enough; there is also that special relationship to the staging of language as the production of agency that one must attend to. But the agenda of post-structuralism is mostly elsewhere, and the resistance to theory among metropolitan feminists would lead us into yet another narrative.

The understanding of the task of the translator and the practice of the craft are related but different. Let me summarize how I work. At first, I translate at speed. If I stop to think about what is happening to the English, if I assume an audience, if I take the intending subject as more than a springboard, I cannot jump in, I cannot surrender. My relationship with Devi is easygoing. I am able to say to her: I surrender to you in your writing, not you as intending subject. There, in friendship, is another kind of surrender. Surrendering to the text in this way means, most of the time, being literal. When I have produced a version this way, I revise. I revise not in terms of a possible audience, but by the protocols of the thing in front of me, in a sort of English. And I keep hoping that the student in the classroom will not be able to think that the text is just a purveyor of social realism if it is translated with an eye toward the dynamic staging of language mimed in the revision by the rules of the in-between discourse produced by a literalist surrender.

Vain hope, perhaps, for the accountability is different. When I translated Jacques Derrida's *De la grammatologie*, I was reviewed in a major journal for the first and last time. In the case of my translations of Devi, I have almost no fear of being accurately judged by my readership here. It makes the task more dangerous and more risky. And that for me is the real difference between translating Derrida and translating Mahasweta Devi, not merely the rather more artificial difference between deconstructive philosophy and political fiction.

The opposite argument is not neatly true. There is a large number of people in the Third World who read the old imperial languages. People reading current feminist fiction in the European languages would probably read it in the appropriate imperial language. And the same goes for European philosophy. The act of translating into the Third World language is often a political exercise of a different sort. I am looking forward, as of this writing, to lecturing in Bengali on deconstruction in front of a highly sophisticated audience, knowledgeable both in Bengali and in deconstruction (which they read in English and French and sometimes write about in Bengali), at Jadavpur University in Calcutta. It will be a kind of testing of the post-colonial translator, I think.

Democracy changes into the law of force in the case of translation from the Third World and women even more because of their peculiar relationship to whatever you call the public/private divide. A neatly reversible argument would be possible if the particular Third World country had cornered the Industrial Revolution first and embarked on monopoly imperialist territorial capitalism as one of its consequences, and thus been able to impose a language as international norm. Something like that idiotic joke: if the Second World War had gone differently, the United States would be speaking Japanese. Such egalitarian reversible judgements are appropriate to counter-factual fantasy. Translation remains dependent upon the language skill of the majority. A prominent Belgian translation theorist solves the problem by suggesting that, rather than talk about the Third World, where a lot of passion is involved, one should speak about the European Renaissance, since a great deal of wholesale cross-cultural translation from Graeco-Roman antiquity was undertaken then. What one overlooks is the sheer authority ascribed to the originals in that historical phenomenon. The status of a language in the world is what one must consider when teasing out the politics of translation. Translatese in Bengali can be derided and criticized by large groups of anglophone and anglograph Bengalis. It is only in the hegemonic languages that the benevolent do not take the limits of their own often uninstructed good will into account. That phenomenon becomes hardest to fight because the individuals involved in it are genuinely benevolent and you are identified as a trouble-maker. This becomes particularly difficult when the metropolitan feminist, who is sometimes the assimilated post-colonial, invokes, indeed translates, a too quickly shared feminist notion of accessibility.

If you want to make the translated text accessible, try doing it for the person who wrote it. The problem comes clear then, for she is not within the same history of style. What is it that you are making accessible? The accessible level is the level of abstraction where the individual is already formed, where one can speak individual rights. When you hang out and with a language away from your own (*Mitwegsein*) so that you want to use that language by preference, sometimes, when you discuss something complicated, then you are on the way to making a dimension of the text accessible to the reader, with a light and easy touch, to which she does not accede in her everyday. If you are making anything else accessible, through a language quickly learnt with an idea that you transfer content, then you are betraying the text and showing rather dubious politics.

How will women's solidarity be measured here? How will their common experience be reckoned if one cannot imagine the traffic in accessibility going both ways? I think that idea should be given a decent burial as ground of knowledge, together with the idea of humanist universality. It is good to think that women have something in common, when one is approaching women with whom a relationship would not otherwise be possible. It is a great first step. But, if your interest is in learning if there *is* women's solidarity, how about leaving this assumption, appropriate as a means to an end like local or global social work, and trying a second step? Rather than imagining that women automatically have something identifiable in common, why not say, humbly and practically, my first obligation in understanding solidarity is to learn her mother-tongue. You will see immediately what the differences are. You will also feel the solidarity every day as you make the attempt to learn the language in which the other woman learnt to recognize reality at her mother's knee. This is preparation for the intimacy of cultural translation. If you are going to bludgeon someone else by insisting on your version of solidarity, you have the obligation to try out this experiment and see how far your solidarity goes.

In other words, if you are interested in talking about the other, and/or in making a claim to be the other, it is crucial to learn other languages. This should be distinguished from the learned tradition of language acquisition for academic work. I am talking about the importance of language acquisition for the woman from a hegemonic mono-linguist culture who makes everybody's life miserable by insisting on women's solidarity at her price. I am uncomfortable with notions of feminist solidarity which are celebrated when everybody involved is similarly produced. There are countless languages in which women all over the world have grown up and been female or feminist, and yet the languages we keep on learning by rote are the powerful European ones, sometimes the powerful Asian ones, least often the chief African ones. The 'other' languages are learnt only by anthropologists who *must* produce knowledge across an epistemic divide. They are generally (though not invariably) not interested in the three-part structure we are discussing.

If we are discussing solidarity as a theoretical position, we must also remember that not all the world's women are literate. There are traditions and situations that remain obscure because we cannot share their linguistic constitution. It is from this angle that I have felt that learning languages might sharpen our own presuppositions about what it means to use the sign 'woman'. If we say that things should be accessible to us, who is this 'us'? What does that sign mean?

Although I have used the examples of women all along, the arguments apply across the board. It is just that women's rhetoricity may be doubly obscured. I do not see the advantage of being completely focused on a single issue, although one must establish practical priorities. In this book, we are concerned with post-structuralism and its effect on feminist theory. Where some post-structuralist thinking can be applied to the constitution of the agent in terms of the literary operations of language, women's texts might be operating differently because of the social differentiation between the sexes. Of course the point applies generally to the colonial context as well. When Ngugi decided to write in Kikuyu, some thought he was bringing a private language into the public sphere. But what makes a language shared by many people in a community private? I was thinking about those so-called private languages when I was talking about language learning. But even within those private languages it is my conviction that there is a difference in the way in which the staging of language produces not only the sexed subject but the gendered agent, by a version of centring, persistently disrupted by rhetoricity, indicating contingency. Unless demonstrated otherwise, this for me remains the condition and effect of dominant and subordinate gendering. If that is so, then we have some reason to focus on women's texts. Let us use the word 'woman' to name that space of para-subjects defined as such by the social inscription of primary and secondary sexual characteristics. Then we can cautiously begin to track a sort of commonality in being set apart, within the different rhetorical strategies of different languages. But even here, historical superiorities of class must be kept in mind. Bharati Mukherjee, Anita Desai and Gayatri Spivak do not have the same rhetorical figuration of agency as an illiterate domestic servant.

Tracking commonality through responsible translation can lead us into areas of difference and different differentiations. This may also be important because, in the heritage of imperialism, the female legal subject bears the mark of a failure of Europeanization, by contrast with the female anthropological or literary subject from the area. For example, the division between the French and Islamic codes in modern Algeria is in terms of family, marriage, inheritance, legitimacy and female social agency. These are differences that we must keep in mind. And we must honour the difference between ethnic minorities in the First World and majority populations of the Third.

In conversation, Barrett had asked me if I now inclined more toward Foucault. This is indeed the case. In 'Can the Subaltern Speak?', I took a rather strong critical line on Foucault's work, as part of a general critique of imperialism.[14] I do, however, find, his concept of *pouvoir-savoir* immensely useful. Foucault has contributed to French this ordinary-language doublet (the ability to know [as]) to take its place quietly beside *vouloir-dire* (the wish to say – meaning to mean).

On the most mundane level, *pouvoir-savoir* is the shared skill which allows us to make (common) sense of things. It is certainly not only power/knowledge in the sense of *puissance/connaissance*. Those are aggregative institutions. The common way in which one makes sense of things, on the other hand, loses itself in the sub-individual.

Looking at *pouvoir-savoir* in terms of women, one of my focuses has been new immigrants and the change of mother-tongue and *pouvoir-savoir* between mother and daughter. When the daughter talks reproductive rights and the mother talks protecting honour, is this the birth or death of translation?

Foucault is also interesting in his new notion of the ethics of the care for the self. In order to be able to get to the subject of ethics it may be necessary to look at the ways in which an individual in that culture is instructed to care for the self rather than the imperialism-specific secularist notion that the ethical subject is given as human. In a secularism which is structurally identical with Christianity laundered in the bleach of moral philosophy, the subject of ethics is faceless. Breaking out, Foucault was investigating other ways of making sense of how the subject becomes ethical. This is of interest because, given the connection between imperialism and secularism, there is almost no way of getting to alternative general voices except through religion. And if one does not look at religion as mechanisms of producing the ethical subject, one gets various kinds of 'fundamentalism'. Workers in cultural politics and its connections to a new ethical philosophy have to be interested in religion in the production of ethical subjects. There is much room for feminist work here because western feminists have not so far been aware of religion as a cultural instrument rather than a mark of cultural difference. I am currently working on Hindu performative ethics with Professor B.K. Matilal. He is an enlightened male feminist. I am an active feminist. Helped by his learning and his openness I am learning to distinguish between ethical catalysts and ethical motors even as I learn to translate bits of the Sanskrit epic in a way different from all the accepted translations, because I rely not only on learning, not only on 'good English', but on that three-part scheme of which I have so lengthily spoken. I hope the results will please readers. If we are going to look at an ethics that emerges from something other than the historically secularist ideal – at an ethics of sexual differences, at an ethics that can confront the emergence of fundamentalisms without apology or dismissal in the name of the Enlightenment – then *pouvoir-savoir* and the care for the self in Foucault can be illuminating. And these 'other ways' bring us back to translation, in the general sense.

### TRANSLATION IN GENERAL

I want now to add two sections to what was generated from the initial conversation with Barrett. I will dwell on the politics of translation in a general sense, by way of three examples of 'cultural translation' in English. I want to make the point that the lessons of translation in the narrow sense can reach much further.

First, J.M. Coetzee's *Foe*.[15] This book represents the impropriety of the dominant's desire to give voice to the native. When Susan Barton, the eighteenth-century Englishwoman from *Roxana*, attempts to teach a muted Friday (from *Robinson Crusoe*) to read and write English, he draws an incomprehensible rebus on his slate and wipes it out, withholds it. You cannot translate from a position of monolinguist superiority. Coetzee as white creole translates *Robinson Crusoe* by representing Friday as the agent of a withholding.

Second, Toni Morrison's *Beloved*.[16] Let us look at the scene of the change of the mother-tongue from mother to daughter. Strictly speaking, it is not a change, but a loss, for the narrative is not of immigration but of slavery. Sethe, the central character of the novel, remembers: 'What Nan' – her mother's fellow-slave and friend – 'told her she had forgotten, along with the language she told it in. The same language her ma'am spoke, and which would never come back. But the message – that was – that was and had been there all along' (p. 62). The representation of this message, as it passes through the forgetfulness of death to Sethe's ghostly daughter Beloved, is of a withholding: 'This is not a story to pass on' (p. 275).

Between mother and daughter, a certain historical withholding intervenes. If the situation between the new immigrant mother and daughter provokes the question as to whether it is the birth or death of translation (see above, p. 192), here the author represents with violence a certain birth-in-death, a death-in-birth of a story that is not to translate or pass on, strictly speaking, therefore, an aporia, and yet it is passed on, with the mark of *un*translatability on it, in the bound book, *Beloved*, that we hold in our hands. Contrast this to the confidence in accessibility in the house of power, where history is waiting to be restored.

The scene of violence between mother and daughter (reported and passed on by the daughter Sethe to her daughter Denver, who carries the name of a white trash girl, in partial acknowledgement of women's solidarity in birthing) is, then, the condition of (im)possibility of *Beloved*:[17]

> She picked me up and carried me behind the smokehouse. Back there she opened up her dress front and lifted her breast and pointed under it. Right on her rib was a circle and a cross burnt right in the skin. She said, 'This is your ma'am. This,' and she pointed . . . 'Yes, Ma'am,' I said . . . 'But how

will you know me? . . . Mark me, too,' I said . . . 'Did she?' asked Denver. 'She slapped my face.' 'What for?' 'I didn't understand it then. Not till I had a mark of my own.' (p. 61)

This scene, of claiming the brand of the owner as 'my own', to create, in this broken chain of marks owned by separate white male agents of property, an unbroken chain of re-memory in (enslaved) daughters as agents of a history not to be passed on, is of necessity more poignant than Friday's scene of withheld writing from the white woman wanting to create history by giving her 'own' language. And the lesson is the (im)possibility of translation in the general sense. Rhetoric points at absolute contingency, not the sequentiality of time, not even the cycle of seasons, but only 'weather'. 'By and by all trace is gone, and what is forgotten is not only the footprints but the water and what it is down there. The rest is weather. Not the breath of the disremembered and unaccounted for' – after the effacement of the trace, no project for restoring (women's?) history – 'but wind in the eaves, or spring ice thawing too quickly. Just weather' (p. 275).

With this invocation of contingency, where nature may be 'the great body without organs of woman', we can align ourselves with Wilson Harris, the author of *The Guyana Quartet*, for whom trees are 'the lungs of the globe'.[18] Harris hails the (re)birth of the native imagination as not merely the trans-lation but the trans-substantiation of the species. What in more workaday language I have called the obligation of the translator to be able to juggle the rhetorical silences in the two languages, Harris puts this way, pointing at the need for translating the Carib's English:

> The Caribbean bone flute, made of human bone, is a seed in the soul of the Caribbean. It is a primitive technology that we can turn around [trans-version?]. Consuming our biases and prejudices in ourselves we can let the bone flute help us open ourselves rather than read it the other way – as a metonymic devouring of a bit of flesh.[19] The link of music with cannibalism is a sublime paradox. When the music of the bone flute opens the doors, absences flow in, and the native imagination puts together the ingredients for quantum immediacy out of unpredictable resources.

The bone flute has been neglected by Caribbean writers, says Wilson Harris, because progressive realism is a charismatic way of writing prize-winning fiction. Progressive realism measures the bone. Progressive realism is the too-easy accessibility of translation as transfer of substance.

The progressive realism of the west dismissed the native imagination as the place of the fetish. Hegel was perhaps the greatest systematizer of this dismissal. And psychoanalytic cultural criticism in its present charismatic incarnation sometimes measures the bone with uncanny precision. It is perhaps not fortuitous that the passage below gives us an account of Hegel that is the exact opposite of Harris's vision. The paradox of the sublime and the bone here lead to non-language seen as inertia, where the structure of passage is mere logic. The authority of the supreme language makes translation impossible:

> The Sublime is therefore the paradox of an object which, in the very field of representation, provides a view, in a negative way, of the dimension of what is unrepresentable... The bone, the skull, is thus an object which, by means of its *presence*, fills out the void, the impossibility of the signifying *representation* of the subject... The proposition 'Wealth is the Self' repeats at this level the proposition 'The Spirit is a bone' [both propositions are Hegel's]: in both cases we are dealing with a proposition which is at first sight absurd, nonsensical, with an equation the terms of which are incompatible; in both cases we encounter the same logical structure of passage: the subject, totally lost in the medium of language (language of gesture and grimaces; language of flattery), finds its objective counterpart in the inertia of a non-language object (skull, money).[20]

Wilson Harris's vision is abstract, translating Morrison's 'weather' into an oceanic version of quantum physics. But all three cultural translators cited in this section ask us to attend to the rhetoric which points to the limits of translation, in the creole's, the slave-daughter's, the Carib's use of 'English'. Let us learn the lesson of translation from these brilliant inside/outsiders and translate it into the situation of other languages.

### READING AS TRANSLATION

In conclusion, I want to show how the post-colonial as the outside/insider translates white theory as she reads, so that she can discriminate on the terrain of the original. She wants to use what is useful. Again, I hope this can pass on a lesson to the translator in the narrow sense.

'The link of music with cannibalism is a sublime paradox.' I believe Wilson Harris is using 'sublime' here with some degree of precision, indicating the undoing of the progressive western subject as realist interpreter of history. Can a theoretical account of the aesthetic sublime

in English discourse, ostensibly far from the bone flute, be of use? By
way of answer, I will use my reading of Peter de Bolla's superb scholarly account of *The Discourse of the Sublime* as an example of sympathetic reading as translation, precisely not a surrender but a friendly
learning by taking a distance.[21]

P. 4: 'What was it to be a subject in the eighteenth century?' The
reader-as-translator (RAT) is excited. The long eighteenth century in
Britain is the account of the constitution and transformation of nation
into empire. Shall we read that story? The book will at least touch on
that issue, if only to swerve. And women will not be seen as touched
in their agency formation by that change. The book's strong feminist
sympathies relate to the Englishwoman only as gender victim. But the
erudition of the text allows us to think that this sort of rhetorical
reading might be the method to open up the question 'What is it to be a
post-colonial reader of English in the twentieth century?' The representative reader of *The Discourse of the Sublime* will be post-colonial.
Has that law of the majority been observed, or the law of the strong?

On p. 72 RAT comes to a discussion of Burke on the sublime:

> The internal resistance of Burke's text . . . restricts the full play of this
> trope [power . . . as a trope articulating the technologies of the sublime],
> thereby defeating a description of the sublime experience uniquely in
> terms of the enpowered [sic] subject. Put briefly, Burke, for a number
> of reasons, among which we must include political aims and ends, stops
> short of a discourse on the sublime, and in so doing he reinstates the
> ultimate power of an adjacent discourse, theology, which locates its own
> self-authenticating power grimly within the boundaries of godhead.

Was it also because Burke was deeply implicated in searching out the
recesses of the mental theatre of the English master in the colonies that
he had some notion of different kinds of subject and therefore, like
some Kurtz before Conrad, recoiled in horror before the sublimely
empowered subject? Was it because, like some Kristeva before *Chinese
Women*, Burke had tried to imagine the Begums of Oudh as legal
subjects that he had put self-authentication elsewhere?[22] *The Discourse
of the Sublime*, in noticing Burke's difference from the other discoursers
on the sublime, opens doors for other RATs to engage in such scholarly
speculations and thus exceed and expand the book.

Pp. 106, 111–12, 131: RAT comes to the English National Debt.
British colonialism was a violent deconstruction of the hyphen between
nation and state.[23] In imperialism the nation was subl(im)ated into
empire. Of this, no clue in *The Discourse*. The Bank of England is

discussed. Its founding in 1696, and the transformation of letters of credit to the ancestor of the modern cheque, had something like a relationship with the fortunes of the East India Company and the founding of Calcutta in 1690. The *national* debt is in fact the site of a crisis-management, where the nation, sublime object as miraculating subject of ideology, changes the sign 'debtor' into a catachresis or false metaphor by way of 'an acceptance of a permanent discrepancy between the total circulating specie and the debt'. The French War, certainly the immediate efficient cause, is soon woven into the vaster textile of crisis. *The Discourse* cannot see the nation covering for the colonial economy. As on the occasion of the race-specificity of gendering, so on the discourse of multinational capital, the argument is kept domestic, within England, European.[24] RAT snuffles off, disgruntled. She finds a kind of comfort in Mahasweta's livid figuration of the woman's body as body rather than attend to this history of the English body 'as a disfigurative device in order to return to [it] its lost literality'. Reading as translation has misfired here.

On p. 140 RAT comes to the elder Pitt. Although his functionality is initially seen as 'demanded . . . by the incorporation of nation', it is not possible not at least to mention empire when speaking of Pitt's voice:

> the voice of Pitt . . . works its doubled intervention into the spirit and character of the times; at once the supreme example of the private individual in the service of the state, and the private individual eradicated by the needs of a public, nationalist, commercial empire. In this sense the voice of Pitt becomes the most extreme example of the textualization of the body for the rest of the century. (p. 182)

We have seen a literal case of the textualization of the surface of the body between slave mother and slave daughter in *Beloved*, where mother hits daughter to stop her thinking that the signs of that text can be passed on, a lesson learnt *après-coup*, literally after the blow of the daughter's own branding. Should RAT expect an account of the passing on of the textualization of the interior of the body through the voice, a metonym for consciousness, from master father to master son? The younger Pitt took the first step to change the nationalist empire to the imperial nation with the India Act of 1784. Can *The Discourse of the Sublime* plot that sublime relay? Not yet. But here, too, an exceeding and expanding translation is possible.

Predictably, RAT finds a foothold in the rhetoricity of *The Discourse*. Chapter 10 begins: 'The second part of this study has steadily examined

how "theory" sets out to legislate and control a practice, how it produces the excess which it cannot legislate, and removes from the centre
to the boundary its limit, limiting case' (p. 230). This passage reads to a
deconstructive RAT as an enabling self-description of the text, although
within the limits of the book, it describes, not itself but the object of its
investigation. By the time the end of the book is reached, RAT feels that
she has been written into the text:

> As a history of that refusal and resistance [this book] presents a record of
> its own coming into being as history, the history of the thought it wants
> to think differently, over there. It is therefore, only appropriate that its
> conclusion should gesture towards the limit, risk the reinversion of the
> boundary by speaking from the other, refusing silence to what is unsaid.

Beyond this 'clamour for a kiss' of the other space, it is 'just weather'.

Under the figure of RAT (reader-as-translator), I have tried to limn the
politics of a certain kind of clandestine post-colonial reading, using the
master marks to put together a history. Thus we find out what books
we can forage, and what we must set aside. I can use Peter de Bolla's
*The Discourse on the Sublime* to open up dull histories of the colonial
eighteenth century. Was Toni Morrison, a writer well-versed in contemporary literary theory, obliged to set aside Paul de Man's 'The Purloined
Ribbon'?[25]

> Eighteen seventy-four and white folks were still on the loose... Human
> blood cooked in a lynch fire was a whole other thing... But none of that
> had worn out his marrow... It was the ribbon... He thought it was a
> cardinal feather stuck to his boat. He tugged and what came loose in his
> hand was a red ribbon knotted around a curl of wet woolly hair, clinging
> still to its bit of scalp... He kept the ribbon; the skin smell nagged him.
> (pp. 180–1)

Morrison next invokes a language whose selvedge is so frayed that
no *frayage* can facilitate full passage: 'This time, although he couldn't
cipher but one word, he believed he knew who spoke them. The people
of the broken necks, of fire-cooked blood and black girls who had lost
their ribbons' (p. 181). Did the explanation of promises and excuses in
eighteenth-century Geneva not make it across into this 'roar'? I will not
check it out and measure the bone flute. I will simply dedicate these
pages to the author of *Beloved*, in the name of translation.

NOTES

1 The first part of this essay is based on a conversation with Michèle Barrett in the summer of 1990.
2 Forthcoming from Seagull Press, Calcutta.
3 'Facilitation' is the English translation of a Freudian term which is translated *frayage* in French. The dictionary meaning is:

> Term used by Freud at a time when he was putting forward a neurological model of the functioning of the psychical apparatus (1895): the excitation, in passing from one neurone to another, runs into a certain resistance; where its passage results in a permanent reduction in this resistance, there is said to be facilitation; excitation will opt for a facilitated pathway in preference to one where no facilitation has occurred. (J. Laplanche and J.-B. Pontalis, *The Language of Psycho-Analysis* [Hogarth Press, London, 1973], p. 157.)

4 Jacques Derrida, 'Force of Law: The "Mystical Foundation of Authority"', tr. Mary Quaintance, *Deconstruction and the Possibility of Justice: Cardozo Law Review*, XI (July–Aug. 1990); p. 923.
5 'The Wet-nurse', in Kali for Women (eds), *Truth Tales: Stories by Indian Women* (The Women's Press, London, 1987), pp. 1–50 (first published by Kali for Women, Delhi, 1986), and 'Breast-giver', in Gayatri Chakravorty Spivak, *In Other Worlds: Essays in Cultural Politics* (Methuen/Routledge, New York, 1987), pp. 222–40.
6 Luce Irigaray argues persuasively that, Emmanuel Levinas to the contrary, within the ethics of sexual difference the erotic is ethical ('The Fecundity of the Caress', in her *Ethics of Sexual Difference*, tr. Carolyn Burke (Cornell University Press, Ithaca, N.Y., forthcoming).
7 Sudhir Kakar, *The Inner World: A Psycho-analytic Study of Childhood and Society in India*, 2nd edn (Oxford University Press, Delhi, 1981), pp. 171ff. Part of this discussion in a slightly different form is included in my 'Psychoanalysis in Left Field; and Fieldworking', forthcoming.
8 See Partha Chatterjee, 'Nationalism and the Woman Question', in Kumkum Sangari and Sudesh Vaid (eds), *Re-Casting Women* (New Brunswick University Press, Rutgers, 1990), pp. 233–53, for a detailed discussion of this gendering of Indian nationalism.
9 Max Weber, *The Religion of India: The Sociology of Hinduism and Buddhism*, tr. Hans H. Gerth and Don Martindale (Free Press, Glencoe, Ill., 1958).
10 More on this in a more personal context in Spivak, 'Stagings of the Origin', in *Third Text*.
11 Ifi Amadiume, *Male Daughters Female Husbands* (Zed Books, London, 1987).
12 For background on Akhter, already somewhat dated for this interventionist in the history of the present, see Yayori Matsui (ed.), *Women's Asia* (Zed Books, London, 1989), ch. 1.

13  'More on Power/Knowledge', in Thomas E. Wartenberg (ed.), *Re-Thinking Power* (State University of New York Press, Stony Brook, N.Y., forthcoming).

14  Spivak, 'Can the Subaltern Speak?', in Cary Nelson and Lawrence Grossberg (eds), *Marxism and the Interpretation of Culture* (University of Illinois Press, Urbana, Ill., 1988), pp. 271–313.

15  For an extended consideration of these and related points, see my 'Versions of the Margin: Coetzee's *Foe* reading Defoe's *Crusoe/Roxana*', in Jonathan Arac (ed.), *Theory and Its Consequences* (Johns Hopkins University Press, Baltimore, 1990).

16  Toni Morrison, *Beloved* (Plume Books, New York, 1987). Page numbers are included in my text.

17  For (im)possibility, see my 'Literary Representation of the Subaltern', in my *In Other Worlds*, pp. 241–68.

18  Karl Marx, 'Economic and Philosophical Manuscripts', in Rodney Livingstone and George Benton tr., *Early Writings* (Vintage, New York, 1975), pp. 279–400; Wilson Harris, *The Guyana Quartet* (Faber, London, 1985). These quotations are from Wilson Harris, 'Cross-cultural Crisis: Imagery, Language, and the Intuitive Imagination', Commonwealth Lectures, 1990, Lecture no. 2, 31 Oct. 1990, University of Cambridge.

19  Derrida traces the trajectory of the Hegelian and pre-Hegelian discourse of the fetish (Jacques Derrida, *Glas*, tr. Richard Rand and John P. Leavey, jr. [University of Nebraska Press, Lincoln, Nebr., 1986]). The worshipper of the fetish eats human flesh. The worshipper of God feasts on the Eucharist. Harris transverses the fetish here through the native imagination.

20  Slavoj Zizek, *The Sublime Object of Ideology*, tr. Jon Barnes (Verso, London, 1989), pp. 203, 208, 212.

21  Peter de Bolla, *The Discourse of the Sublime: Readings in History, Aesthetics and the Subject* (Blackwell, Oxford, 1989). Page numbers are given in my text.

22  References and discussion of 'The Begums of Oudh', and 'The Impeachment of Warren Hastings' are to be found in *The Writings and Speeches of Edmund Burke* ed. P.J. Marshall (Clarendon Press, Oxford, 1981), vol. 5: *India: Madras and Bengal*, pp. 410–12, pp. 465–6, p. 470; and in vol. 6: *India: Launching of The Hastings Impeachment* respectively.

23  See my 'Reading the Archives; the Rani of Sirmur', in Francis Barker (ed.), *Europe and Its Others* (University of Essex, Colchester, 1985), pp. 128–51.

24  Ibid.

25  Paul de Man, 'The Purloined Ribbon', reprinted as 'Excuses (*Confessions*)' in de Man, *Allegories of Reading* (Yale University Press, New Haven, 1979), pp. 278–301.

# Words and Things: Materialism and Method in Contemporary Feminist Analysis

## Michèle Barrett

### INTRODUCTION: DISPENSING WITH 'THINGS'

What, in short, we wish to do is to dispense with 'things' . . . To substitute for the enigmatic treasure of 'things' anterior to discourse, the regular formation of objects that emerge only in discourse.

*(Michel Foucault)*

The ambition to dispense with 'things' – and to value 'words' more – has caused some general perplexity and irritation. Many feminists, in particular, have traditionally tended to see 'things' – be they low pay, rape or female foeticide – as more significant than, for example, the discursive construction of marginality in a text or document. In this essay I want to explore how the issue of the relative status of things and words has become a central one in contemporary social theory and philosophy, and why feminists have a particularly strong investment in this question.

Where has this movement of ideas come from? One source would be the group of thinkers and theories often loosely referred to as 'post-structuralism'. In many ways this is a very unsatisfactory label, lumping together a diverse and often contradictory group of ideas on the specious basis of what preceded them in a chronology of Parisian thought. Yet the key thinkers of 'post-structuralism' – Derrida, Foucault and Lacan – have, in combination as well as individually, mounted a devastating critique of the main assumptions on which much social and feminist theory was previously based, and it has proved to be a critique from which neither has emerged unscathed. In social science generally, such unexceptionable concepts as 'social structure', 'role', 'individual' or 'labour market' have become contentious in terms of what they assume about a social totality or infrastructure, or the presumed characteristics of social actors. In cultural theory and the humanities, the critical assumptions about authors, readers and, most important of all, the 'human subject' as such have come under fundamental scrutiny. Contemporary western feminism, confident for several years about its 'sex – gender distinction', analysis of 'patriarchy' or postulation of 'the male gaze' has found all of these various categories radically undermined by the new 'deconstructive' emphasis on fluidity and contingency. These uncertainties of terminology are the effect of the popularization of some central themes, however distorted, of the work of Derrida, Lacan and Foucault.

## Post-structuralism

These post-structuralists offer a critique of both mainstream liberal social theory and philosophy (including psychology, political science and so on), but a perhaps more intimate blow to the working assumptions of Marxist and radical thought. In particular, the claims of materialism – the doctrine seeing consciousness as dependent on matter and the more general assumption that economic relations are dominant – have been decimated. The 'words and things' quotation from Foucault aptly illustrates this point. It is not that Foucault wished to dispense with things altogether: he was not 'denying reality' or some such inanity. But Foucault challenged the familiar hierarchy of value of the materialist perspective, counterposing the 'dumb existence of a reality' with the ability of groups of signs (discourses) to act as 'practices that systematically form the objects of which they speak'.[1] This critique of the importance ascribed to matter, and the corresponding insistence that the importance of meaning has gone unrecognized, has – where it has been heard – had far-ranging effects.

A second thesis worth noting is post-structuralism's challenge to assumptions about causality. The problem of causality is here linked to criticisms of teleological thought and the retrospective assignation of epistemological power to the past. Thus in both Derrida and Foucault we find an extended critique of the search for the origin, for the founding moment that will explain everything. For feminism, which has from time to time been preoccupied with the question of the origins or cause of women's oppression, any side-stepping of the question of cause is both momentous and contentious. Echoes of the critique of an originary, founding cause can also be found in contemporary understanding of Lacan. Instead of the search for a 'real event' in the psychic past that would explain the causes of neurosis or pathology, one looks for meaning to the ongoing inner representation of experience, with current repetitions being seen as more significant than any 'original' moment.

A third element of 'post-structuralism' with an obvious and crucial bearing on the words/things relationship is the approach taken to language. The working assumption about language in social and feminist theory tended to be that language was a vehicle for the expression of ideas. This is most easily illustrated in the issue of translation. Somebody writes a book containing various ideas and propositions, and this can unproblematically be rendered as the 'same book' in another language. If this is a caricature of the innocent pre-post-structuralist view, it was none the less a commonly assumed one in both social and feminist theory until recently. The Saussurian revolution has, at the very least, knocked out this view of language as merely a vehicle of expression, and the attribution to language itself of the power to construct rather than simply convey meaning has been growing. This can be seen in a variety of different ways, some relatively theoretical and others more pragmatic. Roland Barthes opened up this question in relation to varying degrees of 'writerliness' in texts, and his work has made it clear that – to take one example – the classical French ideal of *clarté* (lucidity) was one of various available writing styles. Clarity is a discursive *style* rather than an essential attribute of an author or a text.[2] Central to this view of language is the understanding that meaning is constructed, within language, through a process of differentiation. Meaning is not absolute or fixed in relation to a referent, but is arbitrary in that respect. Meaning is constructed through the counterposition of differing elements, whose definition lies precisely in their difference from each other.

People have accepted to varying degrees the view that meaning is constructed in rather than expressed by language. The strong position has been taken by Jacques Derrida for whom, logically, there can be no such thing as a 'summary' or a 'translation'. Each new text will construct meaning from its constituent elements in a different way and will not be a vehicle – it will be no more and no less than another text. Another influential approach is that of Michel Foucault, for whom the central question was 'What can be said?' The Foucauldian concept of discourse allows us to think about the epistemological power of discursive regimes and how important it is to understand what can be articulated when. As Foucault put it himself: 'It's a problem of verbal-isation.'[3] The implications of these views are obviously far-reaching. Before discussing them, however, I want to indicate another, and related aspect of the relationship of 'words and things', and this is one within feminism.

## Feminism's own turn to culture

In the past ten years we have seen an extensive 'turn to culture' in feminism.[4] Academically, the social sciences have lost their purchase within feminism and the rising star lies with the arts, humanities and philosophy. Within this general shift we can see a marked interest in analysing processes of symbolization and representation – the field of 'culture' – and attempts to develop a better understanding of subjectivity, the psyche and the self. The type of feminist sociology that has a wider audience, for example, has shifted away from a determinist model of 'social structure' (be it capitalism, or patriarchy, or a gender-segmented labour market or whatever) and deals with questions of culture, sexuality or political agency – obvious counterbalances to an emphasis on social structure.

Such academic developments are part of a much more general shift within feminism, at least in Britain and in Europe generally. In publishing, for instance, the sales of fiction have rocketed and non-fiction plummeted. Feminism sells best as fiction, and attempts to write and market modern versions of the classic feminist non-fiction blockbusters have been notably unsuccessful. Interestingly, too, feminist cultural commentary and discussion has often tended to draw on the pleasures of fiction: the things we want to write and read about are romance, crime, melodrama and so on.

These developments raise some complex questions, not least that of the disillusionment and critique that presaged this new direction. In this chapter I shall not explore the political why or the historical when of these changes, although these are highly significant questions. I want to focus instead on the implications, and on the issues at stake, in this move from one cluster of disciplines to another. At the outset, I would suggest that it will not be adequate simply to shift attention in one direction rather than another, or even to apply the critical tools of one discipline to another's traditional subject matter. The issues of what weight to attach to these various subject matters (the economic or the aesthetic, for example) will eventually have to be rethought. Meanwhile, we can certainly say that the words/things balance has been shifted away from the social sciences' preoccupation with things and towards a more cultural sensibility of the salience of words.

Finally, we might ask what it signifies that the post-modern term 'meta-narrative' has become so appealing. Many who do not really agree with the arguments of Jean-François Lyotard are none the less happy to describe large-scale political and intellectual projects as the 'meta-narratives' of feminism, democratism and so on. The interest here lies in our willingness to fictionalize these entities and to regard them as stories (narrative: to tell a tale, give an account). To say this is not to pose a crude antithesis between 'politics' and 'fiction', but it is to remark on how helpful many have found it to use a metaphorical fictionalizing as a critical tool for unlocking the objectivist pretensions of things like rationality, the Enlightenment or even feminism. In what follows I shall be discussing some of the general implications of these changes.

A PARADIGM SHIFT IN FEMINIST THEORY?

I have opened with a discussion of a from-things-to-words move, but there can be no doubt that this forms part of a broader sea change within contemporary social thought. Feminist thought both contributes to and is influenced by these larger developments. As Anne Phillips and I have commented in the introduction to this book, the changes within feminist thought could be seen as something of a 'paradigm shift'. Another way of thinking about this is to cast the question in terms of whether any given problem can be rethought within the terms of reference of one's existing theory, or whether – in order to proceed – one has to develop a new framework altogether. Ernesto Laclau has written about this in terms of whether one can ever, strictly speaking, 'solve' a theoretical problem within the original paradigm. Laclau suggests that one can't: that if a problem is a genuinely 'theoretical' problem (rather than a matter of how you apply a theory, or the empirical support for it) it cannot be solved but can only be 'superseded' in a new theory.[5] It is, of course, quite easy to suggest that the influence of post-structuralism, and the fundamental critique of Enlightenment rationality and classical Marxism, is establishing a new frame of reference that could be described as a shift of paradigmatic order. Seyla Benhabib, for example, refers decisively to a 'paradigm shift in contemporary philosophy from consciousness to language, from the denotative to the performative, from the proposition to the speech-act'.[6] Many feminists might regard the shift from 'equality' to 'difference' models of feminism, which has characterized the past decade of western feminism, as a shift of that order; on the other hand, one might conceptualize the equality–difference debate as itself a paradigm *within* which either position can be taken without undue strain on the model.


## POST-MODERNISM

To explore the question of the relationship between contemporary feminist and social theory is, of course, to address 'post-modernist' as well as post-structuralist arguments. Although there is less confusion in the use of this term than when it first appeared on the scene, it might be worth recapitulating the different contexts in which it is used. In terms of aesthetic strategies and cultural forms, post-modernism refers to an interest in surface rather than depth, to pastiche and parody, to reference to the past and to self-reference, and it focuses attention on a plurality of styles. In terms of philosophy, post-modernism entails a rejection of the grand projects of the rationalist Enlightenment, including Marxist as well as liberal systems of thought. In terms of sociological analysis, post-modernity is a phenomenon of post-industrial capitalism, crucially determined by the micro-electronic revolution and the globalization of communication and information systems. But since most sociology owes much to rationalism, sociologists must choose between a sociology of post-modernity and a post-modern sociology.[7] A different source of confusion operates within the arts and critical humanities disciplines, and this is that the 'modernism' invoked by post-modern critics is much more like nineteenth-century realism than it is like the 'avant-garde' or 'high modernist' experiments that used to be associated with the term modernism in the arts. A further complication lies in the matter of dates, as unfortunately modernity starts at different times in the different academic disciplines. For philosophy and political theory modernity is under full steam by the end of the eighteenth century; in the arts and humanities the modern world starts no earlier than 1890 and, according to Virginia Woolf, as late as 1910. Since Baudelaire's *flâneur* – the mid-nineteenth-century metropolitan loafer – is such a popular trope of post-modernism, one might legitimately observe that in philosophical terms he was inhabiting modernity and in literary terms was distinctively pre-modernist. In addition, as Janet Wolff's question about 'the invisible flâneuse' indicated at an early stage in these debates, the concepts of post-modernism were urgently in need of some gendering.[8]

### *Elements of the current theoretical conjuncture*

It is as well, then, to use the notion of post-modernism with respectful caution. Notwithstanding this, and the comparable problems associated with the term 'post-structuralism', these generic labels direct us to some very important broad trends in contemporary thought. It might be helpful to identify these at this point, in the following terms.

(1)  First, we can see a general critique of *theoretical universalism*. It is not necessary to reiterate here the major political impact of the recognition that western feminism of the 1970s spoke in a falsely universalized voice. The need to register and engage with the implications of differences among women has been the subject of considerable debate. Elizabeth Spelman has quoted the poet Gwendolyn Brooks in this context: 'The juice from tomatoes is not called merely *juice*. It is always called TOMATO juice.' Spelman observes that 'Even the most literal reading of Brooks ought to make us ask whether we're more careful about what we order in a restaurant than we are in thinking of women as the particular women they are.'[9] I'm not sure how far one can push this metaphor for the problem of difference in feminism. Aren't there situations in which one might opt for 'juice' generically, if offered that or alcohol? (Isn't there even something *very* particular about tomato juice that illustrates the commonality of other fruit juices?)

These debates within feminism form part of a much broader current of contemporary thought in which universalistic theoretical discourses have been subjected to sustained and profound critique. The two clearest cases to take are Marxism and psychoanalysis, both of which can be shown to operate in a strongly universalistic mode in terms of their explanatory claims.[10]

(2)  Secondly, there has been an extensive critique of two central aspects of what is usually referred to as 'Enlightenment' thought, or philosophical 'liberalism': the doctrine of *rationalism* and the '*Cartesian*' concept of a human subject. Feminist political theorists and philosophers have built up a considerable body of work on the masculine character of 'rationalism', and these debates are represented elsewhere in this volume.[11] The so-called 'Cartesian subject' is a topic of complex debate, and much of what is written within post-structuralist and post-modern thought touches on this question. At the heart of the issue is the model of the rational, centred, purposive (and in practice modern European and male) subject for whom Descartes deduced '*cogito ergo sum*'.

There are so many things wrong with this model of subjectivity, one scarcely knows where to begin. It displaces and marginalizes other subjects and other forms of subjectivity. It also denies what many would now accept as a central contribution of psychoanalysis – that the self is built on conflict and tension rather than being an essential or given. Yet the critique of this model of subjectivity has brought in its train a whole set of new problems, neatly captured in the title of Kate Soper's article 'Constructa Ergo Sum?' If we replace the given self with a constructed, fragmented self, this poses not only the obvious political question of who is the I that acts and on what basis, but the more teasing conundrum of who is the I that is so certain of its fragmented and discursively constructed nature.[12] Hence the critique of the Cartesian subject has posed a new set of questions about identity and experience, well developed in the arguments of, for example, Chandra Talpade Mohanty and Biddy Martin.[13]

(3) Thirdly, we can speak of *the gendering of modernity* as a new critical enterprise. One can increasingly identify a debate on the implications, for feminism, of the various critiques of modernism and modernity. Griselda Pollock's discussion of the artist, iconic for the modernist project, has illuminated in great detail the cultural meaning of the masculinity inscribed within that figure.[14] The problem remains, however, that feminism is itself too indebted to 'modernist values' and an emancipatory, liberal project to be able to cut loose from the culture and discourse within which it was formed. Susan Hekman points out that one cannot 'simply' suggest that 'the feminist critique extends the postmodern critique of rationalism by revealing its gendered character'.[15] This is because one cannot readily separate out the constituent elements of an integrated theoretical and political 'package'. Hence one may object to Enlightenment dualisms in which the feminine, or women, are always cast as inferior to the masculine, or men, but a thorough-going post-modern abandonment (in so far as this is possible) of these binary structures would be rejected by many feminists.

(4) Fourthly, we can see a new *critique of materialism* in these debates, and it is to these issues that I want to turn in more detail.

## The critique of materialism

Modern critiques of (philosophical) materialism have attracted a great deal of attention and some hostile responses. The greatest anxiety has been generated from those who see what they call 'discourse theory' as an ideologically suspect attempt to deny material reality – which, presumably, would be as futile an enterprise as Canute's if the materialist perspective is, itself, correct. In so far as ideas are powerful, mechanical materialism is wrong. There is no doubt, however, that these responses are the result of the intellectual provocation offered by 'performative' statements such as Derrida's famous *'il n'y a pas d'hors texte'* (there is nothing outside the text). This statement does not literally mean that railway trains do not exist other than as numbers in timetables, but that all knowledge is discursively apprehended. Ernesto Laclau and Chantal Mouffe have explained the general point very clearly in a reply to their critics, giving the prosaic example of a football. The spherical object exists, but it has no significant *meaning* outside the systems of rules and conventions (discourse) by which it is constituted as a football.[16]

Arguments about materialism have a very different purchase in different academic subjects. Materialist assumptions, whether Marxist or not, are common in the social sciences, and flourish particularly in the notion of a determining 'social structure' on which culture and beliefs, as well as subjectivity and agency, rest. Nevertheless, there has long been what one might regard as an alternative tradition within social theory, emphasizing experience and attempting to understand society without the aid of a social structural model. Phenomenology is an obvious case here, as is the work of Simmel. Recent years have seen a rise of interest in various traditions of social theory – phenomenology, hermeneutics, subjectivist sociology and so on – previously somewhat neglected. The materialist model with the greatest epistemological power is the paradigm of classical Marxism, a formative influence within European social theory.

On the other side of the social sciences/arts divide, the problem of materialism has not had an undue impact on disciplines that have taken the text as by definition constituting the object of study. In history, however, the ramifications of a critique of materialist premises have proved extensive. History's ambiguous position has rested on the fact that what was traditionally sought was a reconstitution or reconstruction of 'social reality', but one necessarily based methodologically on a reading of textual evidence. Thus the question of how historiography adjusts to a rethinking of the balance between text and reality is a particularly acute one.

The implications of post-structuralism for feminist historiography have been much debated. The incorporation of Foucault's work had already taken root (for instance, in the work of Judith Walkowitz and

Jeffrey Weeks on sexuality), and the methodological orientation of Mary Poovey's readings is clearly influenced by Derrida. Joan Scott has taken the lead in explicating the new trend, suggesting that Derridian insights could lead to a feminist history that 'undermines claims for authority based on totalising explanations, essentialised categories of analysis (be they human nature, race, class, sex, or "the oppressed"), or synthetic narratives that assume an inherent unity for the past'.[17]

In this context Derrida's ideas can be used to shore up further an already far-reaching critique of conventional historiography developed by Michel Foucault. As he explained in the opening sections of *The Archaeology of Knowledge*, Foucault's ambition was to replace the old linear and teleological history with an approach that sought for such systematicity as might be found in a general context of dispersal and particularity.[18]

It is a moot point how far some of the theoretical refusals characteristic of post-structuralism can be taken in the accomplishment of specific researches. Without offending anyone we can consider this by looking at a statement which appears on the jacket of a book about Foucault. It reads: 'In the most obvious sense Foucault's analyses of the birth of the clinic, the asylum and the prison are historical and raise problems of historical interpretation. But he makes no attempt to reconstitute the past historically and accurately.'[19] This is a slight exaggeration of the book's authors' view that Foucault's relationship to history was 'eccentric', but it illustrates the point in question. How can history dispense with historicality and accuracy? Of course, despite disclaimers that there is no such thing as truth, only effects of truth that are discursively secured, Foucault's substantive analyses themselves propose a *better account* of the history of mental illness, or punishment, or sexuality, than previous histories, and in this sense are loaded with epistemological claims.

Derrida, particularly, of the post-structuralists, has focused attention on the impossibility of escaping intellectual constraints we may object to. To point to the covert reintroduction of metaphysics, or idealism, in his work is thus not likely to surprise him. Nevertheless, there is a tension between the highly particularistic and relativistic view of knowledge adopted in post-structuralism and the epistemological claims necessarily made in substantive instances. This is clearest in the domain of history, where social reality is always in play, but is a problem too in more philosophical discussions that are none the less always historically located. Yet in these writers one often finds a coy hesitation about actually pinning a date on to something.[20]

Such uneasiness is symptomatic of a more general uncertainty about the implication of post-structuralism's critique of materialism. Such a critique has taken many forms: it is played out in debates about the place of evidence, texts and archives in historical research, in debates about social structure or 'interests' as determinants of behaviour and so on. A critique of the mechanical assumptions of materialism underlies the continued 'turn to culture' in feminism, as witness to a concern with representation and symbolization rather than more classically sociological approaches. In this context perhaps one might add that the contestation of cultural meaning is every bit as important as other feminist projects. Foucault's analysis of the exclusions and prohibitions of discourse is extremely pertinent to a feminism that has pioneered understanding of the power of naming and the efficacy of language.[21]

## Disciplinary considerations

Debates in philosophy and social theory, and the parallel discussions in the humanities, take place in an institutional context. I want next to focus on some of the disciplinary aspects of these debates. In the first place, one can note that feminist scholarship has always had the ambition to transcend disciplinary boundaries. Like Marxism, it has tended to regard them as constructions of an unenlightened system that are better ignored. The philosophy of 'women's studies' is very clearly based on this recognition. In practice, however, there are two widely recognized limitations of working under the rubric of 'women's studies': that it leaves the mainstream definition of the academic subjects unchallenged and even denuded of feminist scholars (an aspect of 'ghettoization') and that it militates against developing an understanding of men, masculinity and the interaction of the sexes (the subject matter of the alternative rubric of 'gender'). I am not interested here in these issues, important though they are. I want to focus instead on some of the problems that arise in relation to feminist concerns and the academic disciplines – outside women's studies – in more general terms.

It is not too banal to observe that most feminist scholars have been trained within the conventions of one or the other of the academic disciplines in the arts and social sciences. The marks of these specific trainings are often indelible. They are particularly visible in feminist work, in that one discipline after the next has historically gained a certain 'influence' within contemporary feminism. This often comes up in the context of accusations of using 'jargon', which usually means using another discipline's accepted terminology: I tend not to perceive my own disciplinary vocabulary as jargon.

Disciplines do not simply generate jargon, though; they rest on distinctive assumptions and conventions as to what their objects of study are and what methods are appropriate to study them. Academic debate can reduce itself, on occasion, to a simple trading of assumptions across disciplinary divides. Foucault developed ideas of disciplinary apparatus and discursive policing to describe the practices that regulate what can be said within a discipline, and has shown how Canguilheim's idea of knowledge being 'in the true' can be applied. 'Within its own limits, each discipline recognises true and false propositions; but it pushes back a whole teratology of knowledge beyond its margins.' So unless a proposition is 'within the true' of these requirements at the time, it cannot be accepted as true. Foucault gives the example of Mendel, whose theories were rejected in the nineteenth century, because he spoke of objects and used methods that were alien to the biology of his time. Foucault concludes (surprisingly to those who insist on regarding him as a complete relativist) that 'Mendel spoke the truth, but he was not "within the true" of the biological discourse of his time.'[22]

To speak 'within the true' of a particular discipline is to speak within a complex web of inclusions and exclusions. Differences of time and space are crucial in understanding these requirements in specific contexts. In contemporary western feminist theory there are clearly different conventions of reference as between, say, Australian, European and US feminists – the sense of what you need to know about to be up with your field is very different.[23] Similarly, for instance, there are significant differences between the different disciplines as to how far interdisciplinarity is desirable or necessary, and significant differences between national and regional disciplinary development of subjects in various parts of the world. To understand these patterns in their complexity would require extensive knowledge and – not least – would require an insight into the educational aspects of colonization in the past and the effects of these on the present distribution of academic power.

Another way of thinking about Foucault's notion of the boundaries of particular disciplines might be to consider a licence to ignore. There is, if you like, an informal division of labour in which certain questions are assigned to one subject and can thus legitimately be ignored by another. In particular, I think one can see this process in the informal division of labour between the arts/humanities critical disciplines and the social sciences. One effect of what I have called here a shift from 'things' to 'words' is a destabilization of this informal disciplinary division of labour. However, it seems to me that the form this has taken has been to open up new substantive areas, or topics, of study to scholars from disciplines that had previously regarded them as beyond the range of what could be studied. The more ambitious task of rethinking the appropriate *methods* of study, and developing ways of genuinely working across disciplines, has lagged behind. The kinds of example that one might give here are obviously contentious, and I will try to present them in a constructive spirit.

The 'post-colonial subject', for example, is better known as a phenomenon of the archive or psyche than as an agent in labour migration or a victim of globalizing managerial strategies.[24] The reasons for this are complex. Feminist economists and sociologists have taken up these issues but the lines of communication between them and literary readers and scholars are institutionally poor.[25] There has also been an evident vacuum within feminist social science on these issues, in my view because the social structural model has proved particularly unwieldy in the face of a triple interaction of disadvantage. Ideally, we would be able to complement knowledge of post-coloniality drawn from textual and archival sources and often focusing on subjective and symbolic questions with a richer social, economic and political treatment of this historical theme. These various aspects of the subject are not in competition with each other, and nor should any aspect be given, in the abstract, greater epistemological significance. But they call for a variety of competences, training and knowledges.

In practice, the recent shifting of disciplinary definitions of appropriate subject matter has often meant an export of methods and techniques. The redefinition of 'literary criticism' is a very important case in point. Certainly one can say that the traditional 'canon fodder' approach has been destabilized, although with complex consequences. Barbara Christian, for example, clearly struck a nerve in pointing to the pursuit of theory for its own sake in literary study and the consequent neglect of reading texts of feeling as well as thought.[26] I want to focus here on a different aspect of this destabilization – the relation between critical reading method and the text or object of study.

One development in the intellectual 'crisis' of literary criticism has been to turn critical attention to texts way outside the previously accepted 'literary' range. The school of thought known as 'new historicism' took a lead in reading social, medical, legal and political documents alongside literary texts; Derridian techniques of reading have played an important part in this development. More generally, one can hear at any up-to-date literary critical meeting (the MLA being the ideal type) many a paper in which the most mundanely social of sources are decoded, deconstructed and 'read' using the critical armoury of modern textual interpretation. The question to be asked, however, is whether these exercises are more than a method bored by its usual stamping ground. How, in particular, does the knowledge gained by such readings interact with what we know from social history, or sociology, about Victorian drains or 1950s cross-dressing practices?

If all this is to say that one trend has been the application of literary critical techniques to social historical documents and archives, read as 'texts', another important trend has been to retain the canon of classical literary texts but to 'read' them through a completely different inter-pretative grid. The most influential example of this at present is the application of psychoanalytic concepts as a method of literary criticism. This, too, raises some complex questions. Given that psychoanalysis has a history of being one of the most 'reductive' of perspectives, in that its strong explanatory claims, exclusion of other factors and incipient theoretical universalism are legendary, it is perhaps ironic that (from the point of view of its practitioners) in this process its epistemological status is dramatically altered. It is increasingly apparent that the working assumptions of those who use psychoanalytic concepts as a method of reading texts are strongly at variance with the assumptions of those who practise psychoanalysis in a therapeutic context. Although there is a certain amount of movement from one to the other, there is none the less a distance and sometimes outright conflict between free-floating cultural analysis and the clinical institution. One might pose this as a breach between 'psychoanalysis', where certain assumptions hold true across the schools of Freudians, Kleinians, Lacanians and others, and a *post-psychoanalysis* whose object is exclusively symbolic.[27]

Psychoanalysis is poised at a complex conjunction of 'words and things', some variants facing exclusively towards the symbolic realm of language and representation while others (though stopping short of the 'real event' mentality) would endorse claims that psychic experience carries some sort of causal power in a subjective history.

To refer to these differences of method and epistemology is to raise the question of how objects of study are constituted within the various disciplines. To ignore this question is to work within very narrow confines. There may be some apprehension that to pose the question is itself to endorse or imply a search for a 'general theory' or 'integrated perspective', but I do not think that this is the likely outcome. On the contrary, to address the specific 'truths' of the different disciplines is to discover not the controlling modernism of a fully integrated general theory of knowledge, but precisely the reverse – an incommensurability of knowledges that provokes interesting reflection.

### IN CONCLUSION

It would, I believe, be useful to consider further the implications of what in Foucauldian vein one might regard as 'disciplinary truth apparatuses'. In the examples I have raised here I have tended to focus on the questions of which I have some experience (sociology and literary studies), and this is inevitable since one cannot speak outside these conventions altogether. It is worth noting, however, that these disciplinary apparatuses are not simply relics of the bad old disciplines, but are powerful and living developments within the good new ones too. 'Women's studies', 'cultural studies', 'lesbian and gay studies' have quickly lost their initial openness of perspective and developed highly distinctive assumptions and conventions (disciplinary paradigms) within which each operates. In feminist studies ambivalence about academic privilege may have marginalized these problems. Yet we might perhaps be in a better position politically if the institutional context of particular knowledges, and the varying powers that go with them, were more openly addressed.

As far as the issue of materialism is concerned, it seems likely that it will take a long time before the far-reaching influence and effects of the structure–culture and base–superstructure dichotomies have been registered, still more worked through. Certainly this is true for feminists working within the disciplinary bases of the social sciences and history. In the arts and humanities the impact of post-structuralism, albeit still highly contentious, has been much greater. Feminist theory has been able to take up a number of issues outside that classically 'materialist' perspective: in particular the analysis of corporeality and of the psyche. 'Post-structuralist' theories, notably Derridian deconstructive reading, Lacanian psychoanalysis and Foucault's emphasis on the material body and the discourses of power, have proved very important in this. Feminists have appropriated these theories rather than others for good reasons: these theorists address the issues of sexuality, subjectivity and textuality that feminists have put at the top of the agenda. In considering the debates that now ramify around feminism and post-structuralism, it is clear that the classic materialist presuppositions are increasingly harder to apply usefully.

To say that is not, however, to endorse a wholesale conversion to 'post-structuralism'. The many post-structuralist and post-modernist critiques of liberal and Marxist thought have decisively exposed the fundamental flaws of those earlier theories. Whether, however, they can promise a more useful alternative is a much more vexed question. In the meantime, there are losses attached to a wholesale abandonment of the areas of study traditionally denoted by the academic disciplines of sociology, political economy, economics and politics.

There is another, paradoxical, aspect of modern feminist deployment of the status historically attributed to materiality in an economic sense. While social class is definitely *non grata* as a topic, one may creditably speak of 'proletarianization' and 'exploitation' in the context of global capitalism and racially driven disadvantage (rather like the legal class discrimination that continues in Britain, in education and housing, for example, where analogous cases of sex and race discrimination would be at risk of prosecution). This is surely something of an anomaly, if a politically explicable one.

Finally, I want to conclude with a point about the issue of materialism and the theoretical 'grounding' of political practice. In the debates around feminism and post-modernism some have argued for a 'modernist' conception of rationalism, egalitarianism and autonomy as the basis of an emancipatory practice, in feminism as elsewhere. On this model, the work of Habermas and critical theory, for example, could be seen to rescue feminism from the irrationalism and political limitations of post-modern perspectives. Clearly this discussion is part of a broader debate as to whether feminism is 'essentially' a modernist or a post-modernist enterprise. There are some good reasons for holding either position on this and, indeed, for the third position that feminism straddles and thus destabilizes the modern–post-modern binary divide.[28] It seems to me, however, that we do not necessarily need more and better theories legitimating or justifying feminist political practice. Such a need is based on an assumption that political values are produced by scientific analysis (the type case being the classical 'scientific' as opposed to utopian definition of Marxism). This 'scientism', taken to its extreme, strips values from politics, and this has also been the effect of the blanket anti-humanism that has characterized post-structuralism and certain schools of feminist thought. Debates about ideology and subjectivity have shown that we need a better conception of agency and identity than has been available in either (anti-humanist) post-structuralist thought or its (humanist) modernist predecessors. It may well be that to develop a better account of subjective political motivation we shall have to reopen in new and imaginative ways the issue of humanism. Meanwhile, perhaps, it will be important to assert that political objectives are in an important sense constituted on the basis of values and principles – that they cannot be grounded in a scientific social analysis but spring from aspiration rather than proof.

### NOTES

I am grateful to Isobel Armstrong for commissioning the article ('Feminism's Turn to Culture') which set me off down this track, and to all the members of the discussion group on post-structuralism and feminist historiography that I have gained so much from. Particular thanks to Catherine Hall, Anne Phillips and Ruthie Petrie.

1 Michel Foucault, *The Archaeology of Knowledge* (Routledge, London, 1989), p. 49.
2 It is a pleasure to acknowledge my debt to Gayatri Spivak (Alabama, 1986) for this point.
3 Michel Foucault, 'The Minimalist Self', in *Michel Foucault: Politics, Philosophy, Culture. Interviews and Other Writings 1977–1984*, ed. Lawrence Kritzman (Routledge, London, 1990), pp. 3–16; p. 8.
4 See Michèle Barrett, 'Feminism's Turn to Culture', in *Woman: A Cultural Review*, 1 (1990), pp. 22–4.
5 Ernesto Laclau, *Politics and Ideology in Marxist Theory* (Verso, London, 1977), pp. 60–1.
6 Seyla Benhabib, 'Epistemologies of Postmodernism: A Rejoinder to Jean-François Lyotard', in Linda J. Nicholson (ed.), *Feminism/Postmodernism* (Routledge, New York and London, 1990), p. 125.
7 This telegraphic formulation signals a complex debate on the extent to which sociology, and the social sciences in general, were born of the modernist 'moment'. For discussion of these issues see Roy Boyne and Ali Rattansi (eds), *Postmodernism and Society* (Macmillan, London, 1990); Scott Lash, *Sociology of Postmodernism* (Routledge, London, 1990), ch. 5; Bryan Turner (ed.), *Theories of Modernity and Postmodernity* (Sage, London, 1990); David Frisby's significant study *Fragments of Modernity* (Polity, Cambridge, 1985); Zygmunt Bauman, *Legislators and Interpreters: On Modernity, Post-Modernity and Intellectuals* (Polity, Cambridge, 1989).
8 Janet Wolff, 'The Invisible Flâneuse: Women and the Literature of Modernity', *Theory, Culture and Society*, 2 (1985), pp. 37–48.
9 Elizabeth V. Spelman, *Inessential Woman: Problems of Exclusion in Feminist Thought* (The Women's Press, London, 1990), p. 186.
10 These issues are discussed in some detail in my *The Politics of Truth: From Marx to Foucault* (Polity, Cambridge, 1991).
11 See also, for example, the collection by Carole Pateman and Elizabeth

Gross (eds), *Feminist Challenges: Social and Political Theory* (Allen and Unwin, Sydney, 1986).

12  Kate Soper, 'Constructa Ergo Sum?', in Soper, *Troubled Pleasures: Writings on Politics, Gender and Hedonism* (Verso, London, 1990), pp. 146–61.

13  See Biddy Martin and Chandra Talpade Mohanty, 'Feminist Politics: What's Home Got to Do with It?', in Teresa de Lauretis (ed.), *Feminist Studies/Critical Studies* (Indiana University Press, Bloomington, Ind., 1986), and their essays in this volume.

14  See the essay by Griselda Pollock in this volume; also Pollock, *Vision and Difference: Femininity, Feminism and the Histories of Art* (Routledge, New York and London, 1988); Pollock, 'Feminism and Modernism', in Roszika Parker and Griselda Pollock (eds), *Framing Feminism: Art and the Women's Movement 1970–1985* (Pandora/Routledge, London, 1987).

15  Susan Hekman, *Gender and Knowledge: Elements of a Postmodern Feminism* (Polity, Cambridge, 1990), p. 5.

16  Ernesto Laclau and Chantal Mouffe, 'Post-Marxism Without Apologies', in Ernesto Laclau (ed.), *New Reflections on the Revolution in Our Time* (Verso, London, 1990), p. 100.

17  Joan Wallach Scott, *Gender and the Politics of History* (Columbia University Press, New York, 1988), pp. 7–8; Mary Poovey, *Uneven Developments: The Ideological Work of Gender in Mid-Victorian England* (Virago, London, 1989/Chicago University Press, Chicago, 1988).

18  Foucault, *The Archaeology of Knowledge*, pp. 3–39. Foucault later declared himself 'flabbergasted' at being described one-sidedly as a philosopher of discontinuity and took for the title of his chair at the Collège de France 'Professor of the History of Systems of Thought'.

19  Mark Cousins and Athar Hussain, *Michel Foucault* (Macmillan, London, 1984), jacket copy.

20  See, for example, Derrida's essay 'Structure, Sign and Play in the Discourse of the Human Sciences', which eventually discloses the 'where and when' of a central thesis by choosing the names ('as indications only') Nietzsche, Freud and Heidegger – enabling us to locate it in late nineteenth-century/ early twentieth-century Europe: Jacques Derrida, *Writing and Difference* (Routledge, London, 1978), p. 280.

21  Michel Foucault, 'The Order of Discourse', in Robert Young (ed.), *Untying the Text: A Post-Structuralist Reader* (Routledge, London and New York, 1987) pp. 48–78. On feminism and the power of naming see Adrienne Rich, *On Lies, Secrets and Silence* (Virago, London, 1980).

22  Foucault, 'The Order of Discourse', pp. 60–1.

23  The usual gripe here is that feminists in the USA see much less need to read what Australian or British feminists write (until it attracts a US publisher) than vice versa.

24  Gayatri Spivak, whose work has been crucial for the development of understanding of post-coloniality, provides an exception to this general observation in that her interests and knowledges range across matters of

technology, economics and so on. 'We cannot ask the economists and the sociologists to attend to our speculations about the subject-constitution of the woman in post-modern neo-colonialism if we do it as charming primi-tivists' (Gayatri Chakravorty Spivak, 'The Political Economy of Women as Seen by a Literary Critic', in Elizabeth Weed [ed.], *Coming to Terms: Feminism, Theory, Politics* [Routledge, New York, 1989], p. 228). See also Spivak, 'Scattered Speculations on the Question of Value', in her *In Other Worlds: Essays in Cultural Politics* (Routledge, London and New York, 1987), pp. 154–75.

25   For two examples, see Maria Mies, *Patriarchy and Accumulation on a World Scale* (Zed Press, London and New Jersey, 1986); Haleh Afshar (ed.), *Women, Work and Ideology in the Third World* (Tavistock/ Routledge, London and New York, 1985).

26   Barbara Christian, 'The Race for Theory', *Cultural Critique*, 6 (1987), pp. 51–64.

27   Barrett, *The Politics of Truth*, ch. 5; see also Richard Feldstein and Henry Sussman (eds), *Psychoanalysis and . . .* (Routledge, New York and London, 1990), pp. 1–8.

28   The most useful anthology in this debate is Linda Nicholson (ed.), *Feminism/Postmodernism* (Routledge, London and New York, 1990). Feminists sympathetically critical of 'critical theory' can be found in Seyla Benhabib and Drucilla Cornell (eds), *Feminism as Critique* (Polity, Cam-bridge, 1987); see also Nancy Fraser, *Unruly Practices: Power, Discourse and Gender in Contemporary Social Theory* (Polity, Cambridge, 1989). Susan Hekman's *Gender and Knowledge* gives an excellent account from a position sympathetic to post-modernism. See also Rita Felski, *Beyond Feminist Aesthetics* (Harvard University Press, Cambridge, Mass., 1989), ch. 2.

# Index